EDUCATION AT LARGE

STUDENT LIFE & ACTIVITIES IN SINGAPORE

1945 -1965

EDUCATION AT LARGE

STUDENT LIFE & ACTIVITIES IN SINGAPORE

1945 -1965

Editors

Teng Siao See

Chan Cheow Thia

Lee Huay Leng

World Scientific

NEW JERSEY · LONDON · SINGAPORE · BEIJING · SHANGHAI · HONG KONG · TAIPEI · CHENNAI

Published by

The Tangent
38 Springleaf Rise
Singapore 788018

and

World Scientific Publishing Co. Pte. Ltd.
5 Toh Tuck Link, Singapore 596224
USA office: 27 Warren Street, Suite 401-402, Hackensack, NJ 07601
UK office: 57 Shelton Street, Covent Garden, London WC2H 9HE

Library of Congress Cataloging-in-Publication Data
880-01 Xiao yao you. English.
 Education-at-large : student life and activities in Singapore, 1945-1965 / [edited by] Teng Siao See, Chan Cheow Thia and Lee Huay Leng.
  p. cm.
 ISBN 978-9814405546 -- ISBN 981440554X
 1. High school students--Singapore--History--20th century. I. Teng, Siao See, 1975–
II. Zeng, Zhaocheng. III. Li, Huiling, 1971– IV. Title. V. Title: Student life and activities in Singapore, 1945–1965.
 LA1239.5.X5313 2012
 373.18095957--dc23

                                    2012017573

British Library Cataloguing-in-Publication Data
A catalogue record for this book is available from the British Library.

Cover Designer: Mark Yong

Copyright © 2013 by The Tangent and World Scientific Publishing Co. Pte. Ltd.

All rights reserved. This book, or parts thereof, may not be reproduced in any form or by any means, electronic or mechanical, including photocopying, recording or any information storage and retrieval system now known or to be invented, without written permission from the Publisher.

For photocopying of material in this volume, please pay a copying fee through the Copyright Clearance Center, Inc., 222 Rosewood Drive, Danvers, MA 01923, USA. In this case permission to photocopy is not required from the publisher.

In-house Editor: Lum Pui Yee

Typeset by Stallion Press
Email: enquiries@stallionpress.com

Printed in Singapore by B & Jo Enterprise Pte Ltd

Still youthful

— dedicated to those who left behind imprints of a bygone era.

 The Exhibition Featured as well as the Publication of this Book is Sponsored by the Chinese Language and Culture Fund.

CONTENTS

Foreword: Those Unforgettable Experiences of Youth   xi
Lee Huay Leng
Translated by Chan Cheow Thia

Exhibition Photographs   xix

Historical Photographs   xxix

Part I.   Forum Documentation   1

A Bilingual Forum: Inhabiting Two Different Worlds Dialogue Between Han Tan Juan and Koh Tai Ann   3
Transcribed by Gan Woan Wen
Translated by Tan Hui Yi and Swee Hui Weng

My Project Work Experience   51
Nur Nasuha

My Thoughts on Participating in the Exhibition "Education at Large: Student Life and Activities in Singapore, 1945–1965"   55
Hsin Shu Han
Transcribed by Chan Cheow Thia
Translated by Chiu Wei Li

Some Thoughts on the "Education-at-Large" Exhibition   59
Tan Pin Pin

Perspectives in Student Movement Research   61
Huang Jianli
Transcribed and translated by Chan Cheow Pong

A Very Brief History of Idealism in Singapore   65

Kwok Kian Woon
Transcribed by Chan Cheow Pong
Translated by Low Yen Yen

A Historical Account of the Chinese Book Industry in the 1950s to the 1960s   69

Zhong Hongzhi
Translated by Ng How Wee

Part II. Oral History   81

Brief Biographies of the Interviewees   83

Youthful Wanderings amidst Student Movements   85
An Interview with Lim Chin Joo

Interviewed by Chiu Wei Li, Zhou Zhaocheng and Lee Huay Leng
Transcribed and Compiled by Lee Huay Leng
Translated by Chiu Wei Li and Chan Cheow Thia

Transfer to Chinese School — Taking a Different Road   97
An Interview with Tan Kok Chiang

Interviewed by Lee Huay Leng
Transcribed by Wang Peijie
Translated by Chiu Wei Li and Francis Lim Khek Gee

Those Organised and Unorganised Times of Youth   115
An Interview with Chen Mong Tse and Chai Chu Chun

Interviewed by Zhong Hongzhi and Lee Huay Leng
Transcribed by Zhong Hongzhi
Translated by Low Yen Yen

Observation as Historical Participation   143
An Interview with Lee Leong Seng

Interviewed by Chan Cheow Thia and Teng Siao See
Transcribed by Lee Hui Jun, Ding Lee Yong and Chan Cheow Thia
Translated by Teng Siao See

Growing Up with Literacy Classes   171
An Interview with Tan Teck Keng

Interviewed by Chan Cheow Thia, Teng Siao See
Transcribed by Ku Ka Tsai, Lim Woan Fei, Chan Cheow Thia
Translated by Ho Sheo Be

The Sojourns of a Village Youth   205
An Interview with Chua Hiang Yong

Interviewed by Chan Cheow Thia
Transcribed by Chan Cheow Thia, Chan Cheow Pong
Translated by Lim Meow Nar

Part III.   Appendix   229

The Singapore Chinese Middle School Students' Union: 231
A Lost Echo of an Era

Lim Chin Joo
Translated by Melissa Gay

Thoughts of Exhibition Visitors   259

Transcribed by Lynn Ong

Participating Schools   265

Editors' Notes: A Collective Imagery of Youth in the Island-State   267

Chan Cheow Thia

About the Editors   271

Organising Committee / The Tangent Committee   273

FOREWORD

THOSE UNFORGETTABLE EXPERIENCES OF YOUTH

Lee Huay Leng

Translated by Chan Cheow Thia

Ever since its founding, The Tangent has always welcomed different opinions within the group. Members are divided with regard to the issue of the society keeping to a small-scale operation, or expanding to take on different forms of public engagement. Some have thought that the group should demonstrate greater social commitment and do more to promote the use of Chinese language in discussing current affairs and other issues concerning long-term national development. There are also others who feel that it is reasonable to maintain small-scale activities given our resource constraints. Looking back, the decision to do something different and yet continuative of our spirit was made under amicable circumstances.

The approach can be perceived as continuative because it was not the first time history was selected as the theme of a project. In 2002, the Tangent had organised a forum entitled "(Un)learning the Past" and subsequently published "Voices of History," a special bilingual issue of our journal in 2003. However, the new task we set for ourselves was no longer merely organising forums or closed door discussions, but sustaining a whole series of activities that would culminate in the exhibition "Education-at-Large: Student Life and Activities in Singapore 1945–1965." These activities included a public forum, during which we invited Mr Han Tan Juan and Professor Koh Tai Ann, educated in Chinese and English school traditions respectively, to share personal memories of their school lives; a conscious and concerted collaboration with schools, with educator-researcher, Mr Lim Cheng Tju, invited to give a special talk to participating students on research methodology and the historical background of the period 1945–1965; as well as an appeal to members of the public to donate artefacts and share their stories, during which members of the Tangent also acquired new knowledge in the process of gathering oral histories.

Most members of the Tangent belong to the generation born in the years between 1960 and 1980. Impressions of the 1950s and 1960s, or even the 1970s — a period not too distant — are almost zilch apart from the mainstream discourse of the state-led relentless pursuit of economic survival and growth. If we have retained some memories, they are faint. For several decades, the entire society has focused on solving problems of food and housing, and we grew up amidst a national mindset that has emphasised the nurture of culture and the arts only after fulfilling our visceral needs. Moreover, our island-state is one of the few places in the world where the founding fathers have occupied the political stage for an extensive period of time. An attempt to approach the 1950s and 1960s would thus involve interpreting the origins of current political power. For many years, the governing authorities abstained from accounting for a past still too close for comfort, whereas the people maintained their silence on the same shared historical experience. When we went to schools, the local textbooks on Singapore history usually offered expositions only up to the end of the Pacific War. What we can remember most vividly after the books have been set aside may probably be the gallant figure of Raffles, his arms wrapped in front of his chest.

Such impoverished memories led us to think and ask more questions about our past. They made us even more curious about the times closest to our childhood. A retrospective survey will tell us that this island-state has experienced tremendous changes over the past 15 years, but the monograph that has been profoundly influential and claims to offer a complete account of Singapore's past is perhaps an autobiography published in two parts in 1998 and 2000: *The Singapore Story: Memoirs of Lee Kuan Yew* and *From Third World to First: The Singapore Story 1965–2000*. For the writing of the two books, massive resources were mobilised to conduct a systematic organisation and recording of issues ranging from individual and public participation to significant national matters. Narrating in an authoritative tone, the author presents what he cast as truths about the past. This gesture attracted considerable attention both within and beyond our island-state. Regardless of whether people agreed or disagreed with the contents of the memoirs, historical events and viewpoints became the foci of public discussion and contestation. Even though there have been more narrators, however when narrating remembrances, people still create for themselves categories of what can be said or otherwise. In general, more people started talking about how our island-state became sovereign; about the players in the process and the roles they played; and how the process has impacted on the subsequent development of Singapore, and etc. The more new materials surfaced, the more it became apparent that we cared and knew too little before this.

The island-state requires the gravity of a historical legacy as an anchor for our present circumstances in order to foster self-identity. For the same reason, the state and society have come to treasure history even more. However, the significance attached to history should not only be demonstrated through the interpretation of a particular figure or an exclusive group. Instead, people should be encouraged to see the value in recording the experiences and perspectives of actors and events beyond those thought to have directly contributed to transforming the course of history. Individuals, families, schools and organisations are all important pieces in the puzzle that capture snapshots of a society caught in a particular historical moment. At the same time, to re-consider the political history of a state, we have to confront some basic questions: What are our attitudes towards history? Do we have sufficient sources to consult? Why is it possible to discuss some figures and events publicly while it is impossible to do the same for others? Who gets to decide what can be or cannot be discussed? A society that truly treasures history should at least accord fundamental respect to a plurality of perspectives, and accept that controversies are bound to occur in the search for truth. The journey to understand history will nurture our society to become self-reflective and accustomed to self-critique.

Such were the considerations underpinning The Tangent's decision to embark on this explorative journey. The choice was to focus on the 1950s and 1960s, and the historical actors we wished to pursue were the secondary school students — from both Chinese and English schools — of the period. The collective image of students from Chinese-medium schools has always been prominent in state discourses and very closely associated with the political processes relating to the nation-building of Singapore. But what were their lives as individual students really like? How different were the afterschool activities for students from Chinese and English schools? Different responses to these questions remain at large and unincorporated into mainstream accounts, but apart from regurgitations by others and indulging in our own speculations, we hope to hear the students' own voices.

Since the theme was related to students, we hoped that present students could join us in some experiential learning. As the state realised the value of history, the older generation also became aware of the ignorance of younger citizens. However, beyond the rhetoric of blaming young Singaporeans, we need to look into the causes and endeavour to change the situation. In reality, reflections by young Singaporeans on their lack of knowledge are also expressions of their desire to learn more. And school histories ignite a natural interest, offering them the best point of entry into understanding a past more relevant to them. Limited resources notwithstanding, the Tangent invited seven schools with distinctive traditions to join us on our journey. Nur Nasuha, a Malay student participant from Xinmin Secondary School recounted how she and her friends had initially faced great difficulties in finding research materials readily online. It was only after they conducted oral history interviews with members of the alumni and consulting old yearbooks that they managed to begin reconstructing their school's history. Her conclusion was "…we share the pride in being a part of Xinmin's glorious history, of playing a part to compile this history, and also, the pride of wearing this uniform."

There were also teachers who accompanied students on this journey. We were extremely moved when we saw Mdm Hsin Shu Han who taught at Chung Cheng High School (Main) guiding and mentoring the students with quiet passion. She offered this piece of reflection, "As I walk around the Chung Cheng campus now, I see the school through their eyes. I wonder why our lake has become so small, because the Chung Cheng lake was very big in the past. I also wonder what happened to a particular tree. In the campus, I can feel that I am in constant conversation with past students or events. So after this project, my feelings towards Chung Cheng have changed. I'm not merely a passerby, I feel that I have delved into the school deeply and have become a part of it."

When we encouraged schools to participate, we did not prescribe targeted outcomes or the types of desired responses from teachers and students. The only thing we were sure of was that the route of learning and understanding would lead them to different horizons at the end of their treks. The school is where classes are held, and where students and teachers interact every day, but the banality of habitual actions may cause us to lose our feel and imagination for the place. We thought we knew the definition of school activities, but we actually know very little about the schooling experiences of people who studied in the same campus, or of those who studied elsewhere but had sung the same songs wearing the same uniform. How different were their experiences from ours? Why did such differences occur? What gains and losses were incurred to create these differences?

This book includes a transcript of the public forum at which Mr Han Tan Juan and Professor Koh Tai Ann — who attended Chinese and English schools respectively — shared recollections of their student years. In addition, there are also transcripts of several interviews conducted with people who had received their education in the 1950s and 1960s. Do the two worlds represented by the language divide in their accounts evoke a vague sense of familiarity, or are they totally foreign? Despite the fact that some of these activities are impossible to re-enact due to the passage of time, is it still possible that some of those delineated by the older generation students from Chinese-medium schools remain familiar to students from the Special Assistance Plan (SAP) Schools who may have inherited traditions from their predecessors? If students in the SAP schools cannot recognise the past activities in these accounts, what does their schools' tradition and historical development mean to them?

At the same time, Professor Koh Tai Ann who had graduated from Crescent Girls' School spoke about an English world, and time spent on activities such as the inter-house competition during Sports Meets and the services Girl Guides engaged in and etc. All these activities are considered common amongst all schools today, regardless of whether they are traditionally English-medium, neighbourhood schools or SAP schools. Students today participate in these activities and perhaps even harness the opportunities to incorporate creativity, but do they realise that there is a history that can be traced? Over several decades of changes to the national education system and a strengthening of citizen consciousness, the two worlds that had existed in the generation of Mr Han Tan Juan and Professor Koh Tai Ann have now merged to become one. Did one of them disappear in the reformative process? Have we paid attention to it slipping away? What does it mean with the disappearance of one of these worlds?

The second section of the book comprised oral history interviews. Several interviewed subjects touched on how the colonial government's decision to enlist youths for military training brought about the May 13 Incident which saw a violent clash between petitioning students and the riot police. When we conducted our interviews and organised the exhibition, we did not have many references at hand, for works such as *The May 13 Generation: The Chinese Middle School Student Movement and Singapore Politics in the 1950s* edited by Tan Jing Quee, Tan Kok Chiang and Hong Lysa had not been published. On the other hand, because our focus was on students' after-school activities in general, we did not devote special attention to researching the May 13 Incident systematically. What we did include in our exhibition about the Incident was a set of photographs depicting the scenes of violence that circulated after the shocking event. Every photo had a caption at the bottom of the picture. Who produced these series of photographs and distributed them amongst the students? How many sets were printed and disseminated? These are still unanswered questions. However, among the transcripts of the interviews, we have first-hand accounts from Mr Chen Mong Tse and Mdm Chai Chu Chun who remembered how students lined up to join the demonstrations and how they escaped after that. Mr Lee Leong Seng did not participate in the petition directly, but was one of the students attending the Combined Chinese Schools' Sports Meet at Jalan Besar and narrated how students at the stadium received news about "students getting beaten up by the police." Mr Lim Chin Joo was also not a participant, but the Incident gave him a "tremendous jolt."

Mr Tan Kok Chiang was then still a student at the Raffles Institution, and he observed how differently students from English-medium schools reacted compared to those from Chinese-medium schools, "... I wanted to organise a school forum to discuss matters regarding middle school students in the Chinese schools. However, they were completely uninterested in these matters. Hence, there was no support." Tan Kok Chiang did not participate in the petition drive, but his younger brother who attended Catholic High School was expelled after the event and Tan subsequently joined the occupation movement at the Chinese High School. It was the same event, but individuals faced different realities, took up distinct positions, responded differently and bore varied consequences, some of which possibly changed their lives.

Although the theme of the exhibition was on after-school activities, it was the participants who are truly the focus of the exhibition and this book. When interpreting the exhibition endeavor, Associate Professor Huang Jianli from the National University of Singapore was more interested in the political dimension. Earlier on, *The Straits Times* demonstrated a similar orientation when "student activities" was cast as "student activism" in its reports. The truth is, The Tangent never set out to organise an exhibition featuring only student political activities. We are aware that student activism was an important aspect of the after-school activities in which students from Chinese schools were engaged. However, we wanted to know why those student activists participated, how they organised themselves and others, as well as hoped to understand how they made their choices. At the same time, we also sought to understand why other students did not fall into the same ranks, that is, for those who did not belong to the activist group at the heart of the movement, what were their school lives like? We had a yearning for the ordinary as much as for the extraordinary. We wanted to hear the voices of the student leaders, but were also curious about the thoughts of the "student masses."

In the current official discourse, the generalised term "*huaxiaosheng*" (i.e. Chinese-medium school students) effaces all the aforementioned types of students who attended Chinese schools. It even became a label that carries a historical burden of negative connotations. Through the oral history interviews, we present the thoughts, experiences and perspectives of each historical subject. Mr Lim Chin Joo, Mr Tan Kok Chiang, Mr Chen Mong Tse and Mdm Chai Chu Chun were all direct participants of the student movement, but they each had their own unique stories. Mdm Tan Teck Keng and Mr Lee Leong Seng were both members of the public who responded to our appeal for artefacts in *Lianhe Zaobao* and later shared their past experiences in great details. Mdm Tan did not receive formal education, but she shed light on a particular form of social engagement middle school students were then involved in — her late husband taught literacy classes ran by the Singapore Itinerant Hawkers and Stall Holders Association while he was still studying at Chung Cheng High School. Mr Lee chose to be an onlooker in those turbulent times as his family was poor, and it is likely that he was not part of the minority. Though born slightly later than the previous interviewees, Mr Chua Hiang Yong provided us with an interesting account of how he and his friends shared a love for painting and initiated an art exhibition in school. They all made different choices, or were compelled to choose their paths, but from the vicissitudes of these disadvantaged *huaxiaosheng*, we witness how they were swept away by strong currents of the times which left a common imprint in their psyches.

Amongst the student endeavours in the 1950s and 1960s, the Singapore Chinese Middle School Students' Union (SCMSSU) established in 1955 had a short shelf life. Historians have yet to assess its influence on nation-building efforts of our island-state. Mr Lim Chin Joo has penned a detailed account containing significant insights on the genesis, organisation, development and eventual dissolution of the Union. With his permission, we have included it in this book. Mr Tan Kok Chiang's interview was originally conducted for the oral history project on Nanyang University (Nantah) convened by the Centre for Chinese Language and Culture, Nanyang Technological University. Associate Professor Lee Guan Kin, the Centre Director, has kindly loaned us the section in which Mr Tan spoke about his middle school life. It has certainly allowed *Education-at-Large* to feature the rare experience and standpoint of a student who transferred from an English-medium to a Chinese-medium school.

As our manpower was really stretched, we could only conduct limited interviews. We also realised that our interviews included only students from Chinese schools. Is it a stereotypical construction that students studying in English schools were apathetic about current affairs and politics? What did they do after school? These were some of our guiding questions for our exhibition and we started by inviting Professor Koh Tai Ann to give a talk at the first forum we organised. Apart from that, we also went through some yearbooks and alumni magazines of English-medium schools, as well as tried to contact some former students. Dr. Lim Hock Siew spoke lightly of his times in secondary school, he said the focus then was on academic studies and he became politically active only after he went to university. Nonetheless, one of the weaknesses of our exhibition was indeed the inadequate treatment of the English-educated students.

The wait must be a long one for readers who have been looking forward to reading our collated materials and it is indeed regrettable that The Tangent could only publish this book half a decade after the exhibition. However, the local scene of rejuvenating historical awareness has been diverse and vibrant over the past five years. For instance, at the end of 2008, more than 20 Chinese school alumni organisations collaborated to put up the "Joint Exhibition on the History of Chinese Schools." There was also "SCENES: The Exhibition" which reviewed the developmental history of Singapore Chinese language theatre at the *Huayi 2010 Festival*. The schools' drama societies were at that time the mainstay of theatrical activities in our island-state. *The May 13 Generation*, mentioned earlier, attracted such a huge turnout at its launch that there was not a single empty seat. Towards the end of last year, when we started proofreading for *Education at Large: Student Life and Activities in Singapore 1945–1965*, the Kangle Music Society, started in 1954 by several high school students who attended Chinese middle schools, published *The Footsteps of History* and contributed to the accretion of historical materials for posterity. All these efforts to explore the history of our island-state have not only enriched us, but also have the effect of urging us to get our act together and share the materials related to the 2007 exhibition.

As I would think, to juxtapose these fragments of the 1950s and 1960s is not a mere process of approaching the original contours of history. Looking at these middle school students who had then pledged their youth to their motherland, I see the lushest, most magnificent and yet irrecoverable journey of our island-state. In spite of the dire material conditions, the deficient systems and the chaos in the society, the idealism and toil of an entire generation shine through collective labour. Associate Professor Kwok Kian Woon from the Division of Sociology at Nanyang Technological University made a poignant point when he attended the forum organised for the opening of the "Education at Large" exhibition in November 2007, "What are we missing if there is no idealism in our society? What is the cost to a society if there is no idealism? Idealism is an important topic to us, and can actually be a very practical issue, because if we cannot imagine a different future, how can we move towards a better future? To be able to imagine a different future, a different reality, that is the essence of being idealistic. And you don't just imagine — you try to work towards that reality. …1945 to 1965 is a very special period in the history of Singapore. Many young people then had no choice but to imagine a different future." In the course of designing the different sections of the exhibition, the Tangent discovered that regardless of whether it was during the Anti-Yellow Culture Campaign, Chinese students learning Malay voluntarily, or what has been depicted in those photographs of the May 13 Incident, there was a palpable sense of imagination and anticipation about the future underpinning those energies. And for this sense of imagination and anticipation, these students contributed the most glorious years of their youth.

The Tangent hopes to record such idealism in the island-state, for we need to understand it, come to terms with it and always remember it.

A note on names, titles and terms:

We have tried our best to identify a suitable English version of names, titles and terms. Those that have eluded our efforts are rendered in hanyu pinyin in the book.

Exhibition Photographs

↑ The memory lane began here.

Exhibition board on student activities, featuring "formal" school extra-curricular activities.

↑ Collecting comic illustrations from magazines and newspapers — another activity students engaged in.

← Memories for the future — thoughts on the exhibition.

↑ Listening to stories from students of yesteryear.

↑ Loan of trophy from a member of the public.

→ Blackboard, white chalk, wooden tables and chairs, all presented as historical objects.

Exhibition Photographs

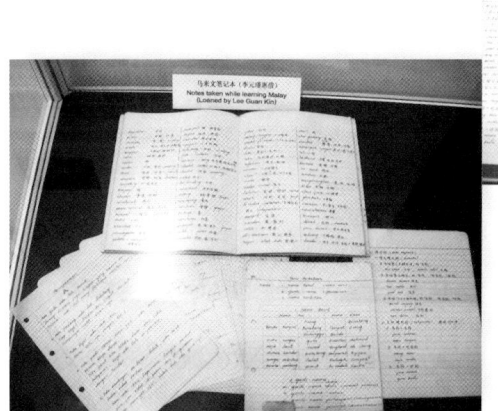

← Textbooks and exercise books that aided the learning of Malay language still kept intact today by former Chinese school students.

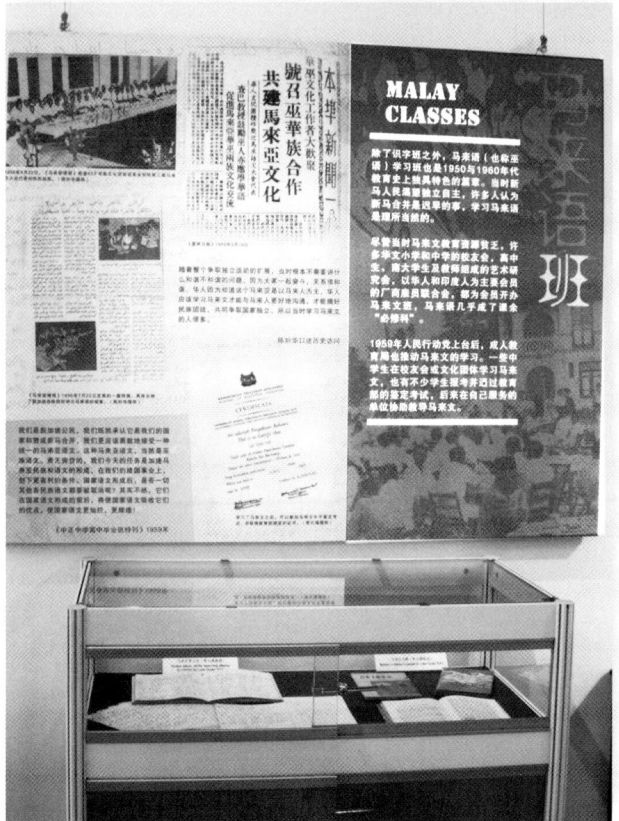

← In anticipation of the new nation in the 1950s, students took the initiative to organise classes hoping to acquaint themselves with Malay language and culture.

↑ In an era when it was materially so much less endowed than the present, the hunger to learn was strong and learning went beyond the classroom.

↓ The greatest commonality between students of Chinese and English-medium schools was the active participation in sports. Their strengths, however, laid in different fields.

Exhibition Photographs **xxiii**

↑ For some people, the exhibition enabled them to revisit the past.

← Former President of the SCMSSU, Soon Loh Boon, came to visit the exhibition.

Current students examining the past. →

Exhibition Area Showcasing the Re-creation of the Past by Participating Schools

Teachers and students from seven schools with long historical traditions participated in the exhibition. The Tangent organised a talk on data collection and research, encouraging students to dig into the history of their schools and gain a better understanding of the past. Students used films and other media to present their interpretations.

Exhibition Photographs

↓ A short film produced by local film director, Tan Pin Pin, was screened at the exhibition venue.

Media Coverage and Responses of Some Exhibition Visitors

The Straits Times – Home, Sep 22, 2006 (Friday)

Group to hold exhibition on student activism next year

By KEITH LIN

A GROUP of young Singaporeans is planning to hold an exhibition next year focusing on student activism of the 1950s and 1960s.

The members of bilingual civil society group The Tangent, which holds regular academic forums, wants to showcase artefacts and texts from a diverse range of student activities during that period.

The six-week exhibition next November will explore alternative voices of history by examining school sports, political and cultural activities, said the group's president, Ms Lee Huay Leng, at a press conference yesterday.

"What we're looking to do through this exhibition is to present different facets of history during that period, instead of what textbooks and other mainstream sources tell us," said Ms Lee, who is local news editor of Chinese daily Lianhe Zaobao.

To facilitate the research, the group is appealing to institutions and the public to contribute relevant objects from the era.

These can include print artefacts, such as school periodicals, photographs, cartoons and diaries, as well as non-print elements like badges, medals and uniforms.

Rare print artefacts will be donated to the National Library at the end of the exhibition, which is estimated to cost $10,000. Research findings from the project will also be published in the group's biannual bilingual journal, Tangent.

The group also hopes to get secondary schools involved and has approached Hwa Chong Institution and Nanyang Girls' High School to engage their students as project researchers.

A forum to discuss the period's history will be held concurrently with the exhibition.

klin@sph.com.sg

Those keen to donate artefacts can do so until December. They can e-mail the group at tangent.the@gmail.com or call 9246-6400.

Lianhe Zaobao article title: The Tangent seeks artefacts reflecting student life in the 1950s and 1960s.

Remembering the extra-curricular activities — Xinmin Secondary School alumni members recall the past.

"Education-at-Large" exhibition fills gap in history.

Chung Cheng High School (Main) takes over the "Education-at-Large" exhibition.

Historical Photographs

↑ Classroom scenario in Chung Cheng High School (Courtesy of Chua Chu Chun).

↑ Choir of literacy class (Courtesy of Tan Teck Keng).

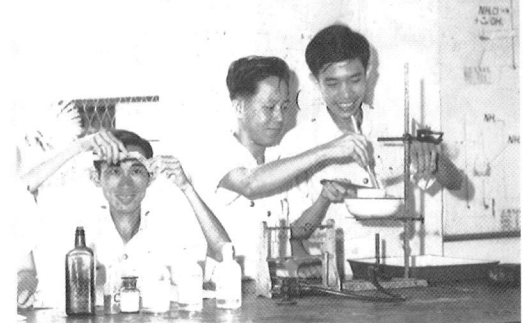

← Lesson in the Laboratory (Courtesy of Tan Teck Keng).

↓ Students in the literacy class photographed in front of the Itinerant Hawkers and Stall Holders Association. (Courtesy of Tan Teck Keng).

Extra-curricular Activities

→ On the road — *Xiao Xiansheng* organised an outing for students of their literacy classes. (Courtesy of Tan Teck Keng).

← Students then like to go on tours together and often go to different parts of Malaya. This photograph was taken in June 1955 on a coach trip made by Chung Cheng High School students graduating from senior middle school. (Courtesy of Chai Chu Chun).

→ Chung Cheng High School was one of the most active schools putting up theatrical performances in the 1950s. In 1953, the school enacted "Our Beautiful Motherland" for its graduation performance and also raised funds through it for the building of Nanyang University. (Courtesy of Chai Chu Chun).

← Male and female students having fun on the waters. (Courtesy of Wu Zhen).

Historical Photographs xxxi

↑ An exchange with a school in Malaya. Students of Senior Middle Class 3B from Chung Cheng High School, posing before the Chinese Hall in Ipoh, Perak in June 1955. (Courtesy of Chai Chu Chun).

↓ Nanyang University was an institution middle school students eagerly looked forward to entering. (Courtesy of Tan Teck Keng).

The May 13 Incident*

After the May 13 Incident, a series of photographs with emotional captions was circulated. Adopting the mode of first person narration, they revealed strong sentiments against the violence of the police. It is believed that quite a number of students came to have this collection of photographs.

↑ At Fort Canning Hill during the May 13 event, the police said we were demonstrating, protesting!

→ Unarmed, we were helplessly beaten like this between the metal fences and the drain!

← The police officer said, "Children, get ready for it!"

→ There's no need to fear! We are not the ones who committed a crime!

---

* The photographs on pages xxxii to xxxiii came with original captions in Chinese.

← Police officers awaiting the brutal orders of their superiors.

→ Fellow students! Run to Nan Chiau Girls' High and we will reassemble there!

← Such was how violence was inflicted on us!

→ Look! This was only the beginning of the violence!

The Singapore Chinese Middle School Student Union

→ The White Paper on dissolving the Singapore Chinese Middle Schools Students' Union

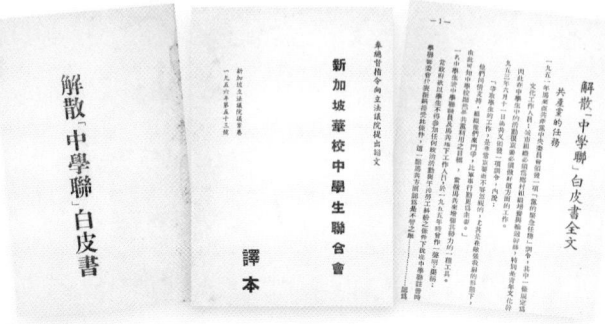

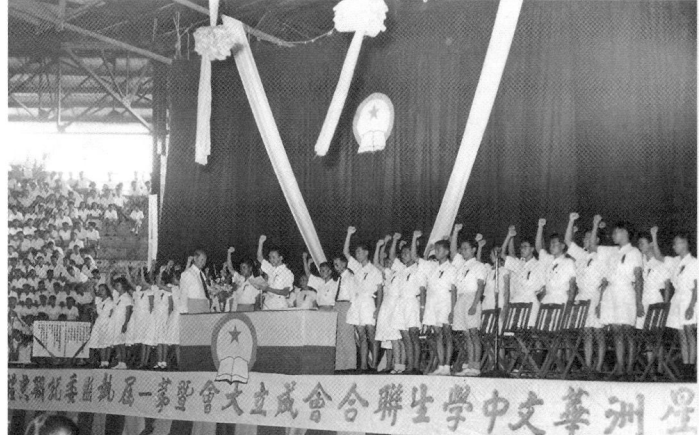

← The SCMSSU was established on 30 May 1955 at the Happy World Stadium, the attendees included more than 10 000 members, teachers, parents, members of public and representatives from other student organisations. (Courtesy of Lim Chin Joo).

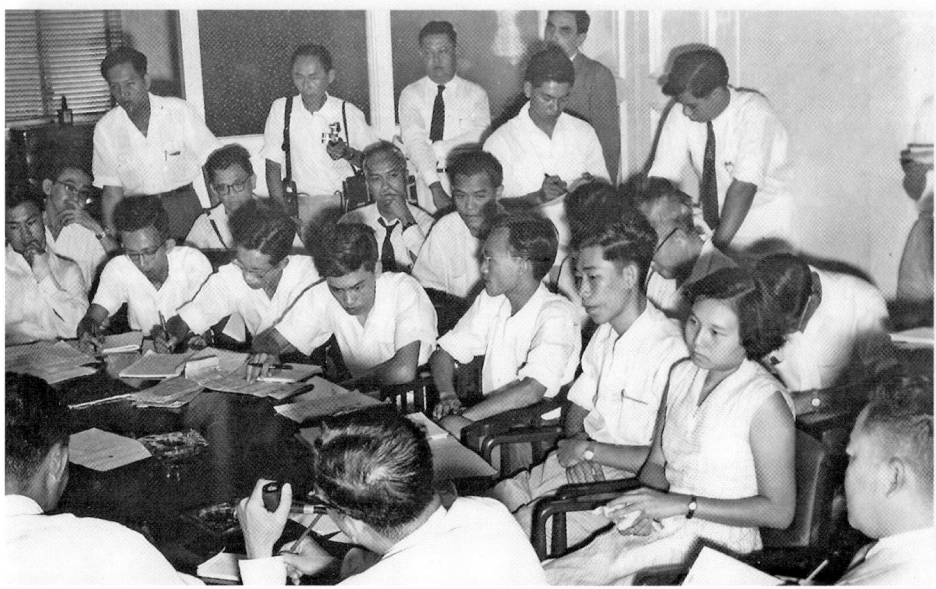

↑ After the government declared the dissolution of the SCMSSU in 1956, students formed a "Anti-Persecution Delegation". On 20 October, the group went to the Chief Minister's office to negotiate with the government. The photograph shows Lim Yew Hock with a pipe, his back facing the camera. Seated from right: Education Minister Chew Swee Kee, student representatives Cai Shijun, Wu Youfa, Wang Hequn, Lim Chin Joo, Chen Zaicong and Li Weizhen (Courtesy of Lim Chin Joo).

Part I
Forum Documentation

A Bilingual Forum[1]
Inhabiting Two Different Worlds
Dialogue Between Han Tan Juan and Koh Tai Ann

Speakers:

Han Tan Juan (Retired journalist and cultural researcher)

Koh Tai Ann (Professor, English Department, Nanyang Technological University)

Chairperson:

Ong Chang Woei (Assistant Professor, Chinese Department, National University of Singapore)

Transcribed by Gan Woan Wen

Translated by Tan Hui Yi and Swee Hui Weng

Ong: Thank you for attending today's talk on student activities during the 1940s to the 1960s. In fact, there are many aspects of students' activities and students lives that we can probe. Doing so not only serves to deepen the collective memory of all Singaporeans, it is also an inseparable part of Singapore's history. Even though it may be difficult for the members of The Tangent to converge on most of the relevant issues, we do agree on one fundamental point: The remembrance and depiction of history should be multi-faceted, and we should look at history from different perspectives. Hence, this is what we at The Tangent have been doing over the past few years. As for today, we have invited two speakers who have lived through this period of time. We hope that the whole process of working together with schools will allow students today to understand more of their school's history.

---

[1] Speakers Koh Tai Ann spoke predominantly English and Han Tan Juan spoke predominantly Mandarin for the entire forum. Chairperson Ong Chang Woei moderated the session mainly in Mandarin. Members of audience spoke in English or Mandarin during the Question and Answer session.

They will also better understand what their seniors had gone through in the past. In addition, either at the end of this year or beginning of next year, we will gather all our research efforts and hold an exhibition on "Student Activities from 1945 to 1965". We hope to gain a more comprehensive and deeper understanding of society and student life during that period. Well, our first speaker today is Mr. Han, and I believe no introduction is needed. He is a famous local researcher on literary history and a former media professional whom everyone is familiar with. Now to get the ball rolling, Mr. Han please.

Han: Thank you, Dr. Ong, for the introduction. A very good afternoon to seniors, teachers, friends and students present. I sincerely hope this will not become a one-man show, Professor Koh will be with us shortly and her presentation should be the main attraction of the day. As for me, I'll help everyone get warmed up first. Firstly, I'll like to engage in some idle chat. The place where I grew up is the area where the National Library is situated now. To put it bluntly, I was the local bully. My house was at Seah Street, and I lived there for several decades. Furthermore, my old home was situated below this new National Library building, there's a street called Carver Street and I lived at 23 Carver Street. I seriously suspect that the exact place where I'm sitting was the place I slept years ago. I feel that there's some sort of confusion between time and space. To sum it up, I am very familiar with this place.

My primary school was Catholic High School, and it was situated just behind my old home. Each time I went to school, I entered through the front gate, this was during the time when we used the old building. After they built a new multi-storey building opposite, which was the new building where Lee Hsien Loong and Lee Hsien Yang studied, I started to enter by the back gate. The walking distance by going through the back gate was much shorter; this is something every student of Catholic High knew. And after six years, I completed my primary school education at Catholic High, and continued another six years of secondary school education at Chung Cheng. Why didn't I continue my studies at Catholic High? The reason was very simple: My English standard was atrocious, I failed. Hence, for today's recollection of my past, I will focus mainly on my secondary school life, and talk a little about my primary school experience. I pondered very long on whether I should talk about my primary school experience, and deemed it necessary to touch on it slightly.

For now, I shall summarise my whole life in a few sentences: Basically, my cohort and I were born in the 1940s; of course, there were a few people who were born in 1938 or 1939. But on the whole, we were born in the 40s, grew up in the 50s, fought vigorously during the 60s, became disillusioned during the 70s, reflected during the 80s and set off again during the 90s. I was born in 1942, the year in which Singapore surrendered to the Japanese. Therefore, I'm 65 this year. When I studied at Catholic High, I was six years old. How can a six year old start primary school education? There weren't many kindergartens around during that time, five and six year olds didn't have the opportunity to attend pre-school education. Kindergartens were rare and only the very rich could afford to send their children to kindergarten. Hence, the minimum age for entry to Catholic High was six years old. However, before I was allowed into the school, we had to answer the principal's queries. When my father brought me to Catholic High for registration, the principal, Mr. Yao Guohua posed a question to my father in Teochew. I was five or six years old then and vaguely remembered their conversation. The principal asked, "Does your son know how to use the toilet on his own?" My father replied, "Yes, he knew how to go to the toilet by himself since last year or the year before, a long time ago." Thereafter, I was allowed to enroll in Catholic High.

There are many stories regarding Catholic High which I can't talk about today as I am focusing on my secondary school experience. However, there is one story that needs to be mentioned, and that is regarding Queen Street where Catholic High was situated. During 1946, 1947 and 1948, that place had a long forgotten name called "*Little Yan'an*". Do you know what is "*Little Yan'an*"? It was a little city in Northern Shanxi where China's Communist Party located their headquarters. Why did our own Queen Street become known as "*Little Yan An*"? This was because the Malayan Communist Party (MCP) had their headquarters situated at that street. Chin Peng[2] once frequented that area to hold meetings. Several important fringe organisations associated with the Malayan Communist Party were also located at that street; there was the New Democratic Youth Party, the Malayan Women Federation and the New Democratic Press. Thus, there were many communists frequenting the street. Other than the communists, there was another group of people, the Catholics. The church of Saints Peter and Paul was situated there, and it was Catholic High's church. Further down was Saint Joseph's Catholic Church. The street was filled with two groups of people, one was the atheists, and the other was the believers. When I was studying in Primary One, I had to cross a narrow stretch of road to enter the school. That road still exists today; beside it was my classroom on the ground level. Primary One students were allocated ground level classrooms whereas Primary Two and Three students had the upper storeys. In my classroom, I often heard singing coming from the opposite building. It was a two-storey building and was where the Communist Party's headquarters was located. A huge signboard hung from the building — The Malayan Communist Party;

---

[2]Chin Peng was the former Secretary-General of the Malayan Communist Party.

another signboard read: The Ex-Service Comrades Association of the Malayan People's Anti-Japanese Army. The signboard was huge and hung from the building. When I was in primary school, I often heard singing coming from the headquarters, hence, I had the privilege of listening to communist songs when I was six years old. You cannot possibly miss the singing; you are sitting in the classroom and the singing just enters your ears. Unless you close all the windows, but we had no air conditioning at that time so we were unable to do so. This was the first unique experience I had in Catholic High that I wanted to share with everyone.

After that, there was another unforgettable incident which happened whilst I was studying at Catholic High. It was 1950; the Malayan Communist Party had gone hiding in the forests and began to use guerilla tactics. In Singapore, the communists committed terrorist acts in the city. Nowadays, people tend to think that Osama Bin Laden started the trend of terrorist attacks in cities. How wrong they are! In 1948 and 1949, Singapore was already under attack from such terrorist activities; there were car bombings, grenade attacks and assassinations of British personnel. When the communists resisted British rule, the Malayan Communist Party took to the forests, but they still had underground organisations operating in Singapore. What did these organisations do? They had a saying: Use Red Terror against White Terror. White Terror was terror caused by the British. When the Emergency was declared in June 1948, control was very strict. The Communist Party was closed, all progressive associations were closed and many people were thrown into jail. But the British behaved very differently from other Western colonial powers. The British were slightly more civilised, they did not execute these people; they also tried not to keep them in jail for too long as it was a waste of resources. What they did was to expel them from the country. Whenever possible, people who were anti-British were expelled; those who were locally born in Singapore and Malaya and cannot be expelled to China were locked up. This was basically what the whole situation was like at that time. When I was studying in primary school, it was a time when MCP used Red Terror against White Terror. An unfortunate incident happened right in my school, and it happened to one of our Physical Education teachers — Mr. Xu Zude. Mr. Xu was teaching students basketball when a man suddenly ran in and asked, "Are you Xu Zude?" After finishing his question, the assailant who was armed with a bottle of acid splashed it at Mr. Xu's face. Mr. Xu's face was completely ruined. "Arggggghhhh....", his scream was terrifying. Among the people who witnessed the crime was a student sprinter, who, putting his sprinting skills to good use, managed to catch the assailant. After that incident, the student's life was threatened by the MCP. The student dared not continue his studies and instead went on to become a plain-clothed police officer, so that he could carry a pistol for self-defence at all times. As for Mr. Xu, he later became the principal of Saint

Teresa's High School. After the attack, Mr. Xu was sent to Singapore General Hospital and they grafted skin from his thighs and legs to replace skin on his disfigured face. However, after the surgery his face was not able to heal completely. He looked liked the protagonist of the movie *Ye Ban Ge Sheng* (Song at Midnight) — Song Danping. This was my memory of a terrorist attack in the city, a scene from my primary school. I shall skip the rest of the details.

I shall talk a little about our primary school life, which I believe many of you will find incredible. At that time, my family was very poor, and most people in my school were from poor families. The rich and wealthy were rare during those days, most people were destitute. However, when a society is comprised mainly of poor people and everyone is equally poor, you won't mind being poor. On the other hand, if the majority of society is wealthy, you won't feel good if you're poor. Take for instance, every household has at least a TV, a computer, and when you don't have either of those, you will feel inferior. However, during those days it was alright to be poor, everyone was poor! You're poor, I'm poor, no one would look down on you. My whole class was poor. Well, poor kids have their own unique way of having fun. After school, we would go to Fort Canning Hill; I have to admit, I have a soft spot for Fort Canning Hill and the National Museum. What did we do there? We went there to catch black spiders, black fighting spiders. If anyone is interested, I'll talk about it some other day, it'll be very interesting. However, I'll have to skip it for today.

Now, I want to share with everyone another story. During those days, we were too poor to buy toys, Mother Nature provided us with a great variety of toys which didn't cost anything. Fort Canning Hill was like a friendly and approachable friend, it didn't matter if you were rich or poor, Fort Canning welcomed everyone to come and play. However, it's very different today; you're required to pay everywhere you go. It was alright to be poor then. Another thing was, we had no pocket money, our parents seldom gave us pocket money. Do you know how much pocket money I was given for each day at school? Ten cents. What could you buy with ten cents? One plate of mee siam cost fifteen cents, but I had only ten cents, I couldn't even afford a plate of mee siam. A drink cost five cents, a cup of coffee or tea costs five cents. Do you know to what extremes poor kids will go in order to increase their income? It sure was incredible. Does everyone know that the old Saint Nicholas school compound had a long corridor which is now the headquarters of SMRT? There was a huge drain which stretched in all directions underground, and reached all the way to Queen Street. The drain extended in all directions, and had very little water in it. Underneath the ground, there was a little lamp which workers would use when they entered. There were a lot of cockroaches running around. We had found an entrance to the underground drain and it had a narrow ladder for workers to use. We used the ladder and entered the underground drain, which was why I am particularly familiar with the underground there. Where was the entrance into the drain? It was at the front of the Raffles Hotel, the side facing Bras Basah Road had an entrance, and we entered the drain from there, once we got in, we used torch lights to shine at the floor. If we saw light reflected, it meant that there was a coin lying around. Usually, there were five cents, ten cents, and when we were lucky, we could even find twenty cents. We picked up money in such a manner. Usually, when people dropped their coins into the drain, they didn't bother to pick it up, how were they going to enter? Five cents, ten cents, twenty cents, if such coins fell through then so be it. At that time, the metal drain covers had numerous holes and the holes were big enough for fifty-cent coins to fall in. We were particularly excited when we found fifty-cent coins, finding one dollar was impossible as notes wouldn't be dropped. We were also very united then, and we practised a form of "communism". What you picked didn't belong to you, it belonged to everyone. At that time, we went into the drain in groups of five or six. Sometimes, when you were unable to find a single cent, you still got earnings as we would share the spoils. What did we do with the extra money? Well, for example, if today we pick up a dollar plus, we would go catch a movie, after the movie we would have *kway teow*, and if there was still some money left, we would use it to play games, such happy times were those. Hence, we picked money frequently and always had an extra 50 cents, one dollar or even two dollars in total. This was pretty good considering the fact that our pocket money was a measly ten cents. Sometimes, we saved the money we picked and went to Emily Hill for a swim on Sundays. To enter the pool we needed to pay 20 cents. I shall tell a little story regarding this, there was a rule on Sundays for swimming at Emily Hill. I think everyone knows about Emily Hill, there was a swimming pool on top of the hill, I don't know if it's still there. They had a really strange rule, for the morning session on Sundays, it was only restricted to female swimmers. Why was there such a restriction? This was because many guys went there to cause trouble and harass the girls. Hence, they had this rule: a female swimmer was allowed to bring in a male partner, if a male swimmer had no female partner, he would not be allowed into the premises. Therefore, female swimmers usually brought their fathers, husbands, boyfriends, brothers to the pool, and they would not dare to make a nuisance of themselves, would they? What about us, Catholic High students? When were there female students in Catholic High? What did we do if we wanted to enter the pool? We didn't have female students to bring us in. So, we had to be thick-skinned, when we saw a large group of female swimmers, we would approach them and ask in Cantonese, "Dear sister, can you bring me in?" We begged the girls for help. Seeing that we couldn't possibly create much trouble as we were all short and small in statue, maybe 10, 11, or 12 years of age, they would usually reply, "Ok, come with me." After one was settled, we would find another girl. Sometimes, when a large group of eight to seven of us went into the pool, we may have one or two people who couldn't find anyone to take them in. In the end, they would have to watch us from outside. While we swam inside, they could only watch from the outside, and we felt sorry for them. So come next week, they would get priority in looking for girls, it was very fair. This was one of the interesting snippets of my primary school life.

Whilst studying in Catholic High School, my English was very bad, how many marks did I get? 60 marks was the passing mark then and I could barely reach 50. Why was my English bad? Let me tell everyone a little joke first. At that time, we didn't speak English at home, nor was English widely used in society. Nowadays speaking English is very common but it wasn't so at that time. Therefore, we had a hard time learning English. Furthermore, I went to Hainan Island for two years and when I returned I had forgotten my ABCs, completely forgotten. There was once when our teacher taught us "January, February, March April……" The next day he taught us names of fruits, "This is an apple", "This is an orange, banana, papaya……" One of my classmates got these two mixed up, and when the teacher asked him for name of the month, he replied, "January, February, March, Apple, Orange, Banana." With English standards like this, I couldn't continue my studies at Catholic High and had to transfer out. Catholic High administrators wrote a recommendation letter to Chung Cheng so that I could continue my studies. At that time, the principal of Chung Cheng was Mr. Chuang Chu Lin who later became the president of Nanyang University (Nantah). Mr. Chuang Chu Lin wanted a school population of ten thousand students, at that time, Chung Cheng's Main and Branch schools had seven or eight thousand students already, he wasn't satisfied with that, he wanted to reach ten thousand. It was under such circumstances that I was transferred to Chung Cheng. In 1956, I began my school life in Chung Cheng; it has been 51 years since. Whilst I was studying in Chung Cheng, it was also a time of great social upheaval in Singapore history, it was the year 1956. Allow me to backtrack slightly, as I'm talking about my own life experiences a while ago, allow me to start from 1954. It was something related to student activism in the 1950s. It's like this, in 1954, when I was a Catholic High Primary 5 student, the May 13 incident happened. One thousand students gathered at Fort Canning Hill to appeal against conscription. At that time, we were under British rule, getting conscripted means fighting against the enemy of the British. Who were the British's enemy? The MCP of course. Asians fighting Asians, many people were thus unwilling to join the British Army. Therefore, many gathered on 13 May 1954 to petition against conscription. It was illegal to petition then. Why so? When the Emergency was declared, an outdoor gathering of five or more people was considered illegal.

Hence, a petition gathering of a thousand people was certainly against the law. Police broke up the crowds using force, which resulted in violent confrontations. Scores of people were caught and more than 10 were tried in court. The defence lawyer for the students was none other then Mr. Lee Kuan Yew.

13 May 1954 was Mr. Lee Kuan Yew's first contact with Chinese-educated students. That same year in November, the People's Action Party was set up. In the following year, April 1955, Singapore held its first Legislative Assembly Elections under the Rendel Constitution. The PAP entered the elections for the first time and secured three seats. One of the three seats was won by Lim Chin Siong in Bukit Timah; another was won by Goh Chew Chua in an electorate consisting of Punggol and Tampines; the last seat was won by Lee Kuan Yew in Tanjong Pagar. During that election, Devan Nair contested in the Farrer Park electorate and lost. At that time, one PAP member contested as an independent, and that was Ahmad Ibrahim. After winning the election, he declared himself a PAP member. Therefore, the PAP was able to secure four seats in the Legislative Assembly. I will just briefly touch on this part of the story. In 1955, Singapore Labour Front came to power with David Marshall as Chief Minister. Just two months after they came to power, the Hock Lee labour strike occurred. The labour strike resulted in a clash between civilians and police. What has the labour strike got to do with students? At the time of the strike, students got together to support and encourage the workers. A lorry would arrive every afternoon, picking up students and ferrying them to the place of the strike. Where was the strike taking place? It was somewhere near present-day Tai Feng biscuit factory at Alexandra. What did the students gather there for? They spoke to the workers, sang for them and performed group dances for them. At that time, a popular song among the students was *The Student Contingent is Invincible*, the gist of the lyrics goes like this:

> The contingent of students is Invincible
> Victorious in every battle, we're unstoppable
> The strength of our unity is steel-like
> At the sight of us, enemies become terrorised…

Another popular song was *We are the Disciples of Lu Xun*. It was afterwards that I found out about a New China song titled *We are the Democratic Youth*, we had used the song's melody but changed its lyrics. These were the most popular songs of that time. Whenever students gathered, these songs would be sung patriotically. Especially *The Student Contingent is Unbeatable* and *We are the Disciples of Lu Xun*, these two songs are a must-sing and became our association's song or school anthem. This was the situation of student activism in the 1950s and 1960s.

Students gave support to the workers on strike which finally ended in violence. When the unrest ceased, the Labour Front government yielded to the workers and the success of the workers added steam to future student and labour activism. In 1956, an island-wide call for independence took place, it was the Merdeka Movement. On 18 March 1956, a 50,000 strong rally for independence was held at the old Kallang airport, more than 10,000 students participated. This was what we lived through, in a time of great change; we were deeply entrenched in political activism.

You might ask, with students so deeply involved in political activism, where did they have time to study? Attending meetings daily, participating in marches daily, how did they find time to study? Let me tell everyone something, back in those days, students had a big bag of tricks when it came to studying. We knew how to get the most out of the shortest time possible; we knew how to make inferences and extrapolate based on a particular case and how to draw out regular patterns. Furthermore, studying in those days was not as stressful compared to these days, we did not have so many standardised examinations. From primary school to senior middle school, we had only one standardised examination, one standardised examination in twelve years of study. Unlike today, students have to tackle numerous standardised examinations. These examinations do not test your ability to study but rather your ability to sit for an exam. We were different, we only had one standardised examination in twelve years, to progress up the different levels wasn't too difficult at all, and we had more free time for extra-curricular activities. Moreover, Humanities was considered more important than Science during those days, and for Humanities subjects, we did not have to attend lessons every day, we could pick up quite a substantial amount of knowledge through self-study. This was an important reason why we could put in more time for extra-curricular activities and student activism.

A series of major events happened in 1956. Mr. David Marshall quitted his post as Chief Minister and Mr. Lim Yew Hock took his place. Mr. Lim Yew Hock behaved submissively to the British, and was ordered to crackdown on anti-colonial activities. The first major crackdown happened in 18 September 1956, many anti-colonialists and student activist leaders were arrested. At that time, there was an association among the Chinese schools in Singapore known as the SCMSSU. The full name was the Singapore Chinese Middle Schools Students' Union. It was established in November 1956. After its establishment, the Union embarked on numerous activities. Within a year, the SCMSSU was dissolved by Mr. Lim Yew Hock on orders from the British colonial government. It was dissolved on 16 September 1956 and the leaders of the union were subsequently arrested. After their arrests, students began to protest intensely. Not long after the SCMSSU was dissolved, students from Chung Cheng and Chinese High gathered in their school grounds on 22 September and took full control of the schools. Why occupy the schools? We implemented internal self-governance, creating a mini government in the school compounds. We had a Provost Unit, a Foreign Affairs Unit, we did not call it "foreign affairs" at that time, it was known as the Reception Unit. Students lived in school classrooms. The situation at that time was like this, thousands of Chinese-educated students assembled at the two schools, all Chinese schools actively participated, except two. They were the most renowned, most well-behaved and most obedient schools — Catholic High and Saint Nicholas. Generally, students from these two schools did not participate. They were well-behaved, did not participate, did not dare to rebel and did not want to rebel. On the other hand, other Chinese-educated students gathered at Chung Cheng and Chinese High. Those who gathered at Chung Cheng were mainly students from Chung Cheng and students from the Singapore Chinese Girls' School and Yock Eng. As for Nan Chiau Girls' School, Nan Hwa Girls' School and Nanyang Girls' School, they gathered at Chinese High. The total number of students gathered at both schools numbered over four thousand.

The Singapore society was very different then. Hawkers and workers were sympathetic towards the students and supported them. Every morning, there would be truck-loads of fresh fruits and vegetables for the students gathered in those two schools. Bags of rice were transported to the schools, there was plenty of food and we need not worry about meals. In the school grounds, we held meetings every morning after breakfast, after which we got into different groups and classes for studies. Seniors were responsible for teaching juniors, the school operated as per normal. Senior Middle Three students would teach Junior Middle students, we had a 3-3 system at that time, Junior Middle School lasted for three years and Senior Middle School another three years. Senior Middle Three students taught Junior Middle Three Students, Senior Middle Two Students taught Junior Middle Two students, and Senior Middle One Students taught Junior Middle One students. This was known as the peer teaching system and we used this system to conduct lessons as per normal.

In the afternoons, we rehearsed for performances. Let me tell everyone something, in such circumstances, human intelligence and talent flourished. We had to come up with performances every afternoon — dances, skits, poems. What activities did we have at night? We held cultural performances every night. We congregated for over 20 nights and held over 20 performances, and the performances were basically different each night. Wouldn't you be bowled over by the talent of these students? The performances were rather good considering the fact that the students had little time for rehearsals. They rehearsed in the afternoon and performed at night, and the next night would be another different performance. Honestly speaking, I miss those days very much. How I wish I can relive those experiences! Sad to say, I can only relive them in my dreams. Although students were in charge and had autonomy in school, it wasn't total chaos. This was the situation of student activism at that time. Then came 26 October, beyond the school grounds, many workers went on strike. The people were protesting against colonial oppression and strikes were commonplace. The society was in complete chaos. The British colonial government and Mr. Lim Yew Hock's government was determined to use force against students gathered in the schools. In the early morning of 26 October, armed military police were dispatched to Chung Cheng and Chinese High. It is very easy to remember 26 October; there are two important dates to remember for student activism in the 1950s. One is 5.13 and another is 10.26. These two dates are extremely easy to remember, 5 times 2 is 10 and 13 times 2 is 26. 10.26 is two times that of 5.13, what a coincidence this is. I will talk briefly about that morning, has anyone in the audience come into contact with tear gas before? We had numerous encounters with it. People in the 1950s had many chances to come into contact with tear gas, especially the students. On the morning of that fateful day, armed military police surrounded the school compound. We were all gathered in the school field as we knew beforehand that the military police would be coming. The night before, Malaya Broadcasting had broadcasted a government notice, requesting parents to fetch their children back from the schools, if they did not persuade their children to return home, the government would not be responsible for anything that might happen to them. Once the notice was broadcasted, many parents hurried to the schools, hoping to persuade their children. However, some parents got persuaded by their children instead and stayed overnight with their children. These parents also got a taste of tear gas. I shall talk about the situation in Chung Cheng where I personally was at. We were gathered at the school field beside the lake when the Gurkha soldiers arrived in the morning, I could clearly see that they were Gurkhas. Gurkha soldiers are easily recognisable; they are dark-skinned, armed with a Gurkha knife and donned gas masks. Once we saw them, we knew that things were going to get ugly. We were subsequently given warnings in English and Mandarin, that we had a few minutes to leave the school compound, if not, they would take action against us. We were not willing to give in and the Gurkhas used tear gas on us. "Pfffft, pfffft, pffft," one by one, the tear bombs exploded; they were just like Pepsi Cola cans, or pop cans. One by one, they landed on our heads, hit our bodies and began to emit smoke. Goodness! Once you inhaled the gas, your lungs felt like they were on fire, tears and mucus flowed non-stop. The feeling was horrible, your eyes became blood-shot, a burning sensation engulfed them, and you could barely open your eyes. What could be most comforting at such a time? It would be to wash your face. We were all prepared; one of the student leaders knew a way to counter the effects of tear gas, and wanted all of us to prepare a wet towel and put it around our necks. When the tear bombs came, we could use the wet towel to cover our faces, making it more bearable. However, the field was filled with so much tear gas that we really couldn't stand it and jumped into the Chung Cheng Lake. We submerged our heads into the water and said in Cantonese, "*Xu Fok Sai!*" (This feel great) Later on, the military police surrounded the lake. "Get out! Get out! Get out!" they shouted.

Seeing that some of us were still young, the police let us off and gathered us at Kong Hwa which was located behind Chung Cheng. Some of the students climbed out and were promptly given a firm beating with the baton. Whack! Once you got up, you would get a taste of the baton. But it was still alright as they didn't aim for our heads, they hit us on the shoulders and we wouldn't get seriously injured. After a whack, we were dispersed, and martial law was enforced for several days. The PAP condemned the British colonial government for such acts of violence. Mr. Lim Yew Hock's government completely lost the support of the people, the island plunged into turmoil and martial law was implemented. In 1957, the PAP took part in the council elections and emerged victorious. At that time, the PAP already had popular support. In 1959, the PAP took part in the self-governance elections and once again emerged victorious, winning 43 seats out of 51. The reign of the PAP had begun.

What role did students play during this period of time? On the whole, we have much more freedom of speech today. In the past, there were many things I wanted to talk about which I dared not voice out. Today, I have to admit, people from my generation still have a lingering fear, since we were bitten once before, we are still shy today. The reason the PAP was able to come into power in 1959 was — according to my understanding, I do not know if everyone agrees with me — basically due to the support garnered from Chinese-educated students. It couldn't be due to support from English-educated students that the PAP got into power. The first reason is that, English-educated students were far fewer numerically. The second reason is, English-educated students were rather pampered at that time. I agree with this viewpoint. English-educated students at that time were more pampered, favoured, led a life of luxury and privilege, had higher social status and were fewer in number. Why were there fewer English-educated students? Firstly, English-educated students were a select few which the British government wanted to groom into future leaders to serve the British colonial government. Moreover, they had to ensure that English-educated students enjoyed a higher social status. If there were too many English- educated students, it would be difficult for all of them to have high earning jobs. If there were too many of them, some of them were bound to become taxi drivers, hawkers and road sweepers. Right? How could everyone become high ranking officials if there were too many English-educated students? It's practically impossible! Hence, English-educated students were the minority elite, while Chinese-educated students were the impoverished majority. Under such circumstances, who would you depend on for support during elections? The English-educated or the Chinese-educated? Logically speaking and in reality, the Chinese-educated masses helped the PAP come into power, it couldn't be any other way. It is a historical fact. Of course, there were English-educated students who supported the PAP, but they formed the minority.

What was the mindset of Chinese-educated students during those times? I would like to take this opportunity to talk about this. Intellectually, they matured very quickly, but emotionally, they didn't mature till very late. When people get oppressed and exploited, they will mature very rapidly. They want to rid themselves of a position that is oppressed and exploited; they want to find a way out. They become concerned with societal issues, world affairs, collective well-being and the well-being of all Chinese-educated people. As you get immersed in so many external issues, you begin to neglect your personal emotions. By the time Chinese-educated students graduated from senior middle school, some were already around 20 years old. This was due to the Japanese Occupation when people stopped going to school for two to three years. Therefore, many students were already young adults; however, as their emotional side did not mature till very late, couples were rarely seen at that time. We learnt philosophy at a very young age; I think most of you will find it incredible. In my first year at junior middle school, we learnt philosophy as part of our extra-curricular lessons. We learnt about dialectical materialism, quantitative change to qualitative change, law of negation and the law of the unity of opposites. As Secondary One students at the age of 13 to 14, we learnt about the latest developments in global affairs. We learnt about the cause of the Hungarian Incident of 1956. When it came to global affairs, Secondary One and Two students were well versed in it. However, when it came to affairs of the heart, they had no clue what it was about. Students of that time had a unique trait, their minds matured very early on while their emotional side didn't mature till very late. They were concerned with global affairs, with the fate of the people, the fate of the country. Another thing about students then was that they had exceptional organisational skills. This was something Lee Kuan Yew sang praises about in his memoirs; he was in awe of the organisational capability of Chinese-educated students. Holding an assembly in the badminton hall, a 15, 16 year-old teenage girl gave instructions to thousands of students in the hall, everyone in the hall stood up in unison, sang in unison and sat down in unison. A girl barely 16 years of age was able to give instructions to everyone in the hall, and each and every one of them would follow her instructions. There's more, after such an assembly, the hall was left in prime condition, not a piece of litter was to be found. Mr. Lee Kwan Yew was amazed at what he saw; you can read the details in his memoirs. The amount of discipline surpassed that of military standards. The organisational capability and discipline of Chinese-educated students left him in great admiration. As for how he used this to his advantage is another matter, I shall talk about that another time.

Another matter I want to address is: how did students organise themselves during those times? Once the Emergency was instituted, it was very difficult to register as a student organisation. You had to apply for a permit for outdoor gatherings of more than five people. Under such strict control, how did student activism develop? I shall answer it with regard to my personal experience. Firstly, student leaders of that time were adept at finding legal loopholes. This is like burying a seed in ground and covering it with many rocks. The seedling is able to find its way through gaps in the rocks, and finally grows into a big tree which bears plenty of fruit. How does one find gaps in rocks? Firstly, students were very poor at that time and school fees cannot be lowered as the government was not willing to subsidise Chinese schools. Under such circumstances, what could one do if he had no money to continue his studies? Hence, students started a movement to help impoverished students. Therefore, Chung Cheng, Chinese High, Nanyang, Nan Hwa Girls' School — which is today's Nan Hua Secondary School — Nan Chiau Girls' School and Singapore Chinese Girls' School had Financial Assistance Societies. The government couldn't ban Financial Assistance Societies and schools greatly encouraged their establishment. The societies solicited donations via various ways — putting up plays, cultural performances and even screening movies. We already had movies from China screening here in 1956 and 1957. Let me digress a little, in 1955, they showed the first movie from China — *Liang Shanbo Yu Zhu Yingtai (The Butterfly lovers)* at the site of today's Prince Cinema. There was once another cinema in that area and the Cantonese film was showed for 90 consecutive days. Usually, after the first or second screening of a film, the Financial Assistance Societies would rent the second or third screening of old films from the cinemas. What other films did the Financial Assistance Societies Screen? The old version of *Song Hua Jiang Shang (Along the Sungan River)*, *Yi Jiang Chun Shui Xiang Dong Liu (Tears of the Yang Tse)*, *Wuya yu Maque (Crows and Sparrows)* and other old films. For each screening, they could raise one to two thousand, or seven to eight hundred dollars. That was a huge sum, and it was used to pay students' school fees. In addition, the Financial Assistance Societies opened bookstores in school. They sold books which were considered "progressive" at that time, books by Ba Jin, Lu Xun and Bing Xin. Schools also had fund-raising events, through the Financial Assistance Societies which would stage plays. For example, the Chinese High Financial Assistance Society staged *The Tale of Troy* and *The True Story of Ah Q* to raise funds. The Chung Cheng Drama Society staged many plays, like *The Cowherd and the Weaving Maiden* and *Sheng Guan Tu*. And so we have a legal organisation. All students automatically became members of the Student Financial Assistance Societies, and each class had their own Student Financial Assistance Group. There was also a Student Assistance Council and they held Student Assistance Society general meetings every day. Through such channels, the schools virtually had a legal student organisation. This is one example of such student organisations. Another was the Farewell Society. What is the Farewell Society? Chinese schools had a tradition, at the end of each year, when each semester came to a close, a farewell party would be held and students would serve tea to the teachers as a form of respect and gratitude. Later on, performances, singing and dancing were incorporated into the farewell party. However, the dances of that time were very different from today's. Group dancing in the past had zero body contact; instead dancers clapped their hands when dancing. Subsequently, this form of farewell party was considered too simple, and they upgraded it to an evening party instead. This was also legal, how could it be illegal? The government had no reason to oppose it; it's all about showing respect to teachers! And so, how did this farewell party develop from its humble beginnings? Preparations for the year end party began in January, at the start of each semester. The school had a head office for the Farewell Society and each class had a preparation group, another student organisation was thus born. In 1953, 1954, when the Farewell Societies were at their peak, the Singapore Cultural Studies Society was established. Student activism at that time used such legal channels to form numerous student organisations. All students were thus part of some organisation during that time.

Well, my time is about up now. I would like to summarise my talk into a few points regarding the outlook of Chinese-educated students and teachers at that time. Firstly, Chinese-educated students in the 1950s and 1960s, particularly middle school students, were heavily influenced by China. They listened to Chinese songs, watched Chinese films and read Chinese books. The New China of 1956 was under communist rule, and I personally believe that the period of 1955 to 1956 was one of the best years of communist China. The Five-Year Plan was rolled out and after 1954, 1955, the development of China was at its peak. 1957 was the beginning of the Anti-Rightist Campaign, and China's development veered slightly off track. In 1958 and 1959, the situation worsened and the Cultural Revolution which happened in the 1960s was a complete disaster. Nevertheless, I feel that 1955 and 56 were China's best years under the newly formed Communist Party. Economic growth was accelerating, cultural activity was booming, the country flourished and its people were able to enjoy peace and prosperity, it was a much celebrated time, and that was during the 1950s. Naturally, Chinese-educated students in Singapore looked to China for inspiration. This is the first point. The second point I want to make is, the mainstream thinking during that time was still very much rooted in the local region, although we looked toward China culturally, politically, we swore our allegiance to Malaya. During those times, there wasn't the concept of Singapore as an independent nation. There was only independence for Malaya, which included Singapore. We wanted to achieve unification of Malaya and Singapore. We strived to unite both Malaya and Singapore during those years, from today's perspective it must be very difficult to understand, however, this cannot be explained in a brief manner. This is the second point. The third point I want to make is people have a misconception that Chinese-educated students did not think much of unity among races in Malaya and Singapore. In reality, Chinese-educated students placed much importance in the unity of different races. Do not misconstrue Chinese-educated students as being limited to Chinese education. During 1957 to 1959, we encouraged our fellow students to learn Malay and held many Malay language classes. I had also studied Malay culture (*spoken in Malay*). This was what I learnt in school, not in Malaya, but in a Malay language class in Singapore. Why was it so? We knew the importance of unity among races. And during those days, the lingua franca was not English but Malay. We could use Malay to converse with other races, not necessarily English. Today it is different; we use English as our main communication tool.

I have a little more to add, and I do not think that this is unnecessary. As we are talking about Singapore's history, I would like to end my account with a few simple points. History is created by both victors and losers. I admit that Chinese-educated students during my time, from a certain perspective, in a relative sense and not in an absolute sense, we were the losers. The goal which we pursued was not realised, we were beaten to the ground and stepped on, and we had suffered a major setback. However, history is created jointly by both losers and victors. How can history be made solely by the victors? Furthermore, the truth of history can never be altered. How history is interpreted and analysed is usually decided by the victors, or in other words, victors have the monopoly in the narration of history. Therefore, today's history is manipulated and written by the victors. Is their account the true story? I will say that it is only a partial history and not the complete story. The account of losers is not accounted for and their voices are absent, therefore, a single perspective of history is incomplete. Today, we ask for a complete account of history, I do not know if people feel that it is too much to ask for, I personally feel that it is our right to know the complete story.

The second point I want to share is, the German philosopher Hegel once said, "All that is real is rational; and all that is rational is real." How can something irrational exist? Student activism and the passion students expressed in the 1950s and 1960s have their rationality in that setting. We must not deny this. Hence, I myself have not regretted the things I did during those growing up years. In short, things that exist must be rational; if it's irrational, it would cease to exist.

The third point I want to share is, till today, we do not have a fair assessment on the place of Chinese-educated students in Singapore history, and this is a great pity. Do we have to wait till the day when there are no longer any Chinese-educated students around before they give us a fair verdict? I strongly feel, please don't, please don't do that. Please give us a fair verdict while we are still alive and well, this way, we can rest in peace.

I shall end here for today, thank you.

Ong: Thank you, Mr. Han. With regard to what Mr. Han had shared with us, I believe the majority of students and people who didn't live through this period would probably not know much about it. Therefore, what The Tangent plans to achieve this time is to preserve such accounts of history. As what Mr. Han said a while ago, this is an account of history by non-victors. Other than history written by non-victors, there is still another issue, it pertains to unheard voices in history. For instance, as Mr. Han said, there were many schools involved in student activism during those times, and only St Nicholas or Catholic High seldom took part in these activities. Then a question arises, what were students from these schools doing? To add on, what were students from English schools like Raffles Institution (RI), Raffles Girls' School (RGS) or St. Joseph doing at that time? These accounts are missing from our official history, when you read Mr. Lee Kuan Yew's memoirs *The Singapore Story*, you cannot find clues to such accounts. Therefore, what we are trying to do is to at least restore part of the missing links. Once again, let us thank Mr. Han.

Ong: Our second speaker for today is Professor Koh Tai Ann. Professor Koh teaches in the Division of English at Nanyang Technological University, and she is also an eyewitness to the happenings of that time. Without any further delay, let us invite Professor Koh to share her experience with us.

Koh: I take it that all the young people present can understand English?

Anyway, listening to Mr. Han's account, it seems as if we were living in different countries, altogether different worlds. But like him, I came from a poor family, my mother being a single parent (having separated from my father) who was very pro-China and as an immigrant, she did not separate China from its politics. Naturally, I came under my mother's influence, joining her in her workers' union activities and all that. I even gave the workers free English lessons when I was at pre-university. I think Mr. Han read the papers a lot more and was, perhaps, five years ahead of me, so the things that he talks about, I was totally unaware of. And even if I did read the papers, it would have been the very different English language papers — although my mother subscribed to the Chinese newspapers, *Sin Chew Jit Poh* and sometimes *Nanyang Siang Pau*.

Generally speaking, I think much of my experience was quite close to what English school students would have experienced. Although he mentioned it only towards the end, the difference between the English-medium schools and the Chinese, Malay and Tamil schools — it was not until 1987, that the entire school system switched over to English being the medium of instruction — was that the English-medium schools were the multi-racial schools. So my childhood was, you know, mingling with people of all races and not only with fellow Chinese. Moreover, I went to the very rural Pasir Panjang Primary School. "Pasir Panjang" in Malay means "long beach", and before the sea was reclaimed, the beach was very visible from Pasir Panjang Road. I recall there was a Malay fishing village near Haw Par Villa which interestingly also had a Chinese temple to cater to the Chinese residents in the area. Indeed, the whole stretch of Pasir Panjang Road had several Malay kampongs. My best friend in primary school was a Malay girl, Maznah, and we keep in touch till today although she is now a resident abroad. We used to spend a lot of time, many of us, in the nearby Malay kampong [at Jalan Mat Jambol] simply because they had a lot of space between the unfenced homes, with fruit trees growing all round, good for climbing, and bearing the kinds of fruits that we no longer see now in Singapore such as pulasan, jambu, guava, mangosteens, and so on. Hibiscus hedges (now hardly seen) were common everywhere including the boundary of our school compound. [When we were in Malaysia, national day bunting usually featured Malaysia's national flower, the hibiscus; nowadays, Singapore bunting on national day features the orchid.]

The other difference is that the English-medium schools were government schools. As Mr. Han has pointed out, that was another major difference. The Chinese schools were privately supported by the community and were thus less well-provided for. Additionally, the English schools already had the kinds of assistance schemes for poor children that we still have today, and I was one of the beneficiaries — such as waiver of school fees, even though it was only (if memory serves me) $1.50 in those days. There was already in place a free textbook scheme whereby we were able to have the benefit of second-hand books or free textbooks, if the former were not available.

The third difference is that the Chinese schools, as you may know, were very much associated with the left wing, dare I say, communist and anti-colonial struggle elements. So they were under great suspicion by both the colonial government and later, the post-independence PAP government, unlike the English schools. So we were ignorant of the things that were happening in the Chinese schools. Besides, if you were in primary and lower secondary school, you hardly read any newspapers, and of course, in those days, the newspapers were not so kind as to bring out special students' editions for young people, as they do now. So that is another difference. Even a major event like the Maria Hertogh riots in 1954, I believe, we did not much notice. I was then in lower primary school. Nor did we think much about it subsequently [until this became regularly cited as an early racial riot like the ones in the sixties which had also led to curfews.] I vaguely recall getting an unexpected holiday because of the curfew, listening to radio broadcasts about Eurasians and white men being killed by Malays.

So, thinking back, our political consciousness was quite low compared to that of the Chinese-educated — even in secondary school, and even in pre-university (although while in Pre-U Two, I chose to do a research project on Mao Tse-tung which was chosen to be presented in class). But I only became active in student politics, for instance, when I stood for elections to become a member of the University of Singapore Union Executive Committee. It was only then that I went with other Executive Committee members and those from the University of Malaya to express solidarity with the Students Union of Nanyang University (Nantah) who were protesting at the time. I have a picture of the University of Malaya, University of Singapore and Nanyang University Ex-Co members posing in front of the riot squad van stationed on the Nantah campus. But we had gone there to give moral support, not to participate in the riots or demonstrations which had erupted earlier and by then, had already been ended.

So what I will do today, is to focus on my primary school activities and describe what we did to show you how different it was from the experience of the Chinese-educated as recounted by Mr. Han. If there is time, I will talk a bit about life in secondary school during my time. What we did in secondary schools during those days — like debates, quizzes, listening to talks, etc., — is very much what English-medium schools still do today. What is remarkable, looking back, is that these were not the things that interested our counterparts in the Chinese schools. There was also the "China effect" on that generation of Chinese-educated students. China was rising as a major communist power; it was the era of the Cold War; so therefore, more attention was paid to, more pressure, you know, was placed on the Chinese-medium schools. Hardly any of those left-wing elements or activities was to be found in the English-medium schools. And besides, as I must point out, we were very much undergoing still a colonial education — although by Form One (today's Secondary One) the curriculum was gradually changing [under the PAP government]. In primary school, we studied and were more familiar, for instance, with British trees, British flora, British songs, British everything, you know, than with Asian history, or tropical trees like the Angsana and all that. (I will come back to that later.)

Anyway, this morning, I decided, on an impulse, to go and look at my old primary school in Pasir Panjang, located at the end of Yew Siang Road. (Incidentally, it happened to be, I only found out recently, the old school of Senior Minister Goh Chok Tong. But I wasn't aware of his existence, anyway, as we may not have been there at the same time.) I had last visited it in 1985 when I thought to enrol my daughter in my old school. But already then, it was unoccupied and derelict, and I noted a new condominium was being built on the slopes behind it. Today, I discovered that the now long-completed condo is Flynn Park condominium. Other condominiums have sprung up along Yew Siang Road. But what delighted me is that the school building is still there although Pasir Panjang Primary School, like many old primary schools, no longer exists because of population shifts. The old, huge school field, amazingly, given that it is such a large vacant piece of land, is still there. And the big old African Tulip tree under which we used to play is also still there. We used the pods of the flowers as cheap water pistols during recess — I don't know if any of you have had this experience. As Mr. Han rightly pointed out, our playthings in school were self-created because we were too poor to buy toys. (I'll come to that later, too.) The old school building now has been painted pink and brown. It used to be a more sombre dark green and cream. It's now been converted into a rehabilitation centre called Red True Mission, I think. Young men were to be seen providing a car wash service under a make-shift shelter constructed on the former playground and car park. Going there just now was literally a trip down memory lane, or Yew Siang Road, which is a lane off Pasir Panjang Road. The old house belonging to the famous Tan family of national swimmers and water polo players — such as Tan Eng Hock, Tan Eng Liang — the latter went on to become a PAP MP — is still there, also amazingly, but locked up and vacant. However, all the kampongs along Jalan Mat Jambol, the little village shops and little lanes off Yew Siang Road, have all gone. And of course, the seaside which was ever present in our view from the bus, has gone too, because of land reclamation.

On weekends or after school, we would go swimming in the sea, and it was common to see many Malay children and families enjoying the breeze at the seaside or further up, among the sandy groves of coconut trees, especially during the "mandi safir" cleansing rituals (now no longer practiced). A big treat during major holidays, especially during Chinese New Year, was a visit to the nearby Haw Par Villa, also on Pasir Panjang Road. Can you imagine, Haw Par Villa was a major treat, and it was free admission! Whole families and couples would go there both to visit the attractions and to eat at the food stalls inside, and at the stalls outside.

But back to my primary school. First of all, it was a co-ed school which meant a greater variety of activities. The school building was two-storey, built around an open grassy square bordered by flower beds. The hill slope behind (now occupied by the condo) was also our playground where we went to pluck pitcher plants, which we knew as "monkey cups". The stall holders in the school canteen would also climb up there to pick the large flat leaves they needed to hold rojak servings or to strip the wild banana trees for their bark, which they used to wrap the fried kway teow in for "take-aways". This saved them from having to buy plates. For what they could charge us, their profit could not have been much. Our standard pocket money per child was 10 cents. 5 cents was enough to buy 3 sweets, while 10 cents will buy a plate of mee siam. And of course, it was heaven, if you had 20 cents pocket money. But not many of us had that much.

I also remember the kinds of punishment that you fortunately don't find in schools anymore. One of the punishments was for us to be put in the grassy square that stood in the middle of the school, right in the view of every classroom, and cross our hands over our chests and pull our own ears while repeatedly squatting down and rising in the hot sun for the whole school to see you from the corridors upstairs and downstairs. And if it was a group of us who were naughty, boys and girls together, regardless, we would have to take a tuckshop bench, and all would have to carry the bench above their heads, and be forced to go up and down, up and down, until the teacher thought they had been punished enough. Sometimes, one in the group would lose his grip and the bench would fall over or even hurt the others when it fell. One of my own frequent punishments was to be asked to leave the class and stand outside, often for reading story books and not paying attention to dull lessons. Or, we could be made to stand on our chairs as punishment during the lesson (for instance, for talking in class). Only the Principal could cane you, but that did not prevent the teachers from using rulers to beat us in various ways, like being forced to hold our palms out and being smacked with the ruler, sometimes with the sharp edge. I was one of the few children, perhaps the only one in the class who could read and write English before I went to school, and so my school experience may be a little different from the usual. That's because my mother thought English was the wave of the future. I had attended Sunday school even though it meant that I had to learn verses from the Bible. But I learnt how to read in English and we had to speak English because the missionaries were all English. So I found Primary One very boring: each day the class would learn to write and pronounce one letter of the alphabet — A, today, and B, tomorrow and so on for 26 days, and when the class started to read by the end of the term, it was, 'A is for Apple' and later, "the cat sat on the mat", boring things like that. So I would always be reading under my desk, comics and story books, which would cause me to be sent out to stand outside, in the corridor, for not paying attention.

The other thing I vividly remember, was the lack of modern sanitation. The whole of Pasir Panjang being rural, our school did not therefore have modern sanitation. I do not know how many of us trace our kidney problems to that time because we were often very reluctant to go to the toilet (or "jamban" as it was commonly called in Malay). Each cubicle had a few steps which led up to an open hole for squatting over, with a bucket below, and if the night soil carrier was lazy, which was often, he did not replace the cover over the hole at the back. So when the wind blew up the hole, the stench was unbearable. We, the girls, would always be in fear that the boys would come peeping through the hole, although I cannot recall that it ever happened. The other nasty thing that I remember, was that most of us had head lice which spread rapidly. So we had to queue up and have our hair washed in some dreadful, smelly, cold disinfectant, while a common recess activity saw us, like monkeys, sitting down and removing lice and eggs stuck along each strand of hair, by pulling them out from each other's heads. Itchy ringworm and boils were also common. Many children also had childhood illnesses, now fortunately rare, like smallpox, chicken pox, diphtheria, mumps and polio. One of my classmates, in fact, was crippled as a result of polio. So we were very much then living in a "Third World" country, even though the English schools seem to be privileged. Perhaps, we were a rural school — what we today might call a neighbourhood school — so the school amenities and everything else were not as modern as you would find today, even in the neighbourhood schools.

But there were also some delights such as the regular visits of a mobile library. Not so delightful an experience was a mobile dental van which would come round once a year, as well as a mobile clinic dispensing medicine and treating minor ailments like tummy aches and sores. Sores or boils, a result of malnutrition and poor hygiene, were very common, too. We even had to take a subject called Hygiene on the curriculum.

The other activities that we enjoyed, apart from the childhood games we played which you may not be familiar with were saga seeds. There were a lot of saga trees around then, shedding hundreds of bright red seeds, but we rarely find them now. We collected and played with the saga seeds, using our fingers to push pairs of them together and building up our collections, supplemented by hours picking them up beneath the trees; five stones; "*tua peh kun*", or *hopscotch*, and sometimes as a penalty one had to carry someone piggy back while hopping from square to square; "*chatek*" [made from the rubber of old tyres and feathers] , and "*goli*", or marbles which could be made of white stone or coloured glass. Being poor and unable to afford store-bought toys, we also made up other games like catching, hide and seek, skipping with rubber-band ropes, and other popular games in those days. "*Tikam-tikam*" was also a popular mild form of gambling.

How different and "colonial" the English-educated environment was could be seen from one of the highlights of our lives, which was to go to the Indian sundry goods shop and wait for the monthly shipment of comics from Britain. Some of you may have heard of "Dandy" and "Beano" comics. We would hang around, to be the first to buy, and later share or exchange the precious copies among ourselves. I doubt the Chinese-educated indulged in anything as frivolous and "colonial" as that, but that's what we did.

In those days, reading comics and storybooks was a real pleasure as pleasures were few, and TV had not arrived and there were no pocket radios. Each classroom had its own cupboard full of story books and so we read a lot. One of the things that we enjoyed, which I regret very much has been long discontinued in schools, (and given the fact that I am now Chairperson of the Speak Good English Movement) were the regular English broadcasts. Everyday around a certain hour, the then Broadcasting Service would have a programme consisting of English lessons, singing lessons and story-telling which reinforced our spoken English (This continued for some while although I remember when my children were in primary schools in the 1980s, the broadcasts were for Chinese lessons.) Because we did a lot of reading and writing to lay a good foundation in English, and because our mother tongues were all Chinese dialects, we didn't start learning Mandarin till Primary Four. The English language foundation laid was therefore very strong and thorough. For example, we learnt phonetics in Primary Three and even had to take phonetics dictation. As a result, we could open a dictionary, look at any unfamiliar word for its meaning, and at the same time, merely by looking at the phonetic symbols, we would know how to pronounce it as well, and which syllable to stress. Somewhere along the line, the schools, regrettably, ceased teaching this and English pronunciation today has deteriorated. But in those days, it was assumed that we had to learn English from scratch, so we learnt it very properly, grammar, pronunciation and all. Consequently, the generations that are now in their 60s and above, 50s and perhaps, late 40s, write English with hardly any grammatical errors. Nowadays, among those who are younger, there are not many who can consistently speak or write grammatically although there are many more using the language.

The school curriculum, unlike that of today, was also more humanities-based and we did not start Science lessons till Primary Five or Six, and it was mostly Biology, no Physics or Chemistry. So we did a lot of reading and writing. Can you imagine, from Primary Three, we were doing History and Geography? We did not have any multiple-choice questions; every question in the exam had to be answered in complete sentences. Even in the Primary School Leaving Examination, no multiple choice questions. And what were we doing for History in Primary Three? Our textbook was *The March of Time*, which was Roman and Greek history, European history, and of course, British colonial and Empire history told in the form of stories or which focused on historical figures such as Alexandra the Great or the English kings. But I should give credit to the colonial educationists in that there were efforts to introduce readers with local content when we were in Primary Four and Five. I can recall textbooks, which some of you in my generation may remember, which had accounts and pictures of local figures such as the satay man who was depicted carrying wooden stools and his table at one end of his pole, and on the other end hung the charcoal grill, his pot of satay sauce and bowls and so on. And in Primary Five and Six, we also did the ancient history of Southeast Asia. Nowadays, if you ask young people, let alone Primary Six pupils, what were Langkasuka, Funan, Srivijaya, the concept of the God King, Angkor Wat, Borobodur, and so on, they would not know a thing even though Singapore is part of Southeast Asia and was once part of the Srivijaya and then the Javanese Majapahit empires. Many wouldn't even know modern Malayan or Indonesian history. Such was our common humanities or liberal education that by the time I completed my education in pre-university, I had covered the entire world history, including that of Russia and China. I had also covered world geography over the same period because of the focus on humanities. So we had a very strong humanities background even though I was to become a science major when I was streamed into the so-called "Pure Science" class. Because we did not start learning a second language till Primary Four or begin doing science till Primary Six, we had all the curriculum time available to read, and to write long essays. In lower secondary, we also learnt something which I also regret has also been discontinued — précis or how to write a summary. That meant you learnt how to reduce a long passage of say, 250 words, to only 50 words without loss of the main points. This was very good training for note-taking and for expressing the same meaning in fewer words. So you see that our preoccupations and even learning experiences were very different from what yours might be today.

The English-educated child's learning experience would also be very different from that of the Chinese schools. While we learnt about the European, Imperial and Southeast ancient history, and English literature, they learnt Chinese History, Confucian or even, extra-curricularly, left-wing values, and Chinese literature and culture.

However, among the things which Mr. Han mentions, with which I agree, is we were not at all worried about or by exams. Our parents were so grateful that we got into school and most of them didn't know English anyway, so they did not know how to read our report books. As long as we passed each year, were promoted and were not held back, they were contented. I don't know about the top schools such as Raffles Girls' and the Convent schools where double promotions were not uncommon, as to whether they were more competitive.

So, I did not have a very eventful, stressful primary school life. The teachers were firm and organised, but teaching was very relaxed. I never studied for exams, not even for PSLE. I don't know why. I only started studying for my O-Level, because everybody impressed us that it was an important exam. I do not know whether I was typical or not. But I think all my classmates also played a lot. The only thing we would think of after school, during recess was to go out and play games, hang around, look at comics, go to the library or whatever, but never to study. And private tuition was unheard of. Nobody could afford to take private tuition. I don't think there were even private tutors. But then I did not go to elite schools like Raffles Girls', Singapore Chinese Girls', and so on. I am sure the pupils there must have had private tutors. They were mostly the schools of the middle class. We were very much a kampong school.

As for our very colonial education — even a rural school such as Pasir Panjang was a colonial school and had until just before I was admitted, a British principal. Our first Chinese Principal was called Major Fam Foong Hee and he was dressed smartly, always with a tie, and held himself in a very British way. I started primary school in the 50s, and we did not get self-government till 1959, when I was in lower secondary. So the sums that we did were in pounds, shillings and pence although daily, we were using dollars and cents — and the readers were about British children such as Dick and Jane, and English life such as life on an English farm with Dobbin the horse. So it was a bit unreal. We were learning about the characteristics of robins, wrens blackbirds, ash trees, oak trees, birch, lilies, roses and daffodils, and never a mention of the Angsana or hibiscus even though there were hibiscus hedges all around us, but oh no, we were not learning about them. We sang the British public school songs such as "40 years on, when afar and asunder/ Parted are those who are singing today" and even an oft-repeated song in Latin — "*Gaudeamus Igitur, Juvenes dum sumus*"(Let us then rejoice, While we are young.) [It was only many years later that I discovered that the former was the Harrow School song, while the latter was a medieval students' song!] We were also singing songs such as "Land of hope and glory, mother of the free", completely without a sense of irony or knowledge of its context as, surely, we were not free, right? We were colonials and yet we were singing this British patriotric favourite [the Finale to Elgar's Coronation Ode] cheerfully to commemorate the Coronation of Queen Elizabeth in 1953, and on occasions such as Empire Day or to celebrate the Queen's birthday, etc. And of course, on every important occasion we "patriotically" sang, "God save our gracious Queen".

However, I was unexpectedly a beneficiary of the Queen's coronation celebrations because of Mr. Tan Jiak Kim, a wealthy Peranakan businessman [and a founder of the Straits Chinese British Association whose members considered themselves loyally, "the King's — or Queen's — Chinese".] To mark the occasion (as well as his loyalty to the Queen) he established the Tan Jiak Kim Coronation Year Scholarship. My school must have nominated me and I became the happy recipient of the royal sum of $600, a lot of money in those days for anyone, let alone a primary school child. This pleased my mother very much, of course, as it represented more than half a year's wages.

Now, what other activities? Remember, we were a rural school and much of Singapore being rural and poor at the time, we had a wonderful item on our time table called Gardening, and another, Swimming/Sewing. These, however, seen in retrospect, were implemented in a very sexist way. The boys grew and tended the large vegetable patch at the back of the school and so, in time, usually just before end of term, they would harvest *jagong* [maize], brinjal, long beans, *chye sim*, and so on to take home gleefully. And what did the girls do? We tended the school flower beds, and of course, we were not allowed to pluck the flowers to take home. The other item was swimming on Friday mornings — one whole beautiful morning — and the boys would go to the Haw Par swimming pool in Pasir Panjang within walking distance (it has long since ceased to exist). And we girls? What did we do? It being deemed immodest for girls to be seen in swimming costume and being in the same pool as boys, with male swimming instructors and lifeguards, we stayed back to learn sewing and embroidery, women's work. So, combined with sewing classes in lower secondary, I learnt how to sew my own clothes and am a very good embroiderer. I can recognise and do all those stitches — satin stitch, back stitch, chevron stitch, and all that. (In those days, girls did not even wear shorts, but bloomers.) Sports was a very big thing because the British were great believers in the dictum, "a sound mind in a sound body". So to build rugged students, the biggest event on the school calendar (after another British invention: the School Speech Day) was Sports Day and sports/games competitions the whole year round. Heats, inter-house games, inter-school competitions, football, netball, you name it (although hardly any basketball, which was more an American-inspired, Chinese-medium high school game). [The "House", usually named after a famous figure, usually British, was borrowed from British boarding or public schools.] That is why, like all schools in Singapore, we had this large school field. And it was not surprising that the famous Tan family whose children went to our nearby school would produce all those national swimmers and also for the water polo team.

When I went up to secondary school, that was when the PAP came into power and was henceforth able to influence the school curriculum and how the schools were being run. Now, I happened to be the top girl in the Primary School Leaving Examinations in Pasir Panjang, and I was looking forward to my dream, and dream of all knowing primary school pupils, at the time — that was to get into Raffles Girls' Secondary (for boys, it was Raffles Institution). At the time, the top PSLE students would be posted to such elite schools. It was believed that one's family had to be Christian, quite rich and parents had to donate money to get into Anglo-Chinese Boys' School or Singapore Chinese Girls' School, the latter being established originally especially for the children of the Peranakan. But when the PAP took over educational matters, they said, "no more elitism". You all go to the school that is nearest to your home. At the time, of course, I was not to know that the new government had to cope with the post-war baby boom, and because of the British colonial authorities' failure to plan ahead, there was a shortage of secondary schools. Since the nearest secondary school was Pasir Panjang Boy's School, the nearest school that I could go to was a new secondary school which had been converted from a primary school along Alexandra Road, at Prince Charles's Crescent, called Crescent Girls' Secondary school, I was among only the second batch to go there. It didn't even have a school song or school badge. Competitions were held and I was one of the winners of the school song competition, my entry becoming the second stanza. What the school did was to combine the three winning entries into one. (A line from my stanza can today be seen above the entrance to the new school building.) We shared a lumpy, uneven sports field with Alexandra Primary School opposite us, while further down the lane, across the other way was Belvedere Primary School. In the 1980s, Crescent Girls' was most fortunate to be given the land occupied by these two primary schools and thus able to combine all three plots to build the grand Crescent Girls' school complex which you see today. It is not anymore the school that I knew before, which was demolished. The school that I had attended was a former primary neighborhood school located in the middle of an aging public housing estate built by the former colonial government. I cried with disappointment that I was not able to attend Raffles Girls' and was utterly miserable during my first week there, having to go to this unknown new school. Being a former primary school building, it lacked all the secondary school facilities such as a proper school hall, its own field, with a tuckshop that was far too small and crowded, no proper science labs, etc. And of course, I did not realise at that time that it was the new policy of a socialist government bent on creating a more egalitarian society such that admission to secondary school was no longer to be distributed according to exam results which before had created these elite schools.

It was therefore a great challenge to Crescent Girls' as a newcomer in a poor neighbourhood, to build a name for itself. But how to make its name, when it was a "neighborhood school" [although that term did not then exist]. Its location meant that all the students were from all the nearby rural "neighborhood" primary schools, the catchment area being relatively disadvantaged enclaves such as rural Pasir Panjang, Alexandra, Bukit Merah and Tiong Bahru, not your usual middle class areas. So, what the sports-loving first principal, Miss Evelyn Norris, did [she was from Raffles] to make the school prominent, was to focus on sporting achievements. And alas for me, I hated sports. I was a bookworm, but I was also ambitious. I wanted to be, (remember, the British dictum?) "sound in body, sound in mind". A "Best All-rounder Award" spurred us on to be good in both studies and on the sports field. Being ambitions, I put all my heart and soul into sports as well — apart from being on the School Quiz team, its Debating Team, editor of the school magazine, class monitor, and Vice President of the National Junior Traffic Safety First Council, prefect and then Head Prefect! But it was terrible. Heats everyday as we had four "Houses" and so there was much inter-house competition. Everyday, we would be out in the field, competing in heats. (As you may know, heats enable the sports teachers to select those who would finally participate in the finals on Sports Day.)

As our science teacher was also the sports master and such was the shortage of science graduates at the time, he was a non-graduate as well, he put all his energies into sports activities and so in upper secondary, we hardly got any science lessons or lab practice because he was on the field most of the time. As the top students were streamed into the Science class, we unknowingly suffered from this relative neglect. Thus when I was, for instance, the top "O" Levels student at Crescent Girls' (and I say this with no particular pride), my aggregate was a mere 60 (which was good for someone from a new school like ours, helped by distinctions in my humanities, but dragged down by our poorer grades in science and maths subjects). Nowadays, an aggregate of 60 would not get you very far. But we had very good English teachers who trained us to win debates and were very rigorous and hardworking in marking our assignments. I also had in Mrs. Dolly Quahe, an excellent English and Literature teacher. I recently came across my lower secondary school composition book. You know, my teachers [such as Miss Wee in Form 2] not only corrected for grammar — in fact, I hardly committed any grammatical errors (as I'd mentioned to you earlier, I was one of those lucky children who had started school able to read and write in English and that gave me a tremendous headstart) — but she also corrected me for style. She improved my phrasing, tightened my sentences if I was wordy, and so on. When I looked at my composition exercise book, I can only conclude, my goodness, how lucky we were to have teachers whose English was so good that they had the confidence and ability to improve our style as well. Our English teachers were also our debating coaches and that was another area in which Crescent Girls' School earned a name for itself. I was on the debating team, and we debated RI, and of course the nearby Queenstown Secondary School, and we always won. Crescent Girls' was always winning, too, in sports and games. Gradually, we became C-Division champion, then the B-Division champion, and finally the A-Division champion. (After I'd graduated and joined the school's Advisory Committee for 10 years, I saw Crescent Girls' become known for its school band and consistently champion in national band competitions too.) Because of its catchment area, it had many Malay students as well as the usual Chinese students, and developed great strengths in both Chinese and Malay. That also helped it to score when it came to ranking and gradually, it became known as one of the top girls' schools in Singapore. But it wasn't the case during our time.

But one thing that I was very grateful for in the old days is that, first of all — to provide another perspective — those of us who went to schools like Crescent Girls' or who also came from poor families, we rarely heard any Mandarin in our lives. We were therefore not stressed out by Chinese lessons and tuition nor did we feel any less "Chinese". Chinese education was for people who aspired to higher culture, higher Chinese, whose immigrant parents wanted their children to retain the old culture, or who could not make it to English schools. We were secure in our identity in the then largely dialect-speaking environment, happily picking up the major dialects needed for ordinary life. Without consciously learning them. I picked up Hokkien, can understand Teochew, can speak best in Cantonese although I am Hainanese. Later, at the university, we were given free Bahasa Melayu classes after Singapore became part of Malaysia as that became the national language. Most of us also spoke in the lingua franca of the time — "pasar Malay". English not being as widely spoken as it is now, we Chinese tended to speak to Indians, Eurasians, the Peranakans and of course, Malays, in "pasar Malay". Among ourselves, we took the cue from our contexts. If the speaker was Hokkien, we switched to Hokkien, if Cantonese, we switched to Cantonese. You cannot survive in Chinatown, for instance, without knowing Cantonese. So we grew up in an environment when the Chinese-educated, the Mandarin speakers, were remote and therefore, we didn't enjoy our Mandarin classes in school, especially when we had to do *wenyan* (classical Mandarin). Some people couldn't believe it that in Form 1 and 2 (i.e., Secondary 1 and 2) after only three years of Chinese in Primary School, we were learning *wenyan* or the ancient classical Chinese. And in those days, the Chinese language teachers were the most horrid, the strictest, the most frightening, most punitive and generally most disliked teachers. They were the ones who did not hesitate to use the ruler to hit you everywhere, right here on the arms, right there on the legs, jabbed their fingers at you, irritated you, scolded you, and we really hated them. And therefore, we also hated Chinese lessons. I am sure they did not have a happy time with us because we were not strongly motivated. We spoke Chinese with a dialect accent or English accent, we played the fool and also played tricks on them such as smearing their chairs with coloured chalk.

That Chinese at the time was not considered important was evident from one of the school practices of the time that was (now that I know better) not very good. Those of us, usually the top students, who were streamed into the "pure science" stream, however good in Chinese, were not able to take Chinese. We could not take Chinese even if we wanted to. The obverse of this is that, unlike what became the case later, "pure science" students in the "A" class were able to take all the humanities subjects, for which I am grateful. I took Geography, I took History, I took English Literature, and English language, of course, apart from Maths, Physics and Chemistry, and was allowed later to drop Additional Maths — seven subjects only. And that was why I was the top student at Crescent, because I had distinctions in my humanities subjects despite B4 or C5 grades in my Maths and Science subjects. I was thus able to switch over to the Arts stream when I entered Pre-U in Raffles Girls' School. Some of us' in fact, willingly went to the "pure science" stream because we wouldn't ever have to take Chinese anymore. Looking back now, that was quite sad. The other things we were prohibited to do in Science stream were, and that was sad, too, Biology, Art and Domestic Science, which were considered suitable only for the academic non-performers. [Eight was the maximum number of O-level subjects allowed during our time, but we were not encouraged even to take that number.] We didn't have a choice. If you were selected for the Science stream, you went to the Science stream. Moreover, being teenagers, that was a prestigious stream, because the new government had come into power and decided that science was the way to go for the brightest and the best. There was this focus on science, because (as I was to discover later) it was believed that an underdeveloped country like Singapore needed more science and other professionals such as doctors and lawyers. Scholarships would be given to science students; the sciences had to be built up and therefore, science students were the elite, and no longer the humanities students. (I was later to pay for my poor Science results at O-level, despite being also the top 'A' Level Arts student at RGS, by not getting the Yang di-pertuan Negara — or President's Scholarship for which I had been nominated.) At that time, at the University of Singapore, the elite students, the best students still took arts subjects, including Economics, even in my time, but the times were changing. So it was a very different world. The British had valued the humanities and the first faculties to be set up at Raffles College and then the University of Malaya were the humanities such as English and History.

Coming back to the topic of what other extra-curricular activities we had at secondary school — Crescent Girls' was among the first schools to support the National Safety First Council, formed because there were more accidents happening on the roads, as Singapore became more affluent, more cars, more crowded. I recall I became the first Vice President of the Junior Safety First Council when Shell started the Shell Safety First Park at the East Coast Park. Is that still in existence? Any of you go there? That was started in the late 50s or early 60s when I was in secondary school. We were the pioneers and what we did was to go there regularly to organise competitions in road safety, or guide younger students in road safety games.

Other things that we did were very much English-medium school activities. I was a Girl Guide, and later on, a Land Ranger when I reached 17. My school, being new, did not have a Girl Guides Company, so I joined an open company, called the 4th Singapore Girl Guides Company based at Guide Hut, Buyong Road, which no longer exists. I think a hotel is now located there or it was demolished for road widening. Next to it was the then new Scout Building, which is also no longer there. They were appropriately located near the Istana (which of course, is still there) as the Chief Scout was the Governor, and later the Yang di-pertuan Negara, and now, is the President. We would meet at the charming single-storey Guide Hut built on pillars above the ground every Saturday, and that was my opportunity to meet friends of my age from other schools. Raffles Girls' had its own company and sometimes they would use the Hut or the large field in front of it, and would bully us because coming from the elite school they felt superior. Indeed, a few of those who bullied us went on to become VPs of Banks and hold high government positions. Such trivial rivalries — as if the English-educated youth had very small concerns compared to the very large national concerns that the Chinese-educated activist teenagers had. And we were not aware that we were so privileged when all those disturbances were going on at the Chinese-medium schools that Mr. Han has described. Partly, we didn't read the Chinese newspapers, we didn't listen to Chinese news, and even if we did listen to the radio we were more interested in listening to *Lei Dai Sor*, stories in Cantonese which featured daily on Rediffusion sets which seemed to be permanently turned on in every poor home and neighbourhood coffee shop.

The Girl Guides and Land Rangers often went camping during the holidays. Looking back, I find it most interesting that my Girl Guide Captain and Lieutenant were, respectively, a secretary and a clerk. See how Singapore has changed. In those days, to have a Senior Cambridge certificate (i.e., completed O-level) enabled you to get a white-collar job as a secretary, a clerk, or teacher, and was the height of educational achievement for most people. Very few people had

A level, even fewer went on to university. However, both my Land Ranger Captain, Mrs. Anna Tham (later the famous principal of Methodist Girls' School) and her Lieutenant, Miss Lim Siew Mei (later to become Director of the Institute of Education) were graduates and we were most fortunate to be under their guidance. (I was to discover much later that only 2000 of us, including those applying to do Law and Medicine, were able to gain admission to the then University of Singapore, but I won't now talk about my university experiences as you may find them in an earlier issue of *Tangent*.) And what did we learn as Girl Guides? Looking back, we learnt a mixture of useful and not so useful skills, but we had fun learning them and enjoying each others' company. We learnt how to tie knots, and other survival skills, such as how to start a fire by rubbing twigs or stones together, even though matches were easily available, how to put up tents, cook, build furniture from tying bamboo or other pieces of wood together with the knots we had learned. There were badges to acquire through which we learned other skills — cooking badge, writer's badge, etc., and after acquiring a certain number of badges we could become a Queen's Guide or Scout, which allowed you to wear this other sought-after badge and a lanyard. I think Girl Guides still engage in these activities although the uniform has evolved and is more comfortable.

What still amazes me is the generosity of those captains and lieutenants. For example, although Mrs. Anna Tham was a teacher, with a family of her own, yet she would give up so much of her time to the Land Rangers. Every Saturday she spent the entire afternoon with us, and after that, we may go to the nearby Koek Road hawker food stalls to have a meal with her and Miss Lim. [This famous eating place, like many such places, has long since disappeared.] Over Easter or other long public holiday, we would go camping, hiking or even visit the beach, and they would be with us. Again, see how our worlds differed from that of the Chinese-educated students of our age. It may seem quite trivial [although supposedly character-building], to go camping, set up tents, play games and practice jungle survival skills, hiking, going on excursions, and other outdoor activities, including joining up with the Rovers. The Rovers were the male equivalent of the Rangers. And that was our equivalent of group-dating. Sometimes they would take us out such as boating to Coney Island, and we had picnics, campfires, Christmas parties, organised fund-raising fashion shows and so on and so forth. And meanwhile, perhaps, the Chinese-educated of the same age-group might be having picnics, sing-a-long and indoctrination sessions, right? In a way, the Girl Guides and Rangers were a colonial legacy. Jungle survival skills, learning how to construct tents from scratch, rubbing two sticks together to start a fire, learning how to tie ten different knots for different purposes, etc. — now seem so irrelevant to the urban lives that we led. The explanation lies in the fact that the Scout Movement, and the Girl Guides, their female counterparts, were started by the British arch-imperialist, Lord Robert Baden-Powell, as character-building associations, based on his experiences with native African trackers during the South African Second Boer War in South Africa at the turn of the 20th century from whom was derived the term, scouts. These local scouts helped the British win the war against the retain original "Afrikaans" or Boers. His wife was instrumental in setting up and heading the Girl Guide movement. Well, they did succeed in keeping the youths occupied and busy.

The other activity that we engaged in a lot of, and again stemming from British love of the stage, was drama, but of a very different kind from the more politically-oriented plays of the Chinese schools. Every school then, including ours, traditionally had an active Literary, Debating and Drama Society (LDDS). There was the traditional annual school concert for which we did short plays or sketches. Or, we would stage the plays we did for Literature such as Shakespeare's plays or an 18th century English play, *She Stoops to Conquer*. Or, we would stage Orientalist, exotic versions of the East like *Lady Precious Stream*, which was actually of British origin. This last was a major co-production between Pasir Panjang Boys' Secondary School and Crescent Girls'. And we were quite innovative. We did both *Macbeth* and *A Midsummer Night's Dream* dressed in Chinese opera-style costumes. These were very much school texts, English-oriented, and not a single political theme there, you know, not a single left-wing thought among us.

The other difference between us, I think, and the Chinese students, was that the Chinese students' secondary education was six years long, because there was *chuzhong* (junior middle school), *gaozhong* (senior middle school), right? In the English stream, only a select few made it to Pre-university after their "O" Level. For instance, at Raffles Girls' School, my sole Arts class, consisted of only 24 of us. Furthermore, the pre-university students functioned separately from the secondary school and many of us would be new to the host school. We joined the secondary classes in activities like Sports Day, Speech Day and all that, but we carried on with our own activities; whereas, I believe, the older senior Chinese students were very much a part of their secondary school. Besides, many of them had delayed their education because of the war, and also because of perhaps, poverty and so on. So they were much older, I think. Older and more mature than the English-educated, hence our immature activities compared to their more mature nationalistic, anti-colonialist struggle activities, perhaps. For instance in May 1954, it was the Chinese schools (and some students at the then University of Malaya) who protested against the British attempt to introduce an early version of National Service. I was then in primary school and unaware of it, nor of the Hock Lee Bus riots a year later, in 1955. Mr. Han mentioned that the Hock Lee bus depot was near the Thye Hong biscuit factory, but my vivid memory of the factory as my

Hock Lee bus passed by it daily — it's being just across the road from my Crescent Girls' School — was the delicious smell of the biscuits baking as it wafted over the whole area nearby. Unlike Mr. Han, I've never smelt, fortunately, tear gas, never even seen it in operation. Because those were the days before TV, so these pictures were not shown, unlike now, when instantly you will see it that evening or on the afternoon news. We depended very much on radio (television did not arrive till I was at university, in black and white), so we were the generation that read and listened, unlike your generation, the MTV generation. You are more visually oriented, and while we were more attentive and focused, you seem to be able to multi-task — work on a PC, while listening to your MP3, and chat on your mobile phone, all at the same time. Now it is your turn to speak. I think I will leave an hour, perhaps, for questions and responses.

Question and Answer

Ong: Listening to Professor Koh's account, I think one thing that has become clear is that the so-called Chinese and English-educated community, is not one that is without internal contradictions. So when we use the term Chinese-educated or English-educated, we have to be extremely careful not to fall into the trap of creating a stereotypical image of the said community. We will now open up the floor for asking questions. What Mr. Han requested just now is to let those who have questions have a go first. If any of you wish to express any views, please kindly wait till our main speakers had answered all the questions, then we will start to open up the floor for opinions.

Koh: I would like to emphasise that it's a personal history. It might not be typical of the English-educated experience. For instance, Rosalind Heng (who became the well-known principal of Singapore Chinese Girls' School) was my classmate. The daughter of a doctor, she got her driving license and drove her own car to school at age 17 — the only student in Raffles Girls' School to do so, although another classmate had the use of her family car. Among the silly things we did, led by her, was to creep out once during school hours to catch a glimpse of Hayley Mills, the young film star, at the Singapore School for the Blind which the star was visiting.

Question: [original question in Chinese] I am one of the participants then. I remember that the Chinese-educated, like us, were not only concerned about politics, but also worried about the hardships faced by the people then. For instance, we donated money and clothes to those victims of the flood in Potong Pasir and the "Bukit Ho Swee Fire". So, it's not purely politics. In terms of social concerns, the Chinese educated students were also rather sympathetic towards this level in society. Do you agree?

Han: I'll answer the question raised by this gentleman. At that time, the Chinese-educated were not only engrossed in politics, in fact, we were also concerned about the public at large and the hardships faced by the masses. During the Potong Pasir flood, our school organised numerous volunteer teams to help provide relief to the disaster victims. I personally took part in the aftermath of the Bukit Ho Swee fire by aiding welfare work. At the time of the Bukit Ho Swee fire in 1961, I was studying in Senior Middle Year Two in Chung Cheng High School. We were at the shelter for refugees for two nights, doing volunteer work and so on. In addition, we even put up a performance to raise funds for the disaster victims. I have to add a point here to be fair, these relief activities did not involve only Chinese-educated students. I remember the English-educated students taking part, as well as the Malay students. On this point, it was not restricted to Chinese schools, English schools, Malay schools or whatsoever school. I can only say, with regard to political activities, the English-educated students were more distant. However, in terms of other undertakings involving social and public welfare, everyone had the same intention regardless of language or racial differences. I feel that this point should be added and put across fairly. Thank you.

Koh: In secondary school, I think we were not as active that way, but what we did do in school for instance, was to raise funds through fashion shows and concerts for which we sold tickets and obtained sponsorships; organised walkathons; sell cookies to raise money to send members of the girl guides to the international Jamboree, usually held in another country. We would have garage sales, for example, to raise money on a smaller scale than now, and for the orphanages and suchlike good causes. But I don't recall any mass fund-raising effort, as people would now for, say, the tsunami, although we all as usual volunteered to sell flags. (Even in those days selling flags was a revered school tradition).

Question: [original question in Chinese] The main speakers today are both Hainanese and educated in Singapore. For instance, [regarding] Lim Boon Keng's exhibition, I read an article written by Mr. Han, saying that many viewers only saw half of what Mr. Lim Boon Keng was like. This year, Xiamen University organised an academic symposium on Lim Boon Keng. In Singapore, a lot of Lim Boon Keng's research has been done in Chinese; I thought the research done in English should have some differing views and so, I went online to check. Professor Koh wrote some articles related to Lim Boon Keng sometime ago. I can't remember the details very well, hence I'm hoping if Professor Koh can tell us more about the articles she wrote and some of her thoughts and views on Lim Boon Keng. We would like to know more.

Ong: This is actually not today's main topic, but it's fine to ask.

Koh: It can be said, that the English-educated in a way, inherited the privileged position of the Straits-born Chinese community because after all, before independence, they were the class among the Chinese who were privileged by the British by virtue of their English-medium education. I have written about the Straits Chinese and my research showed that they took care to differentiate themselves from the so-called *sinkeh* or more recent Chinese immigrants (*sinkeh* means "new guests") on whom they tended to look down. Indeed, they identified themselves socially and politically so much with the British that they formed a Straits Chinese British Association whose members called themselves the "King's Chinese". Thus in one of their early newspapers, one of them expressed anger that the *sinkeh* were pushing for the use of Chinese. Rather, he argued, since they had chosen to come to a British Colony, they should make an effort to learn English, and not insist on using this "foreign language". For the most part, the Straits Chinese were complicit with the British colonial power which gave them their social status and economic clout. It was in their own socio-economic interest to serve the British administration loyally and thus they were among the earliest to take to English education for their children and consequently were quite anglicized. Therefore they were selected to act and acted as the bridge between the Chinese community and the British authority. Apart from his loyalty to the British colonial power, Lim Boon Keng supported what the left-wing Chinese would have regarded as the corrupt Kuomintang and was a strong Confucianist who represented the interests of the Peranakan community and business interests more than that of the Chinese community at large. So with regard to Lim Boon Keng, I have mixed feelings. But to give him due credit, he and his peers [including Tan Jiak Kim] started the Singapore Chinese Girls' School in 1899 to provide an English-medium education, initially for Peranakan girls, with a strong Confucianist bent, educating girls in domestic science, the virtues of being a good wife, and preparing them for the day such that they could be suitable wives for educated Peranakan men. Nonetheless, it was together with the St. Margaret's School, one of the earliest girls' English-medium schools. His life is very much part of the Peranakan story, which I see as a part of British colonial history, which predated modern Singapore history.

Question: ....There was a left-wing club, it is called the Socialist Club. So maybe you can speak a bit more on the left-wing programme in the 1950s,.... maybe

Mr. Han, [the rest of the question was put forth in Chinese] Mr. Han can help us to explain more on this leftist group, probably around 1952 or 1954, theirs was a strong organisation, with student movements……not only involving middle-schools, but also some activities in the University. Thank you.

Koh: I can't say much about the Socialist Club in the 1950s as I was then in primary school. What little I know of its history is from my reading — that among its founders was the now highly respected and renowned Professor Wang Gungwu and another long-retired distinguished historian, Lee Ting Hui (who are now in their seventies, and were in the universities in the 1950s.) It was formed in sympathy with socialist principles. The era of socialism was the 1950s to the 1970s and was a very powerful ideology during that time, chiefly because of its message that wealth should be distributed more equally and everyone in the community should be treated equally. If you were a socialist, then you were also anti-imperialist. The Socialist Club had a publication called *Fajar*, which is Malay for "Dawn". They took the idea from lines taken from the long Persian poem *Rubaiyat of Omar Khayyam* [in Fitzgerald's famous English translation, "Awake! for Morning in the bowl of night / Has flung the stone that puts the stars to flight", lines customarily quoted on *Fajar*'s masthead.] Among the most famous episodes in its history was Edwin Thumboo the editor's being taken into police custody by the colonial government. The Socialist Club had joined forces with the Chinese middle schools to agitate against a proposed introduction of mandatory military service for local youths in 1954 and generally, against the British colonial presence. *Fajar*, the official organ of the Socialist Club, had frequently voiced anti–British sentiments as well. Significantly, Mr. Lee Kuan Yew was his lawyer who got him released such that he was not jailed.

But when I went up to university, the PAP government led by Mr. Lee was fighting against the supposedly pro-communist elements and their associates such as the Barisan Sosialis formed by members of the PAP who had left to form their own party. The Socialist Club at the time was perceived, rightly or wrongly, to be pro-Barisan Sosialis. Some of us at the University of Singapore agreed that we needed a Socialism that went with democracy, while communism was perceived to be authoritarian rather than democratic. At the time, the PAP government strongly stood for democratic socialist principles. Together with a group of seniors and others, we formed the Democratic Socialist Club during my second year at university in 1965 as a counterweight to the Socialist Club. During the 1965 University of Singapore Student Union elections, we fielded members against the candidates of the Socialist Club and we won, taking control of the Union. Elections were not the short tame affairs that I see now at our universities. We really fought very hard and long, staying up overnight, making and putting up posters, making speeches everywhere on campus, at the Union House and in the hostels, bringing out special issues of our publications, etc. The Socialist Club was the older, more established club, and so it was quite a hard fight. Perhaps Mr. Han may know more about it and may have a view on the subject?

Han: Regarding this *Fajar*, if I didn't remember wrongly, this thing happened in 1953. At that time, it conflicted with that Emergency Act, which was implemented by the government then. *Fajar* had probably contravened that Act to be charged [in court]. At that time, other than Thumboo, that is actually Edwin Thumboo, it also involved two other persons. One of them was Sidney Woodhull, another was Puthucheary. These people became very important figures in Barisan Sosialis later on. Woodhull was the Vice-Chairman of Barisan Sosialis, while Puthucheary was in the Central Committee of Barisan Sosialis. They were both leftists amongst the English-educated students. There were quite a few [English-educated leftists], but they were the most famous ones. Subsequently, they also became supporters of the PAP (People's Action Party). Well then let me mention this in passing, they were later jailed and confined at Changi. Then they were moved from Changi to St. John's Island afterwards. Mr. Lee Kuan Yew often visited them [and these included] Lim Chin Siong, Woodhull, Puthcheary, and also Devan Nair, who became our President later. All these people were leftist elements amongst the English-educated. Later on, the PAP split and they were arrested again during the Malaysian Federation period. They were even exiled as some of them were born in Malaysia. Let me share something interesting, that is, some of those who went to Malaysia were invited by the Malaysian government to join their advisory.

Question?... (Question unclear in recording)

Han: This student, here, I would like to know what school were you from?

Student: I was from Chung Cheng.

Han: Chung Cheng? My junior! Hello, Junior. Formerly, during the pre-war years in 1938 or 1939, [Chung Cheng High School] was already established. Not long after that, war broke out and the school was closed. Now I am not going to talk about the history of Chung Cheng High School, or everyone will have to spend the night here. Let me put it simply, there is a reason for Chung Cheng's unique background. That is, it originally was pro-Kuomintang [also known as KMT, or Nationalist]. Chung Cheng High School, does anyone know why is it called "Chung Cheng"? That's because it used Chiang Kai-shek's name, as

Chiang Kai-shek was also known as Chiang Chung-cheng. So, I'm going to tell you a joke now: The greatest contributor to Chung Cheng High School was Dr. Chuang Chu Lin, who was one of its founders. He held the post of the principal for a significantly long time, and achieved a lot. Hence, we called him the "Father of Chung Cheng", which actually meant the founding father of Chung Cheng High School. Later on when we were playing riddle-solving, one of the riddles was "Chiang Kai-shek's father" and the answer to it was "Chuang Chu Lin" because he was the "Father of Chung Cheng". But how odd is Chung Cheng High School? After the war, the school was reopened and many Kuomintang's school teachers who fled from Mainland China were hired. This was because of the failure of Kuomintang in China in 1949 and many teachers could no longer stay there as they were more inclined towards Kuomintang and disliked the communists. Going to Taiwan [was a problem as] they could not take in too many professors. Going to Hong Kong [was also a problem as] they would have to teach lessons in Cantonese and those teachers could not speak Cantonese. Hence, they came to Singapore. When they came here, they did not go to The Chinese High School as it was regarded as being close to Peking's communists, whereas for Chung Cheng, the school's name itself was familiar, as it indicated a connection to Chairman Chiang. Besides, let me tell every one of you here today, the four Chinese characters of Chung Cheng High School were previously written by Chiang Kai-shek, although it does not seem so anymore. What was strange about Chung Cheng is that, most of the teachers were inclined towards Kuomintang, while most of the students were inclined towards the communists. That's all. This was the way I already felt while I was studying in Chung Cheng. Let me just talk about this example, we had a teacher called Huang Lingsheng at that time. We were not allowed to call him Mr. Huang [the way of addressing a teacher], but instead were made to address him as Professor Huang. Why was it so? It turned out that he used to be a Professor in the same Whampoa Military Academy where Chiang Kai-shek was the principal. He told us, "Do you know Chou En-lai (Zhou Enlai) was my subordinate then?" His Mandarin was spoken with an unknown accent, "Do you know who on earth is Chou En-lai? He was just my subordinate then." Subsequently, mischievous students like us would exclaim, "Whoa Mr. Huang, how great you are! Chou En-lai was your subordinate and so, what is he doing now?" Do you get what we meant by asking such a question? That was to make him "lose face". Chou En-lai had already become China's premier then, what are you doing now? There were a lot of similar cases like this amongst the Kuomintang supporters. There was also a Lin Xianjie, do you know who he is? An ex-principal of Whampoa Secondary School — Lin used to teach in Chung Cheng. He was a former military general in the KMT. So you will know how the situation was like in Chung Cheng then. However, our principal — Dr. Chuang

Chu Lin, wanted to follow Cai Yuanpei's principle of establishing schools free from political cliques. Therefore at that time, Chung Cheng High School had pro-communist teachers, anti-communist teachers, as well as pro-Kuomintang and anti-Kuomintang teachers. [He was] incorporating diverse elements and letting a hundred flowers bloom. Hence, a very vibrant kind of academic atmosphere prevailed then. The subsequent achievements of Chung Cheng were largely attributed to our principal — Dr. Chuang Chu Lin, as he had continued Tsai Yuan-pei's style of schools. That is all I wanted to add, Thank you.

Question: [original question in Chinese] I would like to consult Professor Koh again. I know that you were also studying in the University of Singapore then. In our University of Singapore, the students' impressions of ...... DSC (Democratic Socialist Club), erm ...... no, DSC was pro-government. .... The student activities in the University of Singapore were largely unknown to outsiders like us. The students in the University of Singapore were all English-educated and they were also involved in many activities that Mr. Han had mentioned, thus they were not completely indifferent to the people's livelihood. I think Professor Koh should be the most suitable candidate to talk about these student activities in the University of Singapore.

Koh: I thought my brief, originally, was to talk about my primary and secondary school experiences and activities, and not the university and that's why I didn't touch on that in my forum presentation. Yes, as I had indicated earlier, we did support the government's brand of socialism, democratic socialism. As I've mentioned before, my political leanings were much influenced both by my mother and our own social circumstances. My mother, a pre-war Chinese immigrant, was a great admirer of Mao Zedong (Mao Tse-tung). She was nationalistic and socialist in inclination, with a strong sense of social injustice and an active member of the European Employees Union. As I have mentioned before, during the course of my earlier *Tangent* interview, I went with them on their picnics, listened to their songs, and their talks and so on. I also gave them English lessons. And so I was like my mother, very concerned with social injustice, and had nationalistic aspirations for independence from foreign rule. Having lived through the old China as a young adult before coming to Singapore for an arranged marriage, she was impressed by the new China because she said, for once, women were regarded as equals. Secondly, while people were generally poor, nobody starved, and everybody was treated equally in the new China under communism. For people of my mother's generation, they did not separate their [Chinese] nationalism from the political ideology of communism. But she was not consciously a communist, and seemed attracted more to its socialist aspects. So when a classmate and good friend approached me to join the Democratic Socialist Club that a group of students from other faculties such as Law, were forming, it seemed natural to join as I found democratic socialism (as opposed to communism) more attractive. At the time, as a Year One student, I was of course naïve and wasn't aware that it may have been a pro-government Club. I had always, since my school days, joined clubs and societies which promoted things I was interested in. In this case, partly peer influence and an idealistic interest in promoting democratic socialism led me to become firstly, a member, and then its Publication Secretary and eventually, Vice-President. As such, I was the editor of their official organ, *Demos*, and also of their newsletter, the *Socialist Democrat*. In fact, we were not always pro-government. For instance, we opposed the government's plans to introduce so-called "elite schools" which turned out to be the fore-runner of the Junior College, and NJC became the first of these.

Koh: But looking back now, we were also the channel through which the government ministers came to speak to the university students. I saw this as providing opportunities for dialogue as well as education of us undergraduates in political developments and realities. We organised several seminars at which Mr. Lee Kuan Yew and Mr. Rajaratnam came to address students, while Dr Goh Keng Swee, would give scholarly talks and workshops which seemed more like learned lectures and tutorials. At the time, the English–educated undergraduates were regarded and also were made to feel (which they too felt) that they were going to be the future leaders of Singapore. They would be manning the Civil Service, the professions, and they were to be the future ministers, and so on. If that was going to be the case, then it was our duty and in our self-interest to see that Singapore was peaceful, harmonious and so on. As the communists were seen both nationally and globally to be threats to peace and prosperity, those who joined the Democratic Socialist Club were anti-communist. But the interesting thing is that by our time at the University of Singapore in the mid-sixties, the Socialist Club had lost its fire. It was interesting that the people who led the Socialist Club during our time were students who seemed to be comfortably middle-class, who had attended Anglo-Chinese School, and one of them [Raymond Ong] was Peranakan. I saw them as the wealthy students masquerading as socialists. Ironically, the Socialist Club was also perceived to be sympathetic to the Barisan Sosialis and thus pro-communist. We were therefore afraid they would control the Students' Union, so we stood for elections and our candidates (including myself) won the majority of seats.

Nonetheless, in life, things tend to be more complex than they seem. When the Nantah students were protesting and the government sent riot squad vans to control the situation, our student union including me, together with the University of

Malaya Student Union representatives went over to express solidarity with the Nantah Student Union. Because this venue is not suitable for Powerpoint presentations, I could have shown you two pictures which I had intended to, together with some from my school days. One was a *Straits Times* picture of the University of Singapore Student Union members carrying placards, demonstrating on campus for university autonomy and academic freedom. And the other is of the three student unions' Executive Committee members posing in front of the riot squad vans on Nantah campus. When we visited Nantah campus we were really appalled at how privileged we were, and how under-privileged they were. We had air conditioning, we had single hostel rooms to ourselves, servants to — you won't believe it — clean our rooms, even to do our laundry; we had afternoon teas and coffee with cakes served in the hostels, apart from the usual three meals. And they were so poor. There were four to a table to share a meal, and they would sometimes even have five or six to share what's for four people. So the atmosphere over there was very, very different from that over our side at the University of Singapore. Because we felt privileged, some of us also felt bad, and thus we had a mission to advance democratic socialism to address inequalities and to act as a different voice from the Socialist Club which we believed had a more directly politically active agenda. It's true that by our time [the mid-sixties], the Socialist Club was no longer very active or radical, having also been started as an anti-colonial student body. And when the Student Union became very radicalized, it was under a different group, you know Tan Wah Piao, Juliet Chin, and the others who consequently got into trouble with the authorities. They were not from the Socialist Club as far as I am aware; it was a different group altogether. The year after I graduated, 1968, the University had a new Vice-Chancellor, who was significantly, both Chairman of the PAP and the Minister of Science and Technology.

Question: [original question in Chinese] In 1965, Mr. Lee Kuan Yew cried. Televisions may not be that common then, thus I wonder if the two of you happened to see that? As both of you led completely different lives, what were your different individual thoughts when you saw it?

Koh: I saw it but it didn't shock me; all that I was concerned about — I'm really embarrassed to admit this — was I did not have to take my Standard One Malay exam after all! I was then in Year Two at the University. When we joined Malaysia, Malay became the National Language and we had to learn Malay, especially if one was planning to join the Civil Service. So I was studying Malay and was due to take my Standard One exam on 9 August in the afternoon. So I when I heard the news, that was the first thing on my mind, "Oh! No need to take the Malay exam"! We were disappointed by the separation, of course, but not all that much as there were so many problems between the partners. Some of you may have heard this joke: one of the songs that school children sang, began with "Malaysia forever, ten million strong", remember? After separation, it became "Malaysia forever, ten minutes long." So among the English-educated that I knew, most were actually quite glad to leave Malaysia. Intellectually we understood why Mr. Lee.... if you've read Mr. Lee's *Memoirs* — wanted merger and why we separated ... over the fact that Singapore wanted a multiracial, multicultural "Malaysian Malaysia", while the Malays, motivated by Malay nationalism, wanted a Malay-dominated Malaysia with Malay rights and privileges. Mr. Lee had made a very powerful speech in the Malaysian Parliament, indeed in Malay, to argue why don't we help all who are poor equally, regardless of race? Merely giving the Malays special rights and privileges, having Malay as the National Language (I recall his language was quite strong), will not necessarily make the majority of the Malays any more wealthy. It should be about the creation of an equal society.

Han: Now, let's talk about what I felt about seeing this. Firstly, I would like to raise a point to everyone here. I, myself was against the idea of joining Malaysia then. The Singapore Government strongly wanted us to support the vote to join Malaysia, but I was in opposition to it. This dissenting vote cost my citizenship to be revoked after Malaysia was formed. When was my citizenship restored? It was in 1984, when Singapore had already gained independence for a long time that I regained my citizenship. Speaking about this personal experience is very saddening, I think I should not touch on too much of personal experiences. That time when I saw Mr. Lee crying, it proved that my stand against joining Malaysia was correct. If not, why withdraw? Right? Besides, I could understand why he had cried, because withdrawing from Malaysia was a very humiliating and very upsetting affair for some of the leaders in the People's Action Party (PAP). You know there were quite a few ministers who were strongly against withdrawal, Dr. Toh Chin Chye refused to sign on the withdrawal agreement, so did Mr. Ong Pang Boon as well. It was after much persuasion that they reluctantly agreed to the withdrawal from Malaysia. The reason for Mr. Lee Kuan Yew to be very upset at that time was due to a number of factors. Firstly, he originally thought that Singapore would be unable to survive independently. Did anybody read one of his books called *The Battle for Merger* are two paragraphs in it, stating clearly that Singapore would definitely be unable to achieve independence. This is the first reason. Another point is, Singapore was kicked out of Malaysia and was an abandoned orphan, an orphan without any kin, wandering about on the crossroads in the Far East. At that time, China was fiercely against Singapore. Now, I solemnly tell every one of you present here, if there are any fellow friends from China, please remember this: China and Singapore are not always on very good terms all the time. [Words such as] "Lee Kuan Yew is our old friend", I am sorry, but there was a time when we were not friends but foes! China Central Radio Station used to broadcast [messages like] "Down with Lee Kuan Yew, Goh Keng Swee's reactionary regime" everyday. These were not matters that were too long ago! The United States were too far to offer any support, whereas Malaysia was waiting to see how Singapore was going to survive and end up bending over and kneeling down to beg the Malaysian leaders to take you back in again. The Indonesian Confrontation then was not over yet, hence Singapore was an orphan abandoned on the crossroads in the Far East, an orphan without any kin then. Think about it, how can we survive with such an orphan? So I can understand Mr. Lee's mixed feelings of being at a loss then. Therefore, when I saw him cry, I was actually experiencing his mixed emotions as well. My citizenship was revoked, when should it be returned?

Question: ... (Question unclear in recording)

Koh: At the moment, I'm giving a course at NTU for non-Literature students, called "Imagining Singapore", and among the things that my students are required to read are chapters from the two-volume memoirs of Mr. Lee. The students, both local and foreign, were not very familiar with the events surrounding merger while our generation lived through it. When discussing this I recalled the two events which made a great impact on us. One was the Prophet Mohammad's Birthday procession riots in 1964 and the curfew which kept us fearfully at home during my first year at the university. There was tremendous fear among both the Chinese and Malay communities in Singapore that this could happen again. Indeed, the threat of racial riots recurring was one of the reasons Mr. Lee gave for Singapore not being able to remain in Malaysia. It was again this fear that could not be ruled out, and in fact, some years after we'd left Malaysia, the May 13 riots occurred in Malaysia in 1969. The second major fear was economic survival, especially unemployment.

One of the two things that happened as soon as Singapore joined Malaysia, was the arrest of left-wing elements including some Nantah students by the Malaysian central government. Barisan Sosialis and such students had also opposed the merger. Lee Kuan Yew, in his memoirs had noted, "I saw it coming, but it was not my job to warn them." Ironically, just before separation, he was himself in danger of being arrested. He quotes letters from the British government expressing fears that with the continuation of Singapore in Malaysia, Mr. Lee Kuan Yew could one day also be arrested. And he also quotes Tunku Abdul Rahman saying that, "Oh, this troublesome person down there, if he continues, we must do something about him." We had seen what the Malaysian government did to the left-wing elements and those student leaders at Nantah, you know, and that it could happen to Mr. Lee. Therefore the English-educated among us felt that the merger was not working out; it was not going to succeed and we were fearful of more riots, as we had lived through one of the major riots before. After the May 13 1969 riots, one of the questions that I recall people asking was: supposing major riots happened again in Malaysia, and Chinese started rushing across the Causeway, what would we in Singapore do? Do we draw up our gates and say they cannot come in because they are Malaysians? Or do we, to prevent them from being slaughtered, open the gates and let them come in? Those of you who didn't live through the times may not appreciate such fears.

But Mr. Lee and his Ministers did feel Singapore wouldn't be able to survive alone, and the Malaysian government also felt that we won't survive on our own. That gave the Singapore government an added incentive to show them, and work harder, even to choose unorthodox means to pump up the economy. What has happened, as I point out to my students, is that the economy has become a main obsession. To what extent has this obsession with economic survival, and thus political stability, to do with the sense of fear of rocking the boat — the fear that Singapore could suddenly not prosper any more, if there were too many people with different and opposing views — despite a sense that there has now been a relaxation, enabling more flowers to bloom, so to speak, to adapt one of Chairman Mao's best known phrases?

Question: I am a voice from the past. Although these events happened more than forty years ago, the version of events that I recall happening in the then University of Singapore in the early sixties, that led to the formation of Democratic Socialist Club were quite different from the version recounted by Dr. Koh. Every club or society has the right to accept or reject new applications for membership based on the declared goals and programmes of that organisation. The PAP leadership has often made it a point that they are concerned that their party may be hijacked or captured by others who do not share the goals and programmes of their leadership. We who ran the University Socialist Club shared the same concerns, and had the responsibility to defend the proud 10-year history of anti-colonial struggle from the formation of the Socialist Club in 1953, right through to 1963. After the demise of the Malayan Democratic Union, which was the second organisation of English-educated left-wing anti-colonial people. The University Socialist Club was founded in 1953 and took over the panel of anti-colonial struggle among the minority of the privileged English-educated students who saw beyond their self-interests as beneficiaries of the privileged colonial system, to serve society and to demand for independence from British rule. Some of you may not be aware that Singapore in the early 60s was at a political crossroad. The society was deeply divided between those who supported the ruling PAP's leadership's advocacy of independence through merger with Malaysia, based on the terms proposed by the alliance government of Malaysia. Malaysia itself was in fact a British-initiated concept. The Socialist Club and other organisations that shared its views spearheaded the anti-Malaysia campaign based on the terms offered to Singapore for participation in Malaysia. The correctness of this position was subsequently validated by Singapore's exit from Malaysia barely two years later. I was then the Secretary General of the University Socialist Club, when a group of students, some with known relationship with the PAP leadership, came to apply for membership in the Socialist Club, understanding and being concerned about their real interest in the context of the political struggle of that time, we had our reservations and did not support their application for membership. Consequently, they signed a petition among themselves and their friends, and demanded for membership of the club. Without even giving us the courtesy of a response, the next day, there was a press statement which was amply reported in *The Straits Times* announcing the formation of Democratic Socialist Club. So the Democratic Socialist Club was not formed by a group of students who had views different from the Socialist Club. They were formed by a group of students that attempted to capture the Socialist Club, but were unsuccessful in their attempts and consequently formed an organisation that subsequently ruled the undergraduate adjunct of the ruling PAP. PAP ministers and their partners in the then Malaysia Solidarity Convention came with predictable frequency to the campus to speak at DSC forums. The Socialist Club continue to exist for several more years, but eventually closed down in the early 70s as a result of the oppressive climate of that time. Thank you.

Koh: I'm not familiar with that part of the story. [i.e., regarding the unsuccessful attempt by that group of students to become members of the Socialist Club] . May I know your name? Either I don't recognise you or....

Guest: Age has taken its toll. My name is Koh Kay Yew.[3]

Koh: Oh! Koh Kay Yew! Right..... I was not part of those who applied for membership, and in fact, I don't even remember that. I joined because I happened to be friends of those who invited me to join them in the formation of the new Club. But I recall, by that time the Socialist Club was already not an active force in the sense that it was not strongly associated with any kind of activism like the kind that was associated with the anti-colonial struggle of the Socialist Club in the fifties. Anyway it was formed in 1953, when I had just started primary school, so I didn't

---

[3] According to clarification by the speaker, Koh took Economics and was her senior at university.

know that part of Socialist Club history. I'm sorry that when I saw you, Kay Yew, I didn't recognize you. But we were not, I believe, close friends. I don't think we've met since you graduated from university, and I think this is the first time.

But that was not how I saw it. I was not aware of the other agenda, although in retrospect, as I'd already said in my previous *Tangent* interview, it could be that the PAP government did, perhaps, use us in a way, as a student body sympathetic to its ideas, and as I'd also mentioned earlier today, we were indeed the means through which ministers came to address undergraduates on campus, speak at forums, give seminars and conduct workshops and so on. But they came to campus also as elected *Members* of Parliament and Ministers of the government to address the student constituency.

Ong: [Originally in Chinese] Thank you Professor Koh. We also thank the audience for their active participation. Although we would like to continue the discussion, the time is up. Thank you everyone for participating. This event is organised in conjunction with a forthcoming exhibition which will also feature collaborations with various schools. It would be appreciated if members of the public with any valuable objects from that period of time, such as school publications or souvenirs from taking part in school activities and so on, can contact us, to either donate or lend them to us for the exhibition. That's all for today, let us thank the two speakers.

My Project Work Experience

Nur Nasuha[1]

Good afternoon ladies and gentlemen, fellow school mates and teachers. I am here to tell you about me and my group mates' experience in this project. As an introduction, I am Nur Nasuha, a fellow representative from the "Xinminologists", which is our group name. We selected this name because we thought if the people involved in the study of animals are called "zoologists" and those who study plants are "botanists", why don't we call ourselves "Xinminologists"? We are, after all, the group with the responsibility to research and relive our own school heritage — the pride and joy of Sin Min High School, currently 62 years of age.

Let me tell you our back-breaking journey from the beginning. Every Secondary Two student in our school has to do Project Work (PW). It is compulsory as part of our curriculum and we will be given grades. The five of us or "Xinminologists" were specially selected by our history teacher and teacher in-charge, Ms Joan Chia, to take up this external project.

Frankly speaking, we had initially thought this was just another project with nothing particularly significant about it. It could be easily completed by mere research through the Internet, books and so forth, after which we would compile the information in a beautiful sketchbook as a final product. However, a big surprise was in store. There was little relevant information available, and official records or reference materials were also not given to us. We only had three things to start with — a written script on the play "Xinmin Story"; a Xinmin Secondary School 60th anniversary commemorative magazine — *A Tree's Tale*; and the original name of the school, Sin Min High School.

The commemorative magazine and the "Xinmin Story" script only contained brief details about the school's events and its progress over the years, with little specifics and elaboration. Pictures available only had short descriptions about the event with

---

[1] Nur Nasuha participated in the exhibition and researched on her school's history as a student of Xinmin Secondary School.

no dates or further details. With no resources or reference materials, we knew we had to start from literally nothing.

We had a shaky start, spending the first few months with no progress. We went to forums and had many discussions on how to obtain sources of information but the efforts all came to nothing. Interviews with teachers were unsuccessful, the school library had no materials for us, and even the school website had nothing. As the deadline approached, we knew we needed to get find information somehow. A task undertaken must be completed. Thus, we started to think out of the box. If secondary sources were non-existent, we have to look for primary sources.

The first breakthrough in our project was when we contacted and interviewed the old Sin Min High School staff and students. We would like to acknowledge these people for the help they rendered. They shared with us their memories of their school days and gave us a wider scope of the situations and hardships they faced in those post-war years. From then on, we had a picture of the past and it became a stepping stone to greater accomplishments in this project.

Our second breakthrough and most important discovery happened when we found an old handbook of Sin Min High school. It was found among the collection of old and new Xinmin items in the school. Written in Chinese, it formed the backbone of our whole research, by providing data such as the number of classes and facilities. With the help of my group mates, they painstakingly translated this information into English, so that it could be understood by non-Chinese readers. Besides these documents, we also found pictures with specific dates and description of events, giving us an accurate take of the conditions in the past.

With the information from all the sources mentioned, after eight long months of hard work, we created an official account of the history of the old Sin Min High school. This information can now be found on the Internet, both on our school website and also on the Wikipedia website.

There are more stories behind the scenes of the eight months of Project Work: the tears, the heated arguments and the long process of inference and corroborating different accounts to get an accurate picture and compiling those accounts together. We have gained much indeed from this experience. Beside the usual takeaways of developing personal qualities, such as perseverance, we also learnt much more about our own school identity and hence gained a sense of pride. Being part of the school's tradition is one thing, but we felt more deeply for its values from what we have explored, beginning from how it started, how it overcame adversities such as the times when it almost closed down.

For me, throughout this project, I was able to reflect on my experience being in a secondary school with Chinese traditions. Being Malay and a non-Chinese speaker, I faced difficulties in an environment where the majority is made up of Chinese students, particularly due to the language barrier. I am the only Malay student in my class. And sometimes, I do feel slightly awkward because I am in a place where people are speaking a language foreign to me. I am not blaming them for letting me feel this way, because I know it is natural to speak your mother-tongue if you are talking to a person of the same race. However, I do feel insecure, as I could never know whether my friends are talking about me in front of me.

However, though I face such difficulties, I do try to adapt. I am fortunate to have friends who understand my problem and they would try their best to speak in English when I am with them so that I can understand what they say. When they converse in Chinese, they will do translations for me. I really appreciate them for their understanding. On the other hand, when one is in a school with Chinese traditions, it is natural that one will pick up some Chinese expressions. This can be very useful. Once, a Chinese teacher came to my class, not realising that I was there, she greeted us in Chinese. Being polite, I was able to respond in Chinese.

For me, I learn that though I belong to a minority race, I could still be friends with people from other races. It doesn't mean that friends cannot be made when there are differences in culture and perspective. During lessons, I honestly do not see the divide between myself as a Malay and my friends as Chinese. I feel we are all the same, we are all Xinmin students. I also feel that I can serve my school, being Malay doesn't matter. The school needs the contributions of all students. In conclusion, I wish to say that we share pride of being a part of Xinmin's glorious history, and also, the pride of wearing this uniform.

Thank you.

MY THOUGHTS ON PARTICIPATING IN THE EXHIBITION "EDUCATION AT LARGE: STUDENT LIFE AND ACTIVITIES IN SINGAPORE, 1945–1965"

Hsin Shu Han[1]

Transcribed by Chan Cheow Thia

Translated by Chiu Wei Li

As we march forth ceaselessly, we should also occasionally review the paths once trodden.

To get kids of our day and age to research their school's history, we need to make the whole affair interesting, otherwise these kids, who have grown up in a highly materialist world, would not understand the purpose of the effort. So we got them to dabble in web design, shoot videos, participate in external exhibitions, record in studios, interview alumni members and etc.

Some exhibition visitors commented politely that our website is very interesting; actually what's really interesting is not our website but our school history and the stories of our alumni members. The history of Chung Cheng High School is full of character, this really helped us a lot. The Tangent offered a platform for us to explore our history and the students did a great job. Thanks to our passionate and patient alumni members, we were able to learn how down-to-earth the earlier generations of Chung Cheng students were.

After having participated in this project, I feel very strongly that the expression "heroes make great times, great times make heroes" is very apt in describing the

---

[1] Hsin Shu Han is a Chinese language teacher at Chung Cheng High School. She led a team of students to participate in the exhibition and to research into their school's history.

Chung Cheng High School students then. During the 1946 standardised examinations, if my memory serves me right, Chung Cheng was top in the country. It was the best performing Chinese medium school. (If I am mistaken, please correct me, as my source is from our school magazine). Of course, we also know why the school was founded; at that time, Chung Cheng was full of talented people. Even today, we can clearly see that many alumni members have made great achievements in society.

Through our interviews with alumni members, we found that in those times, some of them were full of idealism regarding social reform. They thought that they could refer to China's experience to help Singapore change for the better, so they expended a lot of energy over this matter. Their passion still moves us deeply today. They spent a lot of time organising activities such as fund-raising, farewell parties, tea parties, study groups, mentoring groups; the entire school was like a big family.

We also interviewed some alumni members who did not share the same ideals in social change. Rather, they thought that Singapore could go its own route. So they did not participate in the Chung Cheng mass activities at that time, instead they participated in activities such as basketball, or student activities by the Chung Cheng lake. Whichever type of alumni we interviewed, we could still feel their passion as we talked to them. They felt strongly that as a Chung Cheng student, whatever experiences they had gone through, they still feel a strong sense of pride for having actually experienced that special era.

"To hone one's trade, one needs to sharpen one's tool". For this project, our school's Chinese department purchased a special software; students used it happily in their website design. A reporter asked us what we hoped the students would learn from this activity. I thought that students in the past and present are the same. Each student's personality is different. Some are more mature, some less so; some are more attentive to details, some tend to see the bigger picture. Anyway, as educators, we hope to sow some seeds in their minds. These seeds are like the stories we hear from our parents when we are young. We learn from these stories some traditions and culture, they will not blossom or sprout when we are still young, but maybe when we are of a certain age, they'll start to influence our work, our judgment and our thinking. Similarly, we might not expect students to apply or gain specific rewards from what we have presently taught them. We are just sowing seeds, in the hope that one day they'll blossom and become beneficial to their lives.

Personally, when I started this project, I felt like a bystander. However, as I became more involved, I felt I was slowly falling in love with this project. You'll realise that, as you examine these matters, you'll tend to notice their positive aspects. No matter what the students did then, what you see was their youthful passion. It's difficult to be cool-headed about it, and you will not begin to judge if what they did was right or wrong. As I walk around the Chung Cheng campus now, I see the school through their eyes. I wonder why our lake has become so small, because the Chung Cheng lake was very big in the past. I also wonder what happened to a particular tree. In the campus, I can feel that I am in constant conversation with past students or events. So after this project, my feelings toward Chung Cheng have changed. I'm not merely a passerby, I feel that I have delved into it deeply and have become a part of it.

Early generations plant trees, while later generations enjoy the shade. In contrasting the present and the past, one develops many reflections. Walking in the campus, I can still hear the shrill voices of sixteen year-olds reverberating in the wind; I hear the alumni members reminiscing about a particular youth who could make the entire school fall silent within a minute. In those turbulent times of the 1950s and the 1960s, sentiments of passion, acrimony and excitement were deeply intertwined. The young do not regret, and youthfulness never grows old. In the vast and boisterous campus, amidst the students' laughter, I can still sense his presence.

SOME THOUGHTS ON THE "EDUCATION-AT-LARGE" EXHIBITION

Tan Pin Pin[1]

My job for this exhibition was to document the process of putting the exhibition together. I shot footage of Tangent members interviewing the people who contributed artefacts, the members briefing teachers for the school component of the project, the students putting their group projects together, their teachers gently nudging them along. I was also there to video Han Tan Juan and Koh Tai Ann talk about their disparate experiences of their school days in the English and Chinese streams in a discussion that led up to the exhibition.

This was an opportunity for me to excavate other layers of Singapore society that I was interested in but was unfamiliar with. It amazes me how different one's life can turn out based on arbitrary factors, like whether one went to an English or Chinese school. The people they interviewed were people I would meet everyday but I would never dare ask about their lives, for example, a retired hawker, a shipping clerk, a Chinese book publisher. So this was a precious opportunity to visit another Singapore. I felt very privileged to be present even though I was just tagging along with people who were doing the real work.

Some of these interactions with the older generation were sombre, some lighthearted. I sensed they were glad that there was a receptive younger generation to pass on their stories about their place in Singapore. I am sure the interviewers felt a responsibility to remember what was being said to them. I certainly did, hence the video recordings. The interviews were often enlivened with pictures, artefacts which many kept like precious family heirlooms. Much later, I asked another one of the interviewees how he felt about the whole exercise, he said "I thought that period of our lives was over and done with, buried and forgotten, but I sense that there is now a real interest in it, I am very glad. I never thought I would see this day."

---

[1] Tan Pin Pin is a Singaporean filmmaker who helped document the organisation of the exhibition.

Parallel with Tangent's excavation, the students who were set with the task of exploring their school's history of that period were excavating as well. Their presentations that became part of the exhibition made me laugh. I expected the same respectful tone that some of the interviews had taken, but I was taken aback by the child-like approach (What did I expect!). I remembered Chung Cheng's presentation vividly, it was a website with video clips. One of the clips were two re-enactments of a-day-in-the-life of two students in that era, acted by the same boy who wore cartoon sunglasses. St Nicholas' video had a dream-like quality, news clips were mixed with re-enactments and interviews. All were unintentionally whimsical. They did not have the emotional baggage that came with knowledge and could start their explorations of their past with a blank slate. That was how they saw their school then, I couldn't make them see history my way even if I wanted to. They had to get to the heart of the matter themselves.

While I was documenting all this, I was also shooting footage for *Invisible City* which started as a documentary about spaces in Singapore. Perhaps I was influenced by the Tangent excavations, the documentary gradually moved away from being about spaces to one about photographers, journalists and civil society documenting and searching for a Singapore for themselves, on their own terms. Some footage that I shot for the Tangent was used in *Invisible City*. In the documentary, I explored the labours of remembering, of searching for history, the unreliability of memory, as well as its decay, as vested in artefacts and in one's memory, the role of censorship as well. Trailing everyone around, I observed up-close how time processes facts. I found that there is no history without commitment, duty and purpose. It is also always biased.

PERSPECTIVES IN STUDENT MOVEMENT RESEARCH

Huang Jianli[1]

Transcribed and translated by Chan Cheow Pong

Good afternoon, everyone. Looking at today's forum and the concurrent exhibition, both of which have been titled as "Education at Large, 1945-1965: Student Life and Activities in Singapore", as well as last week's *Lianhe Zaobao* news item promoting the event, we may feel that the organizer has attempted to downplay the political overtones by shifting the focus away from student political activism and towards cultural, sporting and other activities of students. This can be interpreted as a more cautious approach on the part of the organiser to avoid as best as possible the topic of student political movements. This approach is of course reasonable. From the point of historical research, politics is merely one facet of history and we often have neglected other areas, such as society, economics and culture. Therefore, the studying of student leisure activities can help us observe the history of the 1950s and 1960s from more angles, instead of being concerned only with political events.

However, to many of us, our first impression of the 1950s and 1960s is that it was a turbulent era. In other words, the background of that period was intensely political. Therefore, this forum would be seriously flawed if it were to avoid all content of political activities. I have gone to view the exhibition before coming here today and I have listened to the earlier speeches. It is comforting that although the primary focus of this forum is on student leisure activities, student involvement in

---

[1] Huang Jianli is Associate Professor at the Department of History, National University of Singapore.

politics has not been completely neglected in both the exhibition and forum discussion.

This leads me to wonder if The Tangent, the organizer of today's forum and the exhibition, has some other considerations. I am not a member of The Tangent but I have always been paying attention to its activities because I think it is an important civil society group in Singapore. The aim of civil society organisations includes the carving out of a greater space for the community and society. They do not always oppose the government but they usually uphold an ideological consciousness which differs from that of the officialdom. While trying to achieve greater space, civil society groups would have continuous contact and negotiation with the establishment, sometimes resulting in a "tug of war". The Tangent was formed with the mission of maintaining a distance from the centre of power, being a tangential line that touches the rim of the circle, searching for space at the margin, and maintaining a relatively independent and critical stance. Following this line of thought, a question came into my mind. The main Chinese title of the exhibition "*Xiao-Yao-You*" (literally meaning "carefree roaming") does not mention student movements, but I think it is a clever play on words. It can refer to leisurely and carefree activities such as sports, drama and films, but it also encompasses the idea of being at large or getting away scot-free, thus subtly includes the notion of anti-establishment student movements. I am uncertain if the organiser had such similar thoughts when they were initially framing the title for their series of events.

Overall, the exhibition and today's forum complement each other very well. The organiser of the exhibition has collected a large amount of relevant material. Some of them have been sourced from the National Library, the National University of Singapore Library and the National Archives, but the organiser has also gathered a significant quantity from the schools themselves. I think this is an important contribution because we need to have a diverse range of historical materials if we were to delineate the history of the 1950s and the 1960s. Today, the availability of source material poses a major challenge to the study of many historical issues, such as the Nanyang University (Nantah) history project headed by Associate Professor Lee Guan Kin at the Nanyang Technological University. We know that there is quite a lot of relevant official material in Singapore but most of the official documents have yet to be made accessible to the public. Earlier, Tan Pin Pin has also mentioned in her talk about the limited access to sources in the National Archives of Singapore.

Let us take the archival materials on schools as an example. The Chinese High School was one of the hotbeds of student activism. However, in searching through the online catalogue of the National Archives, one will find that accessible material includes 707 photographs and only nine text documents. Similarly, accessible material on the Chung Cheng High School comprises 96 photographs and only 12 text documents. On Nanyang University, there are 2690 photographs but only seven text documents, and these seven documents concerns relatively unimportant issues such as problems relating to the flats of Nantah lecturers. We can be sure that the Ministry of Education has many important documents on these schools but, hitherto, only a very tiny portion has been made accessible to scholars and the general public. This is a barrier to our research work. Therefore, I feel that one big contribution of this exhibition and forum is the collection of historical material.

In doing research on student activism, another important but somewhat rigid perspective is on the binary differentiation of Chinese-educated and English-educated students. Several speakers have mentioned this today, and so did Tan Pin Pin in her documentary film. We must indeed think deeply about whether the Chinese-educated and English-educated students really lived in two isolated and completely different worlds. The discussion today reminds us that although they were segregated to some extent, there was communication and interaction between the Chinese-educated and English-educated students. Based on my impression, today's discussion of their connectivity has been confined only to activities relating to culture and sports. What about political activities — did the students interact, or even collaborate and help each other? If we observe the student movement triggered by the Wang Gungwu Report on Nantah, the participants had not only included Chinese-educated students. Many English-educated students in the University of Singapore, Singapore Polytechnic and Ngee Ann Polytechnic were also involved. Therefore, that wave of student movement was a collaborative effort, and there was cooperation between the Chinese-educated and English-educated students; they were not living in two entirely different worlds. Moreover, the world of the Chinese-educated students was far from being a narrow one. They were not only inclined towards Chinese history and culture; they also watched English drama and their textbooks included content on Western literature, history and philosophy. Hence, they definitely had some understanding of the thoughts and mindsets of their English-educated peers. If we were to split the Chinese-educated and English-educated into two completely segregated groups, we would be stereotyping and oversimplifying the history of student activism in Singapore. Therefore, we must be careful in our management of this perspective.

Thank you.

A Very Brief History of Idealism in Singapore

Kwok Kian Woon[1]

Transcribed by Chan Cheow Pong

Translated by Low Yen Yen

Let me begin by referring to one of the photographs that Mr Yung showed us — the Merdeka Bridge. This leads me to say something about social memory in Singapore. There used to be a pair of lions below the bridge; they were called the "Merdeka Lions". Does anyone here know where the "Merdeka Lions" went? It is now placed at the SAFTI Military Institute. If we ask our youth today whether they know the meaning of "merdeka," most of them would not know, and they would not give a reply like "independence" or "freedom", as they are not familiar with these concepts from an earlier era.

Huang Jianli asked about the student movements of the English-educated, especially those that took place in the 1950s and the 1960s. Actually, among members of the audience here today, there are two people who were involved. First, Michael Fernandez. Michael, can you raise your hand? Is it true, Michael, that you were involved in the University Socialist Club? Yes. And there's Professor Koh Tai Ann. Professor Koh, you were involved in the University Democratic Socialist Club? Yes. So there were two socialist clubs, one Socialist Club, one Democratic Socialist Club, at the then University of Singapore.

I told Sy Ren and Huay Leng that my topic could be "A Very Brief History of Idealism in Singapore". In Singapore, there are periods where young people have shown a great deal of idealism. About over ten years ago, I said this at The Substation:

---

[1] Kwok Kian Woon is Associate Professor at the Department of Sociology, Nanyang Technological University.

in Singapore, if you want to tell somebody off, you can say "You are an idealist! You are idealistic." We use the words "idealism", "idealist", or "idealistic" to tell somebody off. These words are the opposite of "realism", "realist", "realistic" — not "practical". We also tend to tell some young people, "You are not practical, you are *too* idealistic."

What are we missing if there is no idealism in our society? What is the cost to a society if there is no idealism? Idealism is an important topic to us, and can actually be a very practical issue, because if we cannot imagine a different future, how can we move towards a better future? To be able to imagine a different future, a different reality, that is the essence of being idealistic. And you don't just imagine — you try to work towards that reality. I will come to this at the end of my presentation.

1945 to 1965 is a very special period in the history of Singapore. Many young people then had no choice but to imagine a different future. Why? They were confronted by — and had to confront — many "isms". In Singapore — as well as in India, mainland China, Indonesia, Malaya, and later, Malaysia — there were colonialism, anti-colonialism, nationalism, communism, socialism, and democratic socialism. Of course, now it is all about capitalism! But there were many other "isms" then. It was not a black and white era at all. So for example, what did it mean to be progressive in the "leftist" or "rightist" sense, and were these categories mutually exclusive? Our youths today have little idea about what being leftist or rightist meant then. Again, this is a point about social memory in Singapore, especially the memory of the post-war and pre-independence era. Sometimes I joke that our young do not know the May 13 Incident; they may not even know September 11. But I also think that we cannot underestimate the ability of our young to imagine the future — alternative futures, alternative realities. This is something that is both very fundamental and very practical, because entrepreneurs must have this spirit, and political leaders must also have this spirit. However, we also need to look back and dig deeper to search for our multi-faceted and colourful history.

I also wish to talk about the curriculum in our education system. Sociologists will say that Singapore has a formal curriculum, an official curriculum. There is a lot of content in it and examinations are very important. This system may have its merits, but we also need to think about what its weaknesses are. For example, if you look at the student activities documented in this Exhibition, you can have a sense that the students learned a lot that cannot be acquired in the classroom, especially the leadership ability for independent self-organising. There was also a discussion on bookstores and popular culture, which showed us how popular culture and a more literary culture came together. We say in Singapore that we are a multiracial, multicultural society, but is this true? For example, if we did not have the Chinese bookstores in Bras Basah Complex, we would not have any place to find good Chinese books — every other bookstore you enter is selling English books. We used to learn Malay, but now it is very difficult to find a Chinese who can speak Malay. This is a very big change. Singaporeans used to be very, very multilingual. We did not just have English and Chinese, but we also have Malay and dialects. Now we tend to be bilingual, and it is English first and Chinese second for the Chinese population. So is multiculturalism truly a characteristic of Singapore? There also appears to be two cultures, what might be called "popular culture" and "literary culture". Can we merge them to create a public culture in Singapore? For example, our being here together today might be an opportunity for public interaction and for shaping a public culture beyond race and ethnicity.

The recent National Day celebrations said "Singapore, a City of Possibilities". But how can you have possibilities without idealism? Singapore's leaders encourage young Singaporeans to build something that their parents never imagined, something special and unique. I feel that young people have that spirit, but the culture today is much more complicated. We used to be able to differentiate clearly between "yellow culture" and "healthy culture". But today, culture is becoming more and more complex today, and the lines are increasingly blurred. How do you imagine something different from what you have when you are not even sure about what you do have?

A sociologist named Max Weber said — he said it in German, but I will say it in English — "Politics is the art of the possible". If people do not think about the impossible, ideals will not be realized; if you do not imagine, you will not achieve what you could have. I quote Weber's line to highlight the significance of today's forum — we need to look back and think about the meaning of this brief history of idealism. I think its meaning is to persuade us that the possibilities are limited when we only think about what is "possible"; we need to think, imagine, or even fantasize about a future that seems impossible, and be inspired towards that future.

Thank you.

A Historical Account of the Chinese Book Industry in the 1950s to the 1960s

Zhong Hongzhi[1]

Translated by Ng How Wee

In the field of historical research on the 1950s and the 1960s, scholars are mostly concerned with issues of identity and social transformation. One classic work of this nature would be Choi Kwai Keong's *Transformation of National Identity Amongst Singapore and Malaysian Chinese, 1945–1959*. With regard to cultural research, the focus usually revolves around cultural activities of the period, such as literature, epitomised by Fang Hsiu's *A Preliminary Study of The History of Post-War Malayan Chinese Literature*; the Chinese press industry, represented by the academic works of Ng Hong Teng, *A Study of Singapore Chinese Newspapers (1945–1959)* and *A Study of Editorials in Singapore Chinese Dailies (1945–1959)*; the study of drama activities, and etc. These works focus mainly on textual analyses and studies of writers, leaving much room for research on the production and operation of cultural activities or forms, such as publishing, circulation and consumption. Yet, the research of socio-cultural activities in Singapore during the two decades after the end of World War Two must include these topics, without which cultural research would be found wanting.

The 1950s and the 1960s were not only marked by major social transformations and upheavals, but also constituted an era of unprecedented cultural vibrancy. One

---

[1] Zhong Hongzhi was a PhD candidate at the Department of Chinese, National University of Singapore who was researching on Chinese bookstores in early Singapore. This article is a record of her presentation at the November 2007 forum organised by the Target in conjunction with the exhibition.

interesting question to ask would be, since culture is abstract, then how are books — which make up the fundamental medium of culture — produced, circulated and consumed? This question would naturally lead us to the bookstore, a pivotal factor in the industry of books. What is the significance of bookstores in Singapore Chinese culture? During the tumultuous post-war history of the 1950s and the 1960s, what roles did bookstores play?

The focus of this essay is on Chinese bookstores in the two decades of the post-war era. I will be approaching the topic from three areas. Firstly, the history of Chinese bookstores during the pre-war era, which is pertinent to our discussion; secondly, the relationship between the students and bookstores of the post-war era; lastly, the relationship between bookstores and the political situation.

(i) From Pre-war to Post-war Era
Bookstores during the Pre-war Era: Building a Cultural Bridge through Distribution

The earliest bookstores which were larger in scale and more widely recognised should be the Commercial Press of China and the Chung Hwa Book Company. They were the overseas branches of their parent companies in China. The Singapore branch of Commercial Press was established in 1915, while Chung Hwa's branch came into being in 1917. Later, the World Book Company and Shanghai Book Company were set up respectively in 1924 and 1925. These four book stores have long histories and were commonly known to Singaporeans as the "Big Four". According to records in the *Nanyang Annual*, before 1932, there were only eight Chinese book stores in the industry: besides the "Big Four", there were the Mei Mei Book Company, the New Bookstore, the Cheng Hing Company and the Wing Seng Book Company. Cheng Hing was a subsidiary of the World Book Company and specialised in the sale of pictures and diagrams. It merged with the parent company to form the World Book Company after the War. Mei Mei Book Company was the agent for the *Liang You Pictorial*, while the New Bookstore was a dealer in stationery. Wing Seng was an agent for books from Hong Kong and Canton. Before the war, the Chinese book industry in Singapore was of a considerable scale, with twenty-two players, of which the majority was also suppliers of stationery. In terms of strength and scale, Commercial Press and Chung Hwa were leaders of the pack.

During the pre-war era, the wholesaling of books took centre stage in the book business. Amongst all the bookstores, only Commercial Press and Chung Hwa published books under their company names, the rest did not engage in the publication business. (This lasted till 1938, when the ban on school textbooks espousing new ideas imported from the World Book Company in Shanghai led to the Singapore World Book Company's development and publication of primary school textbooks for public distribution. This endeavor ended with the Japanese Occupation of Singapore).

During the pre-war period, bookstores functioned mainly as business entities. Nevertheless, they also served as a "bridge" for the promulgation and influence of culture between Singaporean and Malaysian Chinese with their motherland (China).

Bookstores during the Post-war era: From Wholesaling to Publishing

After the war ended in 1945, people resumed their normal lives and the Chinese book industry experienced a new beginning. When the British army returned to Malaya, a brief period of political and cultural liberalisation ensued, resulting in an unprecedented flourishing of the cultural publishing industry.

Overview

How many Chinese bookstores were there after the war? According to the *Nanyang Annual*, there were "about over 30 Chinese bookstores in the whole of Singapore in the 1950s". However, no company names were recorded. The tenth anniversary journal of the Book Industry Association of Singapore included a list of its members from 1954 to 1957, some of which were dealers in stationery, paper manufacturers and printers of office documents. This is because "before the war, Chinese book publishers formed a club for Singapore book dealers at Seah Street. When the war ended, the book publishers reestablished a Book Association and merged with paper manufacturers and office document printers, boosting the size of the organisation."

The list of bookstores is as follows:

In 1954, there were 24 bookstores:

Popular Bookstore; Shanghai Book Company; Chung Hwa Book Company; China Book Company; Culture Book Company; Wing Seng Book Company; World Book Company; Zhi Cheng Book Company; Starlight Book Company; Sing Chew Book Store; Nanyang Book Company; Modern Book Company; Kai Ming Book Company; Read Read Bookstore; the New Bookstore; International Bookstore; Kong Beng Book Company; Liao Zhengbin Bookstore; Commercial Press; Malayan Chinese Educational Bookstore; Chung Kuo Trading Company; Black Cat Book Company

Two new players entered the industry in the same year: United Publishing House and Singapore Chinese Stationery Store.

In 1955, six new members joined the industry:

Guang Chang Book Company; The Youth Book Company; Students' Bookstore; Nantah Book Company; Wan Shun Company; Jing Hua Company, etc.

In 1959, there were 72 members in the Book Industry Association of Singapore including paper manufacturers, printers of office documents, of which 38 were registered as bookstores and publishers. (Refer to the address list of Book Industry Association of Singapore members found in *An Index to Singapore and Malaya* published in 1959)

During the post-war era, bookstores which were of a larger scale and more influential included the following: Chung Hwa, Commercial Press, Nanyang, Shanghai, United Publishing, Kai Ming, as well as the Cultural Club, the Redhill Cultural Club, etc. (the presence of these cultural clubs were reflected in their congratulatory notices published in the programmes of performances by artistic groups then), most of which were bookstores set up by a group of like-minded friends who congregated on Saturdays for tea gatherings and functioned as contact points for social interaction. According to the local senior newspaperman-cum-historian Han Juan Tuan, bookstores and cultural clubs were "locales where the literati met up to discuss common interests"; there were bookstores and magazines formed by like-minded cultured literati. Sometimes it only took one or two people to come together to set up a bookstore. These cultural clubs and bookstores would also publish books and independent literary titles.

The Publishing "Craze"

Besides the mushrooming of numbers, the greatest difference between bookstores during the pre-war period and the post-war era is the venturing of post-war bookstores into the publishing business which started with school textbooks. Of course, some publishers had already been publishing these materials prior to this. In fact, the Nanyang Book Company, established in 1936, was the first publisher of textbooks. It had published the *Nanyang Standard English Reader* as early as 1936 and this was the first locally published volume of English language textbooks for Chinese medium schools. However, the publishing "craze" of the local bookshops only occurred after the war.

Singapore was once the publishing centre for textbooks in Nanyang. When the Chinese immigrated to Singapore, and found themselves sojourning in a foreign land, they established schools and taught the Chinese language, using textbooks from China. Before the war, textbooks published by Commercial Press and Chung Hwa were widely circulated, with the latter being more popular of the two. According to memoirs penned by the director of the Shanghai Book Company,

Mr Chen Mong Tse, when a large group of intellectuals immigrated to Singapore, they became very familiar with the living environment of overseas Chinese and felt that textbooks written based on the social context of mainland China were not very suitable for overseas Chinese education. To address this problem, a group of literati in Hong Kong embarked on the writing of a complete set of textbooks. The Shanghai Book Company was very courageous and ambitiously took up this publishing project. This was known as the "modern edition" of textbooks published by the Shanghai Book Company in 1948. Thereafter, the World Book Company also set up the United Publishing House and published textbooks for Singapore, Malaysia and Borneo. In addition, the Nanyang Book Company also joined in this competition; together with Commercial Press and Chung Hwa which jointly published the edited version of textbooks for Singapore and Malaysia, the market was bustling with competition among numerous contenders. In 1959, "the different bookstores in Singapore published textbooks for Chinese medium schools. Primary school textbooks were published in different editions, namely the United edition by the United Publishing House, the Chung Hwa-Commercial Press edition by Chung Hwa and Commercial Press, the Modern Edition by the Shanghai Book Company, the Nanyang edition by the Nanyang Book Company, the World edition by the World Book Company, etc, and the Chung Hwa edition by the Chung Hwa Book Company. After the war, the Chung Hwa edition topped the charts of the Singapore and Malaysia markets, enjoying the highest sales among all editions. However, after the United edition entered the market, Chung Hwa's sales declined and many schools started to use the former for teaching and this helped to enhance its sales greatly throughout Southeast Asia. In 1958, the Chung Hwa-Commercial Press edition was released in the market and became widely used by lower primary levels. However, the United edition was still the authoritative volume for higher primary levels. Some schools used the World edition, the Nanyang edition and the Modern Edition either concurrently or partially. As for middle schools, there were the Chung Hwa Edition, the World Edition, the Commercial Press Edition, the Modern Edition, etc. Presently, schools used a combination of textbooks."

In December 1957, after Chung Hwa and Commercial Press merged to become one entity, World Book Company and United Publishing formed another, while Nanyang and Shanghai maintained their independence, competition finally ceased when these four parties established the "Singapore Educational Suppliers Company", specialising in the publication and distribution of Chinese medium primary school textbooks in Singapore and Malaysia.

The "localisation of school textbooks" may be seen as a highly significant event of the local publishing industry. Apart from that, the publication of all kinds of teaching reference books, supplementary materials and reading materials for teenagers flourished. For example, *World Children* and *World Youth* published by the World Book Company were very popular. Other than these major bookstores, the smaller players such as the Students' Bookstore had also published a series of primary school textbooks for different subjects. In a bid to boost business, the bookstore owner also distributed name cards during picnic gatherings.

Publication of Singaporean and Malaysian Literature

Apart from textbook publication, another important phenomenon would be the publication of Singaporean and Malaysian Literature. Professor Yeo Song Nian has observed that the Nanyang Press, the Youth Book Company and the World Book Company were the most prominent publishers during this period. Especially after 1954, the publication activities of the Nanyang Press gradually quietened while the Youth Book Company and the World Book Company were the most active. Mr. Chen Mong Chea from the Youth Book Company was committed towards the publication of Singaporean and Malaysian literary works since 1950s. Just recently, this eighty-seven year old gentleman embarked on a joint project with Hong Kong Ming Pao Publication Ltd. and published *A Collection of Selected Works by Contemporary Singaporean Writers*, with the objective of introducing local writers to overseas Chinese communities. Other publications worthy of mention are Fang Hsiu's *A Preliminary Historical Study of New Chinese Literature in Malaya* (3 volumes) published by the World Book Company and the *Nanfang Collections* published by the Youth Book Company. Other companies also engaged in similar publication projects.

From the pre-war period to the post-war period, the role of bookstores evolved from mere distribution to publishing. On the surface, this may seem like a transformation and pluralisation of management styles, but more significantly, it was an evolutionary leap for bookstores transforming from commercial entities to becoming cultural entities. Evidently, bookstores are by default a special form of business establishment. Its uniqueness lay in the very nature of books, which constitute a special type of commodity, encompassing the dual characteristics of "merchandise" and "culture". Hence, they not only function as commercial products, but also as cultural and social entities. Once involved in publishing, the cultural function of books acquires a greater sphere of influence. While they have to meet market demands, books also shape the tastes of readers, thereby steering the path of cultural development.

(ii) Bookstores and Students

As we look back at that era, many people would perhaps wish to know, what books did the students read then? What titles were sold? Or perhaps we should ask the reverse: What kind of books did the bookstores sell? What books did students read?

It was a very different era compared to the present time. Experienced journalist Mr. Han Tuan Juan shared that many students saved on their daily expenses to buy books during the 1950s and the 1960s; food for the mind was perceived as more important than food for the stomach. It was thus apparent that there was a vibrant reading culture. Moreover, that was a period marked by global turmoil and anti-colonialist movements, in which young students displayed a strong sense of social responsibility and idealism. They took part in strikes, fought for their rights and were undaunted by the powers-to-be. Students were not only well-read, they were extremely sensitive to the ongoing social developments around them; they were also very concerned about national and global issues. Their progressive orientation was reflected in their reading habits.

The students' reading materials can be classified into three categories:

1. Banned Publications

This was definitely an underground source. Books published by mainland China were in vogue then, and the more leftist the better. Books which espoused revolutionary ideas from a new era of a new China, such as *Tracks in The Snowy Forest* and *Liu Hu Lan*. There were many Chinese school students who sang songs like *The East is Red* and *March of the Volunteers*. These were banned publications. Some bookstores became very well-known for selling such publications which were in strong demand. Many people would recall a bookshop by the name of "Middle School Students" whenever the topic of banned publications is evoked. Some said that this bookstore was initially a provision shop which sold condiments and daily necessities. The eldest son of the shop had good business sense and started to sell banned publications which were more lucrative than daily necessities. It was believed that his supplies came from sailors. After making a profit from the sale of books, and since his provision shop business was facing increasing difficulties, he converted his shop into a bookstore. This showed that the book business was a profitable one during those days. In addition, other bookstores well known for selling banned publications included the Seng Lee Bookstore and the Ipoh Culture Bookshop.

2. Books on Literature, History and Philosophy

During those days, books on literature and philosophy sold very well.

Translated novels made up an integral part of literary works. One example was Romain Rolland's *Jean-Christophe,* which was highly popular among youths who were lovers of literature. Others would include *How the Steel was Tempered, The Gadfly* and *The Story of Zoya and Shura* from the Soviet Union. In addition to translated novels, one other popular literary work sold by the Shanghai Book

Company was *Thinking Twice*, which may be considered a must-read for the progressive youths of Singapore and Malaysia. This was an inspiring love novel which motivated people to pick themselves up from failure, and was thus seen as a work of educational value. It had close to thirty print runs and with about 2000 to 3000 copies for each run. It was a best-selling title for ten over years. I still saw the title in a 1970 book sales catalogue. It was equivalent to the *Harry Potter* novels of our present time. The students of Nanyang University (Nantah) also read *Song of Youth, Red Crag* and books written by Ba Jin.

Philosophy for the People was a banned book published by China but enjoyed immense popularity. There were also a few book collections on philosophy written for a wider audience. One editor of such books was Li Yi from the Shanghai Book Company. He penned a series of books on philosophy for popular reading and it achieved good sales in Singapore and Malaysia for 10 years. The students then felt that literary works alone were insufficient to fulfill their quest for knowledge and hence turned to philosophy publications for supplementary reading.

3. Self-Improvement Books and Books about Self-cultivation for Youths

Self-improvement books were also well-received by students. *You are the Genius* and *Ge Luo Shan* were two such books. Books that did not advocate revolutionary ideas, were retrogressive and did not reflect contemporary values were deemed to be unhealthy and shunned by students. Even the books written by Zhang Henshui were considered to be of a corruptive nature.

The activities of students in those days revolved around bookstores — they hung around bookstores, purchased books, read books, met up with their friends and dates there. Below is an extract of his memories by a Nantah alumni:

> "About forty to fifty years ago, in and around the Bras Basah Complex, there was a plethora of bookstores which served as cultural meccas, providing food for the soul. During that time, there was a huge coffee shop near the Shanghai Book Company called the Moon Orchid Pavilion and in it, there was a food stall famous for selling Hokkien noodles and another that sold wanton noodles. Every Saturday, large groups of students from Nantah and middle schools would visit and shop at the bookstores. It was a customary practice for people to first buy books followed by reading them, and only when they had extra time, would they go to the coffee shop to meet friends for tea and snacks."

> "Nantah was formed in 1956. During the years 1956, 1957 and 1958, Nantah students would congregate at bookstores. This was because bookstores such as the Shanghai Book Company, the Commercial Press, Union, Popular and the

Middle School Student, Students' Bookstore were all situated in the same area. The college students would go to these bookstores during the weekends. Naturally, as the college students became very familiar with these bookstores, bookstores became their meeting points and places for social interaction. We stayed in the dormitories then and would go downtown during Saturdays. The majority of meeting places were bookstores."

Another example would be the Union Book Company. While most of the books sold by Chinese bookstores in Singapore were publications from China, Union stood out as a dealer of Taiwanese books. Union opened in the same year as Nantah. Due to the political situation and the Nantah teaching staff who were largely from Taiwan, the textbooks and reference books (especially those for literature, history and philosophy) used were mainly from Taiwan. Hence, the Taiwanese books imported by Union happened to satisfy this market demand.

(iii) Bookstores and the Political Situation

The intimate relationship between bookstores and the political situation may be described as a highly complementary one. The growth and decline of Singapore Chinese bookstores were directly connected to the social, political and culture developments and changes in ideological trends. Due to time constraints, we will illustrate this from broadly the following perspectives:

1. The Establishment of a Bookstore

We will use the Shanghai Book Company as an example. The late director Ms. Linda Chen once said, "Shanghai Book Company is a product of the times." Its founder, Mr. Chen Yoh Shoo has recollected, "I came to Singapore in February 1923. In 1924, I was appointed as the store manager of Chung Hwa, and when I travelled between Singapore and Malaysia, many friends shared with me the difficulties of purchasing new journals and books related to the 'new culture' that originated in China. This was because the Commercial Press and the Chung Hwa Book Company did not sell foreign publications then and other bookstores only sold old thread-bound books and traditional novels. Together with Mr. Wang Shuyang and a few others, we set up the Shanghai Book Company at Number 13, Hill Street, right above Chung Hwa. We started business on 1 Dec 1925 and enjoyed the support and popularity from people in the cultural circle and educational sector, as well as intellectual youths." China was undergoing through the epoch-making May Fourth New Cultural Movement during that period, and reading materials that promulgated new knowledge and ideas were published in great quantities, creating a huge and widespread influence. The impact of the new culture could immediately be felt in Nanyang and increasingly, people were becoming thirstier for new knowledge. With this background, the establishing of the Shanghai Book Company may be seen as a product of those eventful times. Hence, this proves the words of Ms. Linda Chen of the Shanghai Book Company. It was even said that when the Shanghai Book Company started business, many readers went to enquire about the new books and journals even before they have arrived. When they finally arrived, the bookstore staff had to remove the packaging overnight in order to meet the demands of readers.

2. Impact of Anti-war Efforts

Anti-war efforts had a tremendous impact on bookstores. Whenever there is mention of anti-war efforts by the Nanyang Chinese, one tends to think in terms of the anti-Japanese war fund-raising efforts by Tan Kah Kee, as well as the donations, both in cash and kind by Nanyang Chinese. However, anti-war efforts also had a huge influence on local bookstores. Many Nanyang Chinese saw themselves as immigrants, though they were physically in Nanyang, psychologically they were oriented towards China. Hence, when the war broke out, local Chinese were eager to keep up with the events in China and huge shipments of books were imported from China. It is well illustrated in the *Nanyang Annual* that the value of book imports from China were merely about 0.28 billion dollars in 1937 and this increased more than threefold to 0.85 billion in 1938. This trend of increase was maintained throughout the years of 1938 and 1940, until Singapore fell to the Japanese and bookstores closed down.

3. Carpet Ban on Communist Publications

In 1956, under the premise of anti-communist efforts, the British colonial government announced the ban on all publications from 53 publishers in mainland China. Almost 95% of the Chinese books in the market were affected by this carpet ban. This posed a serious threat to the supply of stocks to bookstores. On the other hand, it created an opportunity for local books to be published. Under such circumstances, the Youth Book Company was set up and it started venturing into the publishing of Singapore and Malaysian Chinese literary works. In his recollection, Mr Chen Mong Chea said, "Since we were unable to forecast how long the ban on China books would stay, we decided to give it a try. We started off with publishing The Singapore-Malaysian Literature Series edited by Li Rulin and this was well-received. We went on to publish the second and third series."

4. The Rise of Local Consciousness

After 1956, the anti-colonialist and independence movement was creating huge waves and learning Malay language became a common goal among intellectuals in the Chinese community. Chinese bookstores started to publish Malay language books. One example was the *Abridged Malay-Chinese Dictionary* and the authoritative *Chinese-Malay Dictionary*. When the Shanghai Book Company published its book catalogue for its 45th year anniversary, there was a segment on "Mastering the National Language" which included dictionaries and books on Malay grammar.

5. Change in Education Policies

When Singapore and Malaysia separated, there were changes in Singapore's education policies. When all schools came under one national stream, Chinese bookstores started to struggle. Some bookstores are still trying hard to keep up and will terminate business if they are unable to survive. The Students' Bookstore closed down in 2005; some others managed to evolve with the times, and one such example is the Popular Bookstore which adopted a "bilingual bookstore" strategy. It is still popular till this day. The established Shanghai Book Company has managed to engage the partnership of China National Publication Import and Export (Group) Corporation to form the Shanghai Book (CNPIEC) Company (Pte) Ltd.

With the rise of China, there has been global enthusiasm in the learning of the Chinese language. The flagging Singapore Chinese book industry has inadvertently gotten a new lease of life. Opening a new store downtown, the oldest bookstore, the Commercial Press, is now riding the waves of the times. At one time, the Chinese book industry has almost withered like flowers, its revival now may be likened to that of familiar swallows which have returned. Indeed, such paradoxes of history usually defy easy comprehension.

Part II
Oral History

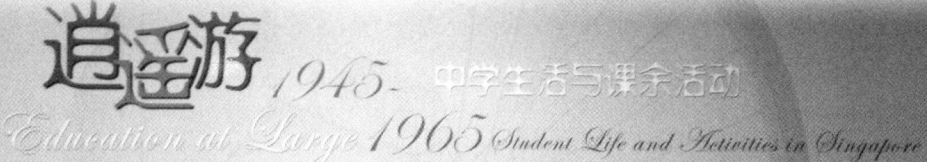

Brief Biographies of the Interviewees

Lim Chin Joo

Born in 1937, Lim came to Singapore from Pontian, Malaysia, when he was a middle school student and joined the Chinese High School. He was active in the Singapore Chinese Middle School Student Union (SCMSSU) as the head of its Academic Division. He shared his recollections on the organisation and activities of the SCMSSU as one of the key figures in the student movement.

Tan Kok Chiang

Born in 1937, Tan went to Choon Guan Primary School, Presbyterian High School and Raffles Institution. After the May 13 Incident, he participated in the occupation of the Chinese High School. Sensing the gap between himself and his peers at Raffles Institution, he transferred to the senior middle school section of Chung Cheng High School. Thereafter, he participated in activities of the SCMSSU, serving as its secretary. As another key figure of the student movement, he recounted not only the activities of the SCMSSU, but also the social and political environment of Singapore during his student days.

Chen Mong Tse and Chai Chu Chun

Born in 1937, Chen lived in the premise of the Shanghai Bookstore managed by his father and attended Catholic High School in the vicinity. He was dismissed by the school in Junior Middle Two due to his involvement in the students' boycott of examinations. He later went to several Chinese-medium as well as English-medium schools.

Born in 1935, Chai is Chen's wife. She is passionate about dancing. Like her husband, she was very active during her middle school days and was a student leader at Nanyang University (Nantah). Together, the couple shared their memories of their happy school days, the May 13 Incident, students' occupation of two

Chinese schools, the Anti-Yellow Culture Movement, the relationship between students and bookstores, and etc.

Lee Leong Seng

Born in 1947, Lee went to the Chinese High School from 1954 to 1959. Although sympathetic toward the student movement, he was not an active participant due to his family's limited financial means; his priority was on his studies. He provided an account of the May 13 Incident, SCMSSU activities, the culture of learning in school and the Anti-Yellow Culture Movement, and etc., offering a more detached perspective of an ordinary student living in turbulent times.

Tan Teck Keng

Born in 1945, Tan was a factory worker at the Khong Guan Biscuit Factory during 1959–1963, and attended literacy classes organised by the Singapore Itinerant Hawkers and Stall Holders Association along Lorong Tai Seng. She talked about the literacy classes and the general classroom environment, as well as lessons and activities that the teachers (also known as "*Xiao Xian Sheng*") and students were engaged in outside classes.

Chua Hiang Yong

Chua, whose pen-name is Cai Xin, is a local writer and member of the Singapore Association of Writers and the May Poetry Society. Born in 1947, Chua entered Sin Ming Primary School in 1955 and graduated from Sin Ming High School in 1963. He went to the Chinese High School for his senior middle school education. With a passion for literature and art, his reminiscences included various extra-curricular activities, the popular culture of those days, social movements and student life, the image of Chinese school students and major occurrences such as self-government and political arrest.

Youthful Wanderings Amidst Student Movements
An Interview with Lim Chin Joo[1]

Interviewed by Chiu Wei Li, Zhou Zhaocheng and Lee Huay Leng

Transcribed and Compiled by Lee Huay Leng

Translated by Chiu Wei Li and Chan Cheow Thia

Family Background

Interviewer: You were active in the 1950s student movements, could you discuss things that happened earlier, for instance your family background, some recollections of your earlier student life and etc.?

Lim: My father was born in Singapore, two of my elder brothers as well, they are authentic Singaporeans. My elder sister and I, and my younger siblings were born in Pontian Kechil, in the state of Johor; however, at that time, the Malayan Federation and Singapore were both British colonies, there wasn't a sense of two separate countries. My primary school and middle school education were completed in Pontian Kechil. Like my two elder siblings, I was conscientious in my studies since young, always amongst the top few in class; my elder brothers were well liked by teachers, but I got into trouble frequently. In primary school I was caught gambling; my palm was hit over ten times in front of the others as punishment until it bled. While I was in Junior Middle One, I wrote a "poem" in my calligraphy book, satirising my form teacher. By the end of the year, my principal expelled me, I stayed at home for a year.

The following year, a new principal, Kuang Guangzhao, came from the Singapore Nanyang Girls' High School. He used to teach in Pontian previously, my eldest brother was his student. My eldest brother appealed on my behalf, and Principal

---

[1] This interview transcript was consolidated from the initial face-to-face interview conducted by Chiu Wei Li and Zhou Zhaocheng in 2007, as well as a follow-up email correspondence in 2008 carried out by Lee Huay Leng.

Kuang allowed me to return; he even allowed me to skip grades and study at a higher level, Junior Middle Three, instead. But I stuck to my mischievous ways, on the eve of my final examination, I wrote a "limerick" in a local tabloid, *The Evening Lamp*, lampooning Principal Kuang. I ought to be expelled, but Principal Kuang wanted me to stay and do the school proud in the year-end examination, and hence marked two major demerits and one minor demerit in my records (one more minor demerit and I'd have to withdraw from the school). When the results were released, only six out of nearly thirty students in class passed. I was one of them, I didn't disappoint my principal.

Pontian didn't have middle schools, our family was poor but my parents still tried to help my elder brothers attend the Chinese High School. My eldest brother could only complete Junior Middle Three, and went to north Malaya to work as a teacher, so that my second eldest brother could study in Singapore. Originally I wanted to go to Rengit which is near Pontian, I wanted to enrol for the teacher training class at Xin Wenlong Middle School. I asked a friend to register for me, but I didn't get in. Later I found out that competition was intense and my friend didn't even submit my application. Some people are unreliable, I learnt my first lesson in life.

Later, it was my eldest brother who spoke up for me again, and my mother allowed me to study at The Chinese High School. One day at the end of 1953, I took a bus from Pontian Kechil to Queen Street. At the green bus terminal, I recognised my second eldest brother. I was surprised by his outfit. He wore pants (I always envied people who wore pants), carried a briefcase and appeared rather mysterious. I heard from my eldest brother that he had already left Chinese High. I didn't know where he was studying or working. My second eldest brother brought me to a wooden hut behind Chinese High and introduced me to a few Chinese High students studying there. That was my accommodation, two to a room, ten dollars a month, which included breakfast and dinner.

Encountering the Student Movement of the Times

Interviewer: So when you came to Chinese High to study in 1954, it was the beginning of the student movement, you were caught up with the turbulent times?

Lim: Before Chinese High, I was not really progressive, I wasn't interested in current affairs, I only liked to contribute to the press, but those were quite trashy articles. Yes, in 1954, I came to Singapore and found myself embroiled with the times. When 16-year old Chong Geok Tin was raped and murdered, middle school students campaigned against yellow culture, bursary committees in many schools organised mass assemblies to burn pornographic materials, they also organised a variety of arts and recreational activities. In 1953, graduates from junior and senior middle schools formed an art research society, its headquarters was at Cairnhill Road, where I first learnt mass dance. I have always been interested in contributing articles, healthy literary journals such as *Wasteland* and *Cultivation* had appeared by that time, I began to realise that writing was a serious affair. In the beginning of 1954, the colonial government promulgated a new law, conscripting youths above the age of eighteen; this led to the May 13 Incident[2]. To me, it was extremely stimulating, but initially I was skeptical about taking part. Maybe because I was not of eligible age, hence I didn't feel an urgency towards the issue, I didn't take part in the petition of May 13. Many students from the Federation of Malaya didn't want to be drafted and wanted to go home, some went back to China in groups.

As this was a matter of vested interest, more and more students felt uneasy. Whether of eligible age or not, we read the papers every day and took part in all sorts of gatherings, keeping up with the developments. We didn't really need others to prod us on and very quickly became part of the student movement. On June 2, a sit-in started at Chinese High, many workers and rural residents came forth to support. After this, we Chinese school students took part in labour strikes and helped out at floods. Some students who took part in the May 13 incident were charged with illegal gathering or obstruction of police efforts, some students of the University of Malaya who sympathised with the May 13 incident were also charged with sedition. During the trials, we gathered outside the courtroom to express support. A political party (The People's Action Party) championing anti-colonialism was formed at the end of 1954. Its founders had close links with leaders of the student movement. We, many of the Chinese school students, attended its inauguration ceremony. Early 1955, I read from the press that my second eldest brother Chin Siong was representing the PAP to run as the Member of Parliament for Bukit Timah. So I went to his union office at Middle Road to look him up. When he saw

---

[2] On 13 May 1954, nearly 500 Chinese middle school students protested against mandatory military conscription introduced by the British colonial government. Students attempted to march to the Governor's premises to submit a petition, but were blocked by the police, resulting in violent clashes. 26 persons (20 students and 6 police officers) were injured in the incident; 45 students were arrested. This marked the first wave of the student movement led by Chinese school students, who on the one hand were disgruntled with discrimination against the Chinese by the British colonial government; on the other hand, they understood that military conscription of 18 year-olds would mean many over-aged students whose studies were delayed due to the Second World War had to disrupt their middle school studies. Appeals were made for exemption from or delayed conscription; the colonial government eventually backed down and aborted the conscription exercise. The student movement aroused the social consciousness of the Chinese-medium school students and led to subsequent waves of student movements in Singapore in the 1950s and 1960s; but in face of intense political struggles and infiltration by communist elements, the movements became highly politicised, eventually leading to their demise.

me, he immediately recruited me as an election volunteer. The campaigning lasted more than a month, we waved the flags of the PAP down the alleyways all over Singapore, one mass rally after another, the crowds grew bigger and the atmosphere more boisterous, those were fiery times, the kind of opportunity in life that many young people dreamed of.

Interviewer: You say that you didn't take part in the petition of May 13, wouldn't you have some recollection or reflections on such an important incident?

Lim: You can't call it recollection, just some thoughts or observations. May 13 is an important incident in Singapore's history, it is of great significance. It will not be inappropriate if we designate that day as Youth Day. The petition march by young students resulted in a breakthrough in the midst of a "white terror" atmosphere after the war. It exposed the weaknesses of the colonial government. Then, many colonies were seeking self-determination, our students successfully opposed the draft imposed by the colonial authorities, this was an open challenge to the legitimacy of colonial rule and was a catalyst to the ensuing movement to end colonisation. This event strengthened the social consciousness of the Chinese middle school students. The Chinese middle school students won the support of all rungs of society (including English-educated tertiary students). The May 13 Incident united students and workers in the society and constituted a critical historical moment. This change led various political forces to take turns wooing the students and shape their orientations, as a result the students paid a heavy price.

Interviewer: What about the Hock Lee Bus[3] strikes later in 1955? What kind of impact did it have on you students?

---

[3] The Hock Lee Bus Incident started on 23 April 1955. The Bus Union was dissatisfied with the duty roster issued by the bus company and the latter's bid to set up a competing pro-government labour union. Hock Lee bus workers responded by striking and picketing; buses were prevented from leaving the depot. The bus company in turn responded by firing workers on strike and hiring new workers, after which the Bus Union requested government mediation. Strikes persisted until early May, and were supported by the Singapore Chinese Middle School Student Union (SCMSSU) and other vocational unions. In the afternoon of 12 May, known in history as "Black Thursday", 2000 Chung Cheng and Chinese High School students rode 20 lorries to the Hock Lee bus depot at Alexandra and met up with 300 striking workers. Around 2 pm in the afternoon, attacks were made on Hock Lee buses all over the island, forcing the buses to stop functioning. The situation soon deteriorated into mass rioting. The police responded with water cannons and tear gas, rioters in turn responded with stones and wooden poles, overturning and burning cars. The authorities imposed a curfew. By dawn, the police succeeded in containing the situation, but the next day, other bus company workers went on sympathy strikes, plunging public transport on the whole island into paralysis. Upon intervention by the government, the Hock Lee Bus Company gave in. Unions were also worried that continued bus strikes would result in further public inconveniences and the loss of popular support, and decided to

Lim: You are referring to the 1955 sit-in, we call it the "Struggle for Resumption of Classes". After the general election in April 1955, the pro-workers Labour Front took power; workers pressed for better conditions, strikes were frequent. The management of the Hock Lee Bus Company prevented workers from joining unions, resulting in strike action, during which we students would travel in lorries to express empathetic solidarity. Many professional unions and people in the society came out in support of the strike. We felt that students and workers were united and mutually dependent. On 12 May, there was an island-wide strike, leading to disturbances. On the following day, the authorities summoned various middle school principals and school deans, ordering the Chinese High School and the Chung Cheng High School to cease classes for a week. Classes would be resumed pending developments, the reason cited being the security of students, in effect it was putting the blame of the disturbances on students. After this sudden development, students went to school the following day. That night, the strikes were resolved, the school directors pressed for resumption of classes. On the 17th, resumption of classes was granted by the Ministry of Education subject to the following conditions: First, the Management Board must expel certain students, a list of which would be provided by the authorities. Second, the Management Board must also, within fourteen days, submit the reasons why the schools shouldn't be de-registered.

News spread, I thought that more serious events were about to happen, that day or the following day, together with a few students, I went to school, found the gates shut and aw many students sitting outside. We requested to meet the principal who came in the evening and relayed the words of Lee Kong Chian, the Chairman of the Management Board that talks were inconclusive and things were not so simple. There were people who told us that Chung Cheng students were having a sit-in in their school and we should join them. The news spread and more than 3000 students gathered by the school lake for a mass meeting that night. Emotions were fervent, we neglected our hunger. My deepest impression was the bowl of fish porridge we ate when it was almost midnight. Our meetings concluded with the demands that the authorities allow the three schools to resume classes unconditionally, those who participated in the meetings were students from Yock Eng, Nanyang

---

stop while the movement was still in their favour. The Hock Lee bus strikes, which became violent, resulting in four deaths and 31 wounded, was a critical incident in the history of Singapore's postwar politics and labour movement. Some commentators believe that the labour strikes were due to agitation by infiltrated elements from the Malayan Communist Party who sought to fan anti-colonial sentiments in order to strengthen the Party's grip on the labour movement. Others believe that the Hock Lee Bus Incident revealed the inherent contradictions between the Chief Minister, David Marshall, and the British colonial government, and it accorded a window of opportunity for the people to fight for independence and autonomy from the British under the leadership of the labour movement.

Girls', Nan Chiau, Chinese High and etc. It was also decided that classes would be boycotted for a day as a sign of protest. The following day we, the Chinese High students, returned to Chinese High for a sit-in, we, the Chinese High students knew that it was the decision of the student leaders, but I cannot remember why we organised separate sit-ins.

Interviewer: You mentioned "student leaders", then, the SCMSSU wasn't set up, right? What sort of organisation did the students have? How were student representatives chosen?

Lim: I can only explain what happened from 1954 onwards. As for what happened earlier, I heard that various schools had student self-governing committees, after the introduction of emergency regulations, these groups were shut down. When I was at Chinese High, there were bursary committees, drama societies, Scouts and other student groups. In 1954, the "Graduates of 1953 Arts Society for Class of 1953" was the main inter-school organisation, it originated from the farewell gatherings of various schools in 1953, its main aim was organising social activities. The May 13 Incident was initially led by a seven-man group, its members were from various schools. After the incident happened, at the suggestion of the school directors, various school representatives formed a 55-man representation group at the Chinese Chambers of Commerce, known as the All-Singapore Chinese Middle Schools Students' National Service Exemption Delegation (hereafter "Exemption Delegation").

If I'm not mistaken, student representatives were chosen from class representatives, who were in turn chosen by each class. The Exemption Delegation was always our representative, our leader, in charge of dealing with the aftermath of the May 13 incident (for instance, how to deal with registration for delayed conscription, petition for students being charged, expressing support for Malayan University students who were charged with sedition for supporting the May 13 incident). The Exemption Delegation was not a formally registered organisation, after being active for a few months, the Registrar of Societies ordered it to be disbanded. During the struggle for resumption of classes, various schools' class representatives elected another inter-school group, the "All-Schools' Committee for the Protection of Chinese Education". Its members were not the same as the Exemption Delegation, I think those guys were busy with organising the SCMSSU. Why was it called "Protection Committee"? I think this was because the Struggle for Resumption of Classes was in essence a struggle to defend Chinese education; on the other hand, the April 1955 election had just ended, the newly-elected Labour Front promised to revise the education policy and give equal treatment to the education of each ethnic group. The Chinese community was planning concrete action to ensure that the government fulfil its election promises. I think that the establishment of the Protection Committee was to coordinate action with the Chinese community.

I was always a class representative, not a member of the Exemption Delegation, I was a member of the Protection Committee, and during the sit-ins I was working at the Chinese High Protection Committee Secretariat Office. Those working at the Secretariat Office were known as "water crows" or "water crow group", I'm not sure why we were known as such.

Interviewer: How long did the 1955 sit-ins last, how did they end?

Lim: The objectives of the 1955 struggle to resume classes were shared by various segments of society, for instance, parents, school directors and various political parties were urging the government to resume classes at the three schools. After barely being in power for a month, Marshall's Labour Front government was already feeling the pressure to fulfill its election promises and accord equal treatment to ethnic education. Resolutely, he ordered the establishment of a multi-party nine-man inquiry committee (Its members were Minister for Education Chew Swee Kee, Minister for Local Government, Lands and Housing Abdul Hamid, Minister for Labour Lim Yew Hock, Assemblymen Lim Chuan Hoe, Wong Foo Nam, Goh Tong Liang, Lim Cher Kheng, Lee Kuan Yew and Nair) to report on the situation of Chinese schools.

The committee moved fast and recommended against expelling students and pressed for the unconditional resumption of classes. The Ministry of Education had to accept the recommendations. Students of the three schools were overjoyed and ended the week-long sit-in, and conducted victory celebrations in the school hall. In the afternoon, a victory parade was held at the parade square of the Chinese High School, consisting of not less than 3000 students and parents. Some raised banners, some banged gongs and played drums, some sang — the euphoria and loud cheering shook the entire hill. Students at the Chung Cheng High sit-in joined in too, it was a joyous moment unprecedented in scale. When the event ended, everyone was sad to leave. The catalyst that sparked off this incident was the brutality and unreasonable attitude of the colonial authorities towards Chinese schools. The struggle to resume classes united the workers, school directors, students and parents. During the sit-in, students, parents and labour representatives attended the student gatherings and gave speeches. During a gathering at the Chung Cheng High School, Lim Chin Siong spoke in support of the students' reasonable requests. He hit out at the colonial authorities for blaming the worker strikes on Chinese school students and for using violence against students. Chinese school students were a threat to the interests of the colonial authorities. He urged the Marshall administration to legislate for equal treatment towards education of every ethnic group, and to ensure that the Labour Front would not betray Chinese education. At the same gathering, Principal Chuang Chu Lin spoke as well, he said that the Chinese-educated students were a notch above the English-educated students, because the Chinese-educated students would analyse in greater detail different types of problems. He suggested that parents organise a group to help solve different types of problems. Before the end of the gathering, students and parents organised meetings at the Chinese High School and the Chung Cheng High School, each selecting six parent representatives to form an All-Singapore Chinese Middle Schools Parents' Association, and appointed legislator Lim Chin Siong and journalist Lien Shih Sheng as advisors. The meeting also urged the Chinese Chambers of Commerce to organise a congress for diaspora organisations to deliberate on the future of Chinese education.

In the 1950s, there were a few organisations related to Chinese education, for instance, the Schools' Management Board Joint Association, the Chinese Schools' Joint Association, the Teachers' Union, the Singapore Chinese Middle School Teachers' Union, the Primary School Teachers' Union, the Singapore Chinese School English Teachers' Union etc. After the Marshall administration took power, these bodies held meetings with the Chinese Chamber of Commerce on convening an All-Singapore Congress of Diasporic Organisations to discuss the future of Chinese schools. During the Hock Lee labour strikes, the Ministry of Education ordered the closure of Chinese High and Chung Cheng High, as well as clampsdown on students' struggle for resumption of classes and the set-up of a multi-party nine-man inquiry etc. These events led to the establishment of the 6 June Congress of Diasporic Organisations. The Congress was held at the Chamber of Commerce, and was well-attended by over six hundred people, representing 503 organisations, (including clans associations, clubs and schools). If I'm not mistaken, I think the Protection Committee sent representatives. It was unprecedented in scale as well as representation. The Congress passed several resolutions: (1) Request the Government to fulfil its promise by abolishing the education policy of the colonial authorities and support mother tongue education of each ethnic group; (2) Request the government to improve school facilities, particularly those of village schools; (3) Equal pay between teachers of English schools and Chinese schools; (4) Chinese school students should enjoy six years of free education. In the past, Chinese schools were organised and sponsored by various clan associations resulting in differences of opinion. In order to coordinate matters, the Congress set up a well-represented 21-man core committee- the Chinese Education Committee. The Committee took swift action and submitted a proposal to the nine-men multi-party committee, and managed to secure ad hoc funds for Chinese schools within a short span of time.

Interviewer: During this time, there was a "Chen Yangcheng Incident". Would you like to elaborate?

Lim: Chen Yangcheng was a history teacher in the 1950s at the Chinese High School and the Nanyang Girls' School, he was my history teacher until he was arrested. He was a serious man. When he spoke both his eyes were always staring at the ceiling shyly. Students liked him because his classes were in-depth yet easy to understand and were interspersed with current affairs commentary. We were all interested in his history lessons. The deepest impression he gave me was when he brought to our attention the founding of the People's Action Party in the papers in late 1954, he also mentioned that some of the founders were his former students. Shortly after the Hock Lee labour strikes and the struggle for resumption of classes, the government detained several labour activists as well as Mr. Chen, under the Public Order Ordinance. Students from two schools (Chinese High and Nanyang Girls') felt that these actions were retaliatory in nature. The Protection Committee issued a press statement criticising the arrests, various schools held protest meetings, requesting the release of Mr. Chen. The Chief Minister Marshall then met the representatives of the Protection Committee from the two schools and explained to them the rationale behind the government action. He said that Mr. Chen has decided to pursue further studies in England, students should put their mind at ease and focus on studies. A few years ago while I was at the Public Records Office in London, I read the notes of this meeting. Marshall's explanation did not satisfy the Protection Committee, but he was very patient, calm and cordial when he explained to the student representatives. Now that I reflect on it, it was really kind of him. Reading between the lines of the notes, I can tell that Marshall was helpless about Mr. Chen's arrest. It was no surprise that Mr. Chen was finally released a few months later. Speaking of the Chen Yangcheng incident, I am reminded of the "Song Zhuoying Incident" and the "Zhou Yuanguang Incident". Song Zhuoying was the discipline master at the Chung Cheng High School (Branch), as he was always at odds with the students, he was branded a "reactionary", and meetings were held continually to denounce him. Under the pressure of the students, the school directors eventually demoted him to just an ordinary teacher. As for Zhou Yuanguang, he was the replacement sent by the Ministry of Education for Wang Changzhi, the former principal of Yock Eng High School, who was banished from Singapore. He opposed student activities and expelled students involved. When the Ministry of Education sent him for training in America, the school directors sacked him and appointed a new principal. The Ministry intervened, the school directors were represented by lawyers from Lee & Lee, the matter fizzled out and he was relieved of his post.

Interviewer: When we talk about the activities of the 1950s middle school students, we cannot leave out the SCMSSU.[4] What were the circumstances behind its establishment?

Lim: The idea of SCMSSU was first conceived during the 2 June 1954 sit-in at the Chinese High School. After the sit-in, the Exemption Delegation convened a meeting to welcome the Queen Counsel D.N. Pritt who would be defending students arrested during the May 13 Incident. At the meeting, the idea to establish the SCMSSU was announced. The organising committee appointed lawyers Lee Kuan Yew and Tann Wee Tiong as legal advisors, the union was registered in the October of the same year. On 15 January 1955, the Registry of Societies wrote to Lee, rejecting the registration of SCMSSU on the grounds that "this organisation will be detrimental to the public welfare and good order of the colony".

The organising committee did not accept the reply of the authorities, Lee Kuan Yew appealed on its behalf, but the application was again rejected. Nearly 10,000 middle school students from seven schools boycotted classes on 30 March in protest. The organising committee issued a statement that it would conduct elections on 2 April and would march towards the Governor's premises to submit a petition on the same day. The authorities swiftly announced that it would not meet with any representatives and summoned the principals of the seven schools, urging them to dissuade students from organising a petition march. The organising committee hence decided to submit a petition via school directors instead.

The Pan-Malayan Students Federation also petitioned the Governor in support of the registration of SCMSSU. The Marshall Labour Front agreed to the registration on condition that it was explicitly mentioned in the Union's constitution that it would not participate in political activities. The organising committee thought that this vague condition was a catch-all and a trap so that the Registry could thereafter find fault with the students easily. Led by lawyer Lee Kuan Yew, the committee met with the Minister for Education, Chew Swee Kee, several times, suggesting that the constitution state it "would not engage in activities contravening its goals and

---

[4] Singapore Chinese Middle School Students Union in full, formed in October 1954, the main organisational force behind the Chinese middle school student movement, allegedly infiltrated by Communist Party forces. As Lim Yew Hock came to power, tough measures were adopted against leftist forces. In September 1956, he gave orders to disband the SCMSSU, resulting in a strong backlash from the middle school students. Students occupied the premises of Chung Cheng High and Chinese High; the protests lasted two weeks. The government issued an ultimatum on 24 October of the same year, compelling the students to disperse, resulting in violent clashes at the Chinese High School. The protests lasted five days, and led to 13 deaths, over a hundred wounded and nearly a thousand people arrested.

objectives". After a few sessions of discussion, the preparatory committee accepted the condition of "not directly or indirectly participating in political activities or labour union strike action". I remember very clearly, the official registration date of SCMSSU was 6 October 1955. When the news spread, fire crackers were set off in various schools, gongs and drums were played, the mood was ecstatic.

Interviewer: As an officially registered organisation, how did the SCMSSU function? What were some of its activities? What role did you play in the Union?

Lim: The SCMSSU had almost ten thousand members. The Central Executive Committee provided the leadership and there was a Supervisory Committee above it. The posts of the Central Executive Committee included President, Secretary, Treasurer, Head of Public Relations, Head of Academic Affairs, Head of Liaison Matters, Head of Recreational Activities and Head of Student Welfare. I was a member of the Central Executive Committee and was in charge of Academic Affairs. What sort of activities? There were too many and (all of them) extremely meaningful! It is hard to completely and clearly describe them in just a few words, I might have to take a few days. However, to put it simply, in a year we conducted activities that people these days might take ten years to accomplish. The influence of SCMSSU over the different sectors of society, as well as the influence of the Union on history was very significant. The effects were both wide and profound.

Interviewer: It appears from materials that have emerged recently, that the capabilities of the Malayan Communist Party (MCP) suffered greatly after the proclamation of the Emergency, and what survived seemed to be the infiltration of the student community. Did you and your friends sense that during the times? Were you a target of the MCP's efforts?

Lim: I did not sense that. What I know is the MCP was also anti-colonial, and the Party fought for national autonomy and independence. It would not be surprising if there were MCP members amongst us. Infiltration? That was the term usually employed by the colonial government. I was not a member of the MCP. I did not know who was and who wasn't in the Party, and I did not need to know. In that large group that was fighting for national independence, each person had the right and opportunity to find a position to make his/her contribution. "A target of infiltration" or "manipulative efforts"? We were young then, we did not have any political ambition or what you people call "agenda" these days. We only had passion and ideals. It is not unusual for young people to be manipulated and betrayed by different forces at different historical stages.

Transfer to Chinese School — Taking a Different Road
An Interview with Tan Kok Chiang

Interviewed by Lee Huay Leng

Transcribed by Wang Peijie

Translated by Chiu Weili and Francis Lim Khek Gee

Date: 27 March 2006

Family Background

Interviewer: Would you like to talk briefly about your family background?

Tan: There are five siblings in my family, I am the middle child, the third one. My eldest sister and eldest brother, myself, and my two younger brothers. We started school only after the Japanese Occupation. We had attended some lessons during the Occupation, and we also learned some Chinese. However, we started formal education only after the War. Therefore, from the very beginning, my father had understood the importance of learning both the mother tongue as well as English in our society, and had therefore insisted that we studied Chinese and English. Though our family was not wealthy, our childhood was filled with happy memories. Partly because our school results were not bad, but mainly because our family members were together and helped one another. At that time my grandmother was still alive, therefore family life was rather meaningful.

Interviewer: Were you born in Singapore?

Tan: Apart from my eldest sister, we were all born in Singapore. We stayed at several places during the Japanese Occupation, the most memorable one was the village with a vegetable market. During the Japanese invasion, we tried to escape. Father was replenishing stock at Liang Seah Street and was wounded by the Japanese bombardments. Hence, we went back to this market village where we lived for a long time. The kids grew up in the village. Although life was very difficult at that time, as I said previously, we lived together, and this helped us to cope. During the latter part of the Occupation, we moved to Purvis Street where Father rented a shop. We lived there, and started a small business. I can still remember…images of the Japanese bombardments, the American planes and the dropping of pamphlets, the return of the British troops. At that time, kids were very curious about such things. Although Father was injured and our family faced turbulent times, on the whole it was still all right, and our situation was slightly better than that of other families.

After the war, Father revived his original business at Naval Base. So our shop at Hainan Second Street was used for this type of business, which was mainly a grocery shop, procuring foodstuff and vegetables for the British and the British troops. Because of this, that single shop was not enough. Father also thought that we children should not be involved in the business, so he rented a house at Katong area, at Haig Road and sent us there. So we settled down there and began to attend school formally. At first it was the Choon Guan School, then I went to Presbyterian High School and slowly progressed. My school results were not bad. I was over-age by one or two years.

Interviewer: In which year were you born?

Tan: 1937. After the war, in 1945 or 1946, when school started, I was already eight or nine years old. At that time, I would have been considered over-age for Primary One. Thankfully, my results were not bad, so I skipped a few levels and caught up in the end. As mentioned previously, there was an emphasis on bilingual education. So, although there were classes the whole day, and we were under greater pressure compared to other students, we did not feel there was anything unusual. Looking back now, we feel that Father had made the best decision.

Interviewer: Was your father himself bilingual?

Tan: No, he wasn't bilingual. My father completed his junior middle school studies at Hainan Wen Chang High School, but only received a Chinese education. He was already grown up when he came here. He only came in his twenties or thirties, and had to work and support the family, and hence did not continue with his education. However, he did learn some English on the job. I think it might be due to this reason that he felt that we also should have some English education growing up here. But, ultimately, he was not motivated solely by pragmatism. He thought that in order to enter the mainstream society, knowing only Chinese was insufficient. I think he realised from the start that although we were migrants, in the end we would settle down here. Especially as my siblings and I began to grow older, he felt that this was our home, and therefore he emphasised the importance of bilingualism. Generally, school lessons were good, while the family still maintained a rather strong Chinese cultural environment.

Although Father was a businessman, his business was not prospering. Sometimes, especially after we were older and in our teens, we had to help our father out a bit. I remember the few of us, the first three kids in particular, namely my elder brother, myself and my younger brother, we tried our best to help him when we were in middle school. At that time he had a small truck, and he would drive around selling Coca Cola and other types of soft drinks, and we would help him. I remember, in those days, selling a whole carton of Coca Cola—24 bottles— would earn you at most twenty cents. This twenty cents would have to cover his transport and labour cost. The profit margin was therefore very slim, but that was how we managed to survive. My fourth brother helped my father after we three elder ones graduated from middle school.

Although life was difficult, on the whole we felt that it was very meaningful doing those things with him. It was also an educational experience, in all aspects, especially with regard to fulfilling familial responsibilities. It had to do with character and moral development. Therefore, we don't feel a sense of regret at all when we think back about those days. This is one aspect. On another aspect, we also started to read all sorts of Chinese novels at home. This had definitely shaped our thinking in some ways. Therefore, on hindsight, that could be one reason why we participated in various student activities later on.

Interviewer: What kinds of novels?

Tan: For example, (the works of) Lu Xun, Ba Jin, all these authors. There was also some Chinese revolutionary literature that was popular in the 1950s. We even read many Russian works and works written during World War II. All these served as formative material for us to a certain degree.

The May 13 Student Movement

Interviewer: Was it your own decision to move from Presbyterian High School to Raffles Institution?

Tan: It was my decision of course. One reason was that, as we had then moved back to Hainan Second Street, Presbyterian High School was further from where we lived, whereas RI was just on the next street. I was also thinking then: RI was a school with a very good reputation, why not give it a try? At that time, the Indian principal was quite good; he understood that it was more convenient for us, and my results were also not bad, so he accepted me. I started at Form 8 and studied for two years at RI, for Form 8 and 9. There is one thing I have to add. During the Japanese Occupation, we did not have any formal Chinese education; there wasn't any Chinese school then.

However, when we lived at Hainan Second Street, we went to St Anthony's School that adopted the Japanese education system at Victoria street. I have forgotten how many months we were there. However, Father still insisted that we learn Chinese. He had a good friend, Mr Ding, who became a primary school principal; his wife was also a teacher. So we learned Chinese under the couple's careful guidance, beginning with the lesson "Clapping Hands".[1] Consequently, when the war was over, when we enrolled in Choon Guan School, we went straight to the third year. Our grasp of the fundamentals was not bad; not just in terms of language, the couple had educated us very well. That's how I developed a strong sense of intellectual curiosity in school and in learning.

Interviewer: When you were at RI, did you feel you were different from your peers, in terms of your thinking?

Tan: I did feel this way. But the difference between RI and Presbyterian High is that RI was a government school. Those who studied in government schools generally had better results, and they were all from English-speaking families. As for myself, I came from a Chinese background, and hence I felt there was some difference. There was definitely a difference.

Interviewer: What were they concerned about?

Tan: They were mainly concerned with graduating from middle school and finding a job after that, to work as a clerk in the public sector or as a sales person. It was basically like that. Of course, there was a minority who wanted to pursue an advanced diploma and enter the university. But for most students, their vision for the future was to find a suitable middle or lower management job, and that would suffice.

Interviewer: Therefore, you didn't discuss with them the events happening outside school?

Tan: Very rarely, though we did discuss them occasionally, especially after the May 13 Incident, when I wanted to organise a school forum to discuss matters regarding middle school students in the Chinese schools. However, they were completely uninterested in these matters. Hence, there was no support. I remember

---

[1] "Clapping Hands" refers to the first lesson of a Primary One textbook published by Chung Hwa Book Company and used by Chinese primary schools in the pre- World War II era.

I was in the same form as Tommy Koh,[2] though we were in different classes. We did discuss these problems; but in the end there was no solution.

Then, after the May 13 Incident, in my family, my brother was expelled from school. We were very unhappy with the school's action. Personally, I also felt it was wrong. Hence, I came forward and supported him in my own way. In this manner, the difference with RI students became even starker. I participated in the rallies at Chinese High, in the day, no, in the afternoon after class, and went back to school again the next day. It was very obvious, our divergent ways of thinking.

Interviewer: Did your school…?

Tan: The school authorities were unaware; I'm not too sure if the school was aware. I think even if they were, they would not have taken any action.

Interviewer: Therefore you were in RI till…

Tan: Till I graduated after Form 9.

Interviewer: Where did you go upon graduation?

Tan: I went to Chung Cheng High School.

Interviewer: Was that a natural choice?

Tan: It was quite natural. That's because I had gotten to know many friends from Chinese High and Chung Cheng when I participated in the rallies. They had all advised me to join them after I graduated from English school. At that time my family was not rich, and hence entering the university was not an option. If I had wanted to enter university, I would have gone to the University of Singapore, called University of Malaya at that time, or gone abroad. It was impossible to go abroad as my family was unable to support me. Because of the difference in thinking between my RI classmates and I, I hadn't thought of going to the University of Singapore. Therefore I switched to a Chinese school to further my studies. This may be considered rather natural, especially after getting to know these friends. In particular, their actions at Chinese High had exerted a great influence on me, and that's why I had a strong urge to join them.

---

[2] Currently Singapore's Ambassador-at-Large, Tommy Koh is also Special Adviser of the Institute of Policy Studies and Chairman of the Centre for International Law National University of Singapore. He has served as Singapore's Permanent Representative to the United Nations, New York, High Commissioner to Canada, and Ambassador to the United States of America and Mexico. Other appointments that he has held include founding Executive Director of the Asia-Europe Foundation, founding Chairman of the National Arts Council, and Chairman of the National Heritage Board.

Interviewer: In those days, did many Chinese school students think this way?

Tan: I think they did.

Interviewer: Why is that so?

Tan: Why? I think the climate was like this: On the one hand, ours was not a stable society. We had just regained peace; the colonial government had also just returned and started a whole series of things to re-establish colonial rule. So everybody felt that this was not quite right. We had gone through a few years of resistance against the Japanese, so how could the British just come back and re-establish their colonial rule? That was one aspect.

On the other hand, there were only Chinese middle school students at that time. That kind of student activism normally should be led by university students, while middle school students should focus on their studies. But our Chinese community did not have any university students, so this matter was naturally taken up by the middle school students. Especially the May 13 Incident. The government wanted to conscript us, and that directly involved the middle school students. Actually, if ours was a stable society, the students might not have protested against this, because the government wanted those 18 and above. Maybe in a stable society, those 18 and above mostly would have graduated, and hence the middle school students would not have been affected. But due to the war, there were many over-age students in the middle schools. Hence this problem affected them in a direct way. That's why mobilisation occurred very naturally to resist the draft, to ask for exemption, or a postponement. It was not...to intentionally fight the government, but these were the students' interests. You should let us finish middle school, and the draft can be considered later.

Of course, as I said, inherently we were against the return of the colonial government; it was wrong to re-establish colonial rule. That's why, at that time, we felt that the conscription issue was also wrong in principle. Why did we have to fight for the colonialists? Who should we fight against? We had no enemies! The enemies were those of the colonial government, not ours. Then why do we have to fight for you, to become your cannon fodder? Right, this was also an important factor. When the issue was stirred up, the British government at the time also did not consider the students' interests. And that's why the disturbance started. The British government did not want to compromise, and did not allow us to focus properly on our studies. Therefore, on our part, we continued to seek postponement to the draft, and that was how the student movement began.

Interviewer: But, why the Chinese middle schools' students, why not gather the others...

Tan: Chinese schools, I think...yes, that's an interesting question. Because the draft involved all young men, and not just those from the Chinese schools. But, on the other hand, there were more students in Chinese schools in those days, let's see...there were Chinese High, Chung Cheng, Catholic High, Yock Eng, all these four were boys' schools, this affected them directly. Of course, the girls' schools were involved as well: Nanyang Girls, Nan Chiau, Chung Hwa and Nan Hwa Girls also established middle schools, but not senior middle sections, only junior middle sections. St. Nicholas also had a middle school section. These female middle school students also had brothers, right? That's why the impact was more extensive.

Another point is that actually the colonial authorities did this secretly, so the English medium school students were not aware. For example, when I was studying at RI, it was only when the Chinese medium school students started protesting that we knew. We had been completely in the dark over this matter. In addition, the English medium schools might have felt—at least a certain proportion of the students felt—that this wasn't an important issue. If you want to conscript me, so be it. The best would be if there was no draft, but if the government wanted me, I would go. And also, many English medium schools, like RI, Victoria, St. Joseph's, they had their own student cadets. Therefore, to these student cadets, it might feel natural to join the regular forces.

Interviewer: So, to people such as Tommy Koh, there was nothing inappropriate?

Tan: At that time, I did not discuss the matter in great detail with Tommy Koh. His view would mainly be that it was a matter that could be negotiated, so let's discuss. Why did the Chinese medium school students oppose the government so vehemently? We can discuss this issue. However, at the time I did not fully understand what his views were on the conscription issue. We did not discuss this matter properly at that time.

Interviewer: But how old were you then, during the May 13 Incident?

Tan: May 13 happened in 1954, I was 17 then.

Interviewer: Hence you would be immediately affected?

Tan: That's right. But at that time I did not feel the personal impact. It was rather, hey, everyone was protesting...But the most important factor was because Catholic High had expelled my brother. As such, they protested and participated in the

Chinese High rallies. I was curious, so I went, and not so much because I personally did not want to be drafted.

Interviewer: At that time, the relations among the Chinese medium schools were…

Tan: Relations were excellent among the Chinese medium schools. In the early 1950s, competition was very intense among Chinese schools. This was especially true in sports. During the annual sports meet, the rivalry between Chinese High and Chung Cheng especially would be very intense. However, everyone was united over the issue of exemption from the draft. At the time, the mobilisation and the gathering for the May 13 movement all originated from the sports meet.

Interviewer: Was it a combined sports meet?

Tan: It was the combined sports meet for all Chinese medium schools in Singapore. At that time, in the sports arena, the cheers were not "Go, Chung Cheng!" or "Go, Chinese High!" etc., instead, it was a rallying cry for unity. So the unity between the Chinese medium schools was also brought about by the quest for exemption from conscription.

Interviewer: According to some British colonial documents, at that time there weren't many middle school students who put up strong opposition; it was just a few schools that stirred up the matter…

Tan: I think that was the case. However, when the matter gained momentum, many students joined in as well. You can't expect the majority of the students to understand the problem right from the start and to take the initiative to participate. No movement happens this way. In the beginning, a small group of people will see the problem, and will then articulate it to mobilise the students to participate. It must happen in this manner. Later, it did happen this way. However, it was able to sustain itself, able to attract almost all of the middle school students. This shows the urgency of the appeal to postpone the conscription.

Interviewer: How was the assembly like at that time?

Tan: At first, I was rather unclear. But, it was a student mobilisation. At that time there was a so-called Chinese Schools Students' National Service Exemption Delegation. This delegation comprised representatives from various schools, including the girls' schools. Some people were arrested during the May 13 Incident and were charged in court. Consequently, the sentiment that the movement had to be stepped up prevailed. Thus, we were mobilised to rally at Chinese High.

Interviewer: You said that the Chinese community also supported......

Tan: The Chinese community supported it, because this sit-in would generate focus on this issue. Initially, the Chinese community was saying, students, don't be so radical, you go back to the schools, let us negotiate with the government. But in reality, there wasn't much point in talking with the government. Because they had been talking for such a long time, and the government refused to budge. So this student sit-in made the Chinese community, especially the press, realise that this problem ought to be dealt with rapidly. What was the sit-in like? At that time, I think it was not the majority of the students that took part. But I think in Chinese High then, there were at least 1000 people. That did not represent the entire student body, it was definitely not the majority of students in the Chinese middle schools. But it was a relatively significant force supporting exemption from conscription.

Interviewer: Then the student leader was….?

Tan: I remember one of them was Robert Soon Loh Boon. Afterwards, the same group of people were selected as the leaders of the Singapore Chinese Middle School Student Union (SCMSSU): Soon Loh Boon, Chen Ziquan, Feng Yihua, Lee Soo Huay, Tay May Nah… boys and girls were included.

Interviewer: What about the Chinese community? For example, did Lee Kong Chian try to persuade the students then?

Tan: He did. I'm not sure if he went directly to Chinese High to do so, or whether a meeting was arranged at the Chinese Chamber of Commerce. I can't recall. He definitely did come out and advise the students not to be too radical, and to let either him or the leaders of the trade associations and the Chinese community negotiate with the government about this. Then the attitude of the students was, it has dragged on for so long, and you haven't resolved this, why is there a need to continue discussion, there's a need for action! At that time, Lee Kong Chian did not leave a good impression on the students. Of course, looking back now, with the benefit of hindsight, the students may not have understood the predicament that Lee Kong Chian faced.

But the issue of exemption from conscription was finally resolved. That is, the government finally relented and agreed to delay conscription, acceding to the strong demands of the students who were backed by the Chinese community. The students could wait till they graduated from middle school before being conscripted… So this matter of delayed conscription was settled, actually it became *de facto* exemption. Conscription was not an issue anymore. Delaying conscription was just a face-saving gesture. In fact, this matter was not raised henceforth. After graduation from middle school, nobody was called up... The government did not call us up for conscription. No more mention of it. Of course in certain ways, due to constitutional developments in Singapore, conscription was no longer a key issue.

Interviewer: When you were at Raffles Institution, was the education oriented towards being loyal to the British colonial government?

Tan: I think, to the majority of students, it was so. Actually this was not a very clear-cut or conscious way of thinking. Everyone accepted the status quo then, the status quo was as such: everything was determined by the colonial authorities. So let's just let it carry on, as long as we can have a secure job, it's enough. In reality, students didn't consider or discuss this matter.

Interviewer: Did you read English novels? Besides reading Lu Xun, you read...

Tan: Yes, I read anything! Haha.

Interviewer: Which English novels did you read?

Tan: I read what was required for English literature in school, as part of the curriculum. Of course many of these were novels from Britain. For instance, the novel *Jane Eyre*. Also, later I read some English novels from Britain and the United States. For instance, Jack London's novels. But I mainly read the works of British novelists.

Interviewer: Coming back to the May 13 Incident, some student representatives were arrested. Then, were you all afraid?

Tan: Not really. For one matter, I wasn't directly involved, I wasn't part of the petition protest. I learnt about it much later; initially we in the English schools didn't know about this incident at all. It was only later that we knew. In fact, even after the incident, we didn't think that this was very important. But later, when my brothers in the family were expelled from school, I thought that something was amiss.

Interviewer: Because it seemed like some teachers in Chinese High were also affected.

Tan: It seemed that some Chinese High teachers were affected. That was not because they took part in the petition, although this was directly related to the student movement. Nevertheless, when they were arrested, the official reasons at least were that they were spreading communism and such, not because they supported the student petition.

Interviewer: For instance, the Malayan communists......there was a central committee directive in the early 1950s that stated that they were planning to infiltrate the student community. So the colonial authorities thought that some students were stirring up other students and this was supported by the Communist Party. At that time, did you feel that other students, those student leaders, had such tendencies?

Tan: Now that I reflect, I think, such tendencies were not present. But I didn't think far ahead then. Soon Loh Boon was a very good orator. What he said made a lot of sense, so we participated. It wasn't whether he was influenced by the Communist Party or not. This question wasn't relevant. Of course, regarding the Communist Party, because they contributed to the anti-Japanese cause and made contributions to Malaya, we definitely had a certain respect for them. Nevertheless, I think very few people would link these two matters together. The Communist Party was accorded respect by the students in general. But can we then say that we were influenced by the Communist Party, and hence we participated in these student activities? I don't think so, it was not so. According to many materials now, actually the Communist Party was not very active then, because their organisation had already been weakened by the colonial government. Even if they might have said these things, in actual fact, they did not really create much of an impact. The impact of the Communist Party on student activities was more imagined than real, and existed in some people's imaginations.

The SCMSSU Days

Interviewer: After transferring to Chung Cheng High School, you began to prepare for the SCMSSU?

Tan: When I was at Chung Cheng, because I transferred over from another school, when school started, I was working hard on my Chinese. Then, among my classmates, my Chinese standard was relatively poor. My highest level was Junior Middle One. When I was at Catholic High, I didn't even complete Junior Middle One when I switched, learning English directly. So my standard of Chinese was very poor. So I concentrated on learning Chinese then.

Interviewer: Then, were you in the Arts or Science stream?

Tan: You mean?

Interviewer: Were you studying the Arts or the Sciences?

Tan: Then there was no distinction between the Arts and the Sciences. No such distinction in school. However, at that time, because I was from an English medium school, my standard of English was basically much higher than the rest in class, so I didn't need to spend much time on my English. I needed to spend more time on my Science subjects. Then the standard of Science subjects in English medium schools was poorer. Particularly Mathematics. Really, we didn't learn trigonometry. So when I arrived at Chung Cheng, hahaha, I couldn't make it. So right from the beginning, I was focusing more on my studies.

Later, I joined the SCMSSU, mainly because everyone knew that my English was better. At that time, some people with a good grasp of English was very much needed in the movement so as to connect with the outside world. So I was selected. So when we were occupying Chinese High School, I took part, I was then a "*Xiao laoshi*" (literally meaning "little teacher", better understood as "young mentor"). So many people knew my situation. So when I entered Chung Cheng, not long after, they needed a student with good English proficiency. So they chose me as the representative of Chung Cheng. After that, during the Executive Committee election, I was elected and became the English Secretary of the SCMSSU.

Interviewer: In SCMSSU, what activities did you guys engage in?

Tan: Because the SCMSSU was just formed, plus the issue of exemption from conscription was not resolved, so basically, it sought to publicise this cause, to continue resolving the problem of the exemption of middle school students from conscription. Of course, at the same time, in school, it was about organising the students. Through organising the students, we tried to stabilise school life. One of the initial slogans then was to "improve one's studies". So, we implemented the mentorship scheme in middle school. Senior students would help junior students in their studies. During this process, there were a lot of cultural activities as well, for example, theatre activities, dance activities etc., all these were flourishing.

Interviewer: From the point of view of the colonial authorities, some of the concepts behind the slogans and songs the SCMSSU used at that time were similar to those of the Chinese Communist Party. They sang accolades to Mao Zedong, borrowing that sort of language, those concepts.

Tan: This interpretation is understandable. Why so? Because then we sang many songs that were popular during China's revolutionary times. However, when we sang, we would adapt the lyrics to suit Malaya's situation. But everyone knew how to sing these songs, so we sang "Unity is Strength". Of course such things were obviously from China. To say that this was singing accolades to Mao Zedong….. of course at that time, we also had a certain admiration for the Chinese Communist Party, this is undeniable. I think that most ambitious youths then simply admired the achievements of the Chinese Communist Party.

Interviewer: Why so?

Tan: Why? Because they managed to stabilise China, it was a good thing they did. Those of us who knew China's history, we all accepted this thing as a positive development. Of course, there were those who did not accept. Some of them in the middle schools were still supporters of the Nationalist Party and insisted on going to Taiwan to study, such things happened too. But those were the minority after all. But I think it was not worshipping Mao Zedong. In fact, at that time, we had already introduced a slogan that is: "Malaya is our Motherland". Maybe when that slogan was just introduced, there was no clear understanding of it. But it was already introduced. The students were already shouting that slogan. So the British colonial government accused our actions of being supportive of the Communist Party, of singing accolades to Mao Zedong, we did not really have any means to convince them otherwise. This was a transition period. I can only explain it as such. However, at the same time, there were some students, I should make this clear, there were some students who still regarded China as their motherland. Some students saw the oppression by the colonialists, and they gave up Malaya and went back to China. The saying then was to "return to country and serve". Many such students were activists. However, some of the students who "returned home" did not do so voluntarily. They were born in China and were thus deported by the colonial government in Malaya after their arrest. It was said that some of these people were protesting as they were forced to board the ships to China; they refused to disembark when they reached the Chinese harbour and insisted on taking the boat back to Malaya. In the end, they remained in China but still regarded themselves as people from Malaya.

Interviewer: You said you became a "*Xiao laoshi*", what was that about?

Tan: When we were occupying Chinese High, we were conducting classes, English classes, Mathematics classes, we were all having classes. I was conducting the English classes, then we were using, what textbook was it… we were using Feng Xuefeng's fables in class. We treated it as if it was a normal English class.

Interviewer: Was any emphasis placed on English? Did the Chinese medium schools place any emphasis on English?

Tan: The English standards of Chinese medium school students were relatively poorer. But everyone wanted to learn. The main reasons for the poor English standards — one was that time wasn't enough, the other was that teaching standards were poor. I remember then, the Chung Cheng teacher, he was Indian. He completely couldn't understand the difficulties Chinese school students faced in learning English. So classes were attended, homework handed in, but in reality nothing was learnt. Before the Indian man came, many teachers graduated from Chinese schools themselves. At that time the emphasis was on grammar, students then were pretty good at grammar. I noticed that when I was conducting classes with them, if we were to analyse a sentence, they did it better than me. English-educated students did not do this, grammar was something very natural.

Interviewer: Did the SCMSSU have legal advisers?

Tan: Legal advisers – Lee Kuan Yew and Tann Wee Tiong.

Interviewer: Why was it considered necessary to have a legal adviser then?

Tan: One reason was because the SCMSSU originated from the National Service Exemption Delegation. The Exemption Delegation faced various legal challenges, particularly that of students being arrested in the later stages, so a legal adviser was needed. The two of them were very keen to help, in particular, Lee Kuan Yew, so naturally he banded with us. To say something self-congratulatory, ha, during the times of the SCMSSU, I was the main person who liaised with Lee Kuan Yew. Because, when some students were arrested, I was the only one left who could speak English. Lee Kuan Yew's Chinese was really bad, so I went to his law firm Lee and Lee in Malacca Street. It was I who liaised with him, I reported to him and sought his help.

Interviewer: At that time, it was you who invited him?

Tan: No, there were earlier arrangements to invite him. Afterwards, when the SCMSSU was set up, when I assumed the role of English Secretary, the Executive Committee delegated the task of liaising with Lee Kuan Yew to me.

Interviewer: How was his attitude towards the students?

Tan: His attitude towards the students was then very good, very good. I remember the few times when I went to Lee and Lee, the firm had already started to be very busy. Every visit, when Mrs Lee Kuan Yew knew I arrived, she would say I needn't queue up and let me in to see Lee Kuan Yew. His attitude towards us was very good. I remember that when the SCMSSU was closed down, I was the last to leave the union. At that time, it was at 14 Wilkinson Road, I was there. Lee Kuan Yew hurried over, it was then about 2–3pm. He drove his, I forgot, his Morris Minor I think, over. He told me, he heard on his car radio that the SCMSSU was forcibly shut, so he came over to have a look. And he met me. After we chatted for a while, he needed to leave. He then asked me whether I needed a lift. Luckily he gave me a lift, otherwise… At that time, there were spies everywhere. He sent me to that place opposite Cathay, to that Rendezvous restaurant and let me get off. He said that I could get off there. Then he went back. I walked about. Our relations were very good. Whatever changed later, I am not clear. I was no longer around at that time. But at that time, he did his best to help.

Interviewer: How was the SCMSSU closed down later, what happened during this stage?

Tan: Actually there was nothing special about it, nothing really. About the SCMSSU being shut down, I think actually when the colonial authorities allowed us to be registered, they were already preparing for this. They were waiting, watching. Actually, they didn't really wait that long, and didn't really see anything, anyway we didn't really do anything. We just fought for delayed conscription, exemption from conscription. In the schools we organised the students, settled the study life of the students. We didn't do anything special. Later it was……of course due to the student movement, the labour movement also emerged. Also, then it was roughly 1955, 1956, Singapore started its feminist movement, the Singapore Women's Federation was set up. Also, the farmers set up their organisation as well. From the point of view of the British authorities, this was very threatening. So they started arresting people, as they saw these as challenges to their authority, they started arresting people. They arrested Linda Chen Mong Hock and others from the Women's Federation. That wasn't enough and they went on to arrest Soon Loh Boon, then one by one these organisations were shut down. The SCMSSU wasn't the only one, it was merely one of many.

Interviewer: At that time, what was the relationship between the SCMSSU and the workers?

Tan: Relations with the workers were very good of course! Because we were occupying Chinese High as we fought for exemption from conscription, the workers lent a huge helping hand. Of course, when workers went on strike we supported them too. This is very natural, isn't it? We didn't need the Communist Party or anyone behind the scenes to teach us what to do. At that time the students thought that the workers who supported us were our big brothers, they went on strike to demand for better working conditions, so naturally we would support them. We didn't just support them individually, we went in as the SCMSSU and organised the students through various schools to support the workers.

Interviewer: Hock Lee Bus Incident...

Tan: Hock Lee Bus... I remember that we all went.

Interviewer: How did that incident happen?

Tan: I'm not sure about the trigger. But during that time, the workers and students became more and more united, so the British authorities thought it was time to act. But what was actually the case, whether anyone was fatally wounded by the police, we were not sure. At that time it was very chaotic, very difficult to say. But there were certainly riots at Alexander Road. I still remember...when was it then....because we organised an activity, a SCMSSU activity, so we travelled from Gay World Stadium down to the city centre. We all sat at the back of a lorry. That lorry was stopped by the police who wanted us to disperse. I remember that incident. Personally I don't remember anything else. I think he wanted us to disperse mainly because the Hock Lee Incident had gotten out of hand.

Interviewer: Afterwards, after being shut down, the SCMSSU committee members were....

Tan: Some were arrested. Some went underground. Going underground doesn't mean engaging in underground activities, but mainly to go into hiding, not to get caught. But a bunch of people were caught anyway.

Interviewer: What about you...?

Tan: I was fine, haha, I was very lucky. Because I had then already enrolled into Nanyang University (Nantah), so I went to Nantah.

Interviewer: By that time, Nantah had already....

Tan: Started school. Nantah started school in March 1956... When Nantah started, I was still in the SCMSSU, though I enrolled, I was still in the SCMSSU Executive Committee, until my term was up in October 1956.

Interviewer: Full time in the SCMSSU?

Tan: Full time. I remember, Nantah had started. The SCMSSU was shut down, we were still occupying Chung Cheng and Chinese High. I was still participating in the Chinese High's occupation. I was already a graduate student then, but I still participated… You know these things….if you start it you have to see it through …

Interviewer: After it was shut down, was there another occupation of schools?

Tan: Yes, another occupation, and the scale was much larger. It was in two locations, one was in Chinese High, another in Chung Cheng. In the end, the one at Chung Cheng was dispersed. They ran to Kong Hwa School. Kong Hwa School was near Chung Cheng.

Interviewer: Did the school authorities take any action?

Tan: All the middle schools were shut. No…the schools did not take any action against us. It was mainly the government.

Interviewer: But the government exerted pressure on the school principals……

Tan: The government gave the principals a lot of pressure, but the student requests were reasonable, so basically the principals supported us. But they couldn't do so openly. But in the end, it was okay, if you want to arrest people go ahead, there was nothing the school could do anyway. This was the position taken by the schools. After you had carried out the arrests, school resumed. Within the school, we would carry on classes. Whatever the students did, if you think they are anti-government, arresting them is your business.

Interviewer: When you were at Chung Cheng, the principal was…

Tan: Chuang Chu Lin…

When I went to enrol, it was Principal Chuang who said yes, you can come. Hahaha. It was very rare then, transferring from Chinese High to Chung Cheng, or Chung Cheng to Chinese High. Also, then I just used an English…I didn't have any certificate yet, I didn't know if I could graduate. My certificate from the Chinese school was at most that of Junior Middle One, so I needed to see the principal. The principal said, okay, okay, okay, you can all come. Principal Chuang's attitude was, anyone could come, but when you go out, you must make the mark.

Interviewer: At that time were there other students like you?

Tan: I'm not sure if there were any, it seemed not.

Those Organised and Unorganised Times of Youth
An Interview with Chen Mong Tse and Chai Chu Chun

Interviewed by Zhong Hongzhi and Lee Huay Leng

Transcribed by Zhong Hongzhi

Translated by Low Yen Yen

Date: 10 September 2007

1. Family and Education Background

Interviewer: Can we first talk about your family background?

Chen: I was born in 1937. During the war we had to flee to Palembang in Sumatra, and we lived in the back end of the second storey of a shophouse; the front part was a private club where the Japanese drank. I only found out later from the books that Yu Dafu was then a translator there. We managed to stay there for a few years until the war ended because Yu Dafu helped cover up for us. Only after the war did my sister, brother-in-law and I return to Singapore. While the Japanese occupied Indonesia, we could not go to school and my eldest sister could only teach us a bit. After returning to Singapore, I could not enter Catholic High, we lived in the warehouse of the Shanghai Bookstore… that old house was standing behind that Odeon cinema. Catholic High was just behind the house. Initially, because I had stopped schooling for several years, I did not know which level I should study at in school, and studied at home most of the time. Eventually we found Yao Guohua, then principal of Catholic High School, and he took me in. I remember starting off from Primary Three.

Interviewer: Why did you choose Catholic High?

Chen: It was nearest my home. I was staying in the Shanghai Bookstore, and there were not many cars then, the school was just across the street. The current SMU is where Catholic High was sited. I studied in Catholic High till Junior Middle Two. When I was in Junior Middle Two, the Junior Middle Three students boycotted the examinations — the then famous nation-wide Examination Boycott. After the boycott, the Ministry of Education started checks on student activists in various schools. Actually I was not involved then, but I was kicked out anyway. During that time, each school expelled and suspended a few hundred students, and I do not know why I was on their list. I suspect it was due to my family — my siblings Mong Chow and Mong Sing were student activists.

My Junior Middle Two year ended. The Ministry of Education then had not decided to continue with the [Chinese-medium] Junior Middle Three examinations, because it was just after the boycott. But all [Chinese-medium] schools in Singapore then effectively did not take in Junior Middle Three students because it was close to the examination time. Through Shanghai Bookstore's links — there were links with the various school principals from the book business — I entered Yock Eng to continue my studies. Yock Eng did not have a senior middle school section then. I studied there for one year but the Junior Middle Three examinations were abolished. After Yock Eng, I moved on to an English school. I studied in several English schools — St. Andrew's in Hougang, Geylang English School in Geylang Lorong twenty-something, and then a Presbyterian school in Katong.

Interviewer: Did you spend only a few months in each school? Why did you go to so many schools?

Chen: Strictly speaking, my English was not good, but I topped my class in Mathematics and the Sciences. The English schools then had a strange system — one teacher to a class, who would teach all subjects including Literature, Mathematics, Science, History, Geography, etc. Most of these English teachers were weak in Mathematics and the Sciences, though they were strong in English, of course. I was weak in English, so they put me in Standard 3 [initially]. I was bored so I moved up to the more advanced classes a few times. My English was still weak, but because I was strong in Mathematics and the Sciences, sometimes when the teacher could not solve the difficult mathematical problems, I would be asked to solve them. So the teacher would try to accommodate me and try to let me pass English. But I still found it very tough, so after a year I decided to go back to a Chinese-medium school. The English classes in English schools were too difficult, and I found them boring.

Interviewer: Then why did you decide to go to an English school?

Chen: At that time, the Chinese-medium schools expelled many Junior Middle Three students who participated in the Examination Boycott, so many of them joined the English-medium schools and it became a trend. I was very familiar with these people and joined them in transferring to English-medium schools. This trend went on for about two years. There were hundreds of students who did so, they were from Chung Cheng, Chinese High, Yock Eng, Nan Chiau, Chung Hwa and Catholic High, six Chinese-medium schools.

Interviewer: What was Catholic High like then?

Chen: Catholic High was quite a good school. When I was there, Yao Guohua was the principal — an easygoing and enlightened man. Of course he was deeply religious, but he was not imposing, because mission schools need to conduct missionary work, so they were basically very civil towards the students. He had a very good memory, that left a deep impression on me. He could call out the name of any student he saw on the streets. I was very weak in English, and Catholic High placed a lot of emphasis on learning English. My marks for all the English subjects — composition, dictation, grammar — did not even add up to 60 marks, ha ha ha, I failed. But because I lived very nearby and my parents did not supervise me, I spent many afternoons playing basketball in school, together with the Junior Middle Three students who were one year my senior. Now I know why I was expelled, because that whole group of basketball players was expelled, ha ha ha, about 80% to 90% were expelled.

Interviewer: Was Catholic High not supportive of students taking part in some social movements?

Chen: Students were not encouraged to take part in social movements. And I am actually still confused about the student movements then. It seemed disorganised, but it also seemed organised. Picnics were then very popular among students in Chinese-medium schools. A group of people would organise one, rent a lorry, and invite students from various schools. Everyone paid two to three dollars, gathered at a specified time, took a ride to the beach where there was space under the coconut trees. We would swim, the organisers would pack lunch, and there would be group games after lunch. The most popular game was "singing to grab a seat", later called "musical chairs". The losers had to sing and tell stories, the organisers would teach mass dance. It was very lively! There was a picnic almost every week.

Interviewer: Were the organisers mostly senior students?

Chen: Yes, they were from the senior middle school section. Those taking part were from various schools. So there was some form of organisation. When we entered senior middle school, we also organised [these picnics], it was a sort of trend to go to many picnics and also to organise them. I remember having organised some with my friends, often at the Punggol beach, Zhang Jin Ling Villa, which belonged to a rich man, it was quite old but people were allowed to go in, there was a swimming pool... I cannot remember if we had to pay. There were many activities, mostly self-organised.

Interviewer: What songs did you sing then?

Chen: We learnt many songs from the picnics. Mimeographed sheets of lyrics were handed out, someone would teach the group to sing. There was a song *Da Jia Chang (Everyone Sings)*, [Hums the song], the songs were all from China. There was also *Gu Guai Ge (The Strange Song)*, *Wu Kuai Qian De Chao Piao (A Five Dollar Note)*... *Cha Guan Xiao Diao (A Tune from the Teahouse)*, etc. There was also a song that the *getai*[1] sang, [Hums tune], they changed it to become a flirtatious song. After the *getai* sang it, we students stopped singing that song.

Interviewer: Catholic High was strong in English language, in school the students...

Chen: All spoke Mandarin. But there was great emphasis on English. I studied English also because ...I was very weak in English then, and Yao Guohua was very observant. He noticed this child playing basketball in school the whole day. Catholic High and St. Joseph's Institution were then related, he gathered those of us who were poor in English and always playing basketball, and informed our parents that we were to attend classes at St. Joseph's in the afternoon. This was the "immersion scheme" run by the Ministry of Education; we were the first cohort. So I was forced by Yao Guohua to attend Catholic High in the morning and St. Joseph's in the afternoon. I was very weak in English, so I joined their Primary One and Two classes... haha, even though I was already in Junior Middle One and was thirteen years old. The teachers there were also young, and weak in Mathematics and the Sciences, so I taught Mathematics.

Interviewer: Where were the teachers from?

Chen: I guess the teachers in the English-medium schools were locals. The first teachers at Catholic High were from China, they came south to avoid the war, there were also many [Catholic] priests who did so. When I was in Junior Middle Two, school management was transferred to the priests, and Yao Guohua stepped down. The new principal was one of the priests. Many classes were taught by the priests. I have a rather good impression of them, they were cultured, knowledgeable, and quite good in teaching.

---

[1] A lively variety stage show, including songs, dances and dramatic skits often comedic in nature, which were held every night at the Gay World, the Great World and the World Amusement Park in the 1950s.

Interviewer: Where were the textbooks from?

Chen: They were textbooks from China, [like] *Zhong Hua Wen Xue (Chinese Literature)*. We had a very good History teacher. He taught China's modern history of the past century, students took notes while he lectured, and by the end of the year, the notes became a book on Chinese modern history. I have a very deep impression of Chinese history in the past century because of this teacher. But it is a pity this teacher was knocked down by a car while waiting at a bus stop; he died from the accident. He had also ventured south from China, and was probably a Catholic church member, so the school employed him.

Interviewer: How did the school emphasise [the learning of] English? All the textbooks were in Chinese.

Chen: (*Emphasis*) English grades, they organised all sorts of English contests. But basically it was still Chinese, the Chinese standard at Catholic High was good. The English teachers were all Indians. English textbooks were from overseas, from England. I remember the book *High School English Grammar*, it was like our Bible! (Laughs) A classic. I later learnt that it was from India, but as a student I kept thinking it was from England.

Interviewer: As for the other activities, Catholic High was similar to other Chinese-medium schools?

Chen: Similar, similar.

Interviewer: But later, such as during May 13, Catholic High …

Chen: During May 13 …

Interviewer: Many student participants were expelled….mainly from Chinese High, Chung Cheng …

Chen: During May 13, I had already left… haha…

Interviewer: Catholic High and St. Joseph's were so near each other, did you interact with the English-medium students?

Chen: No, mainly because of the language barrier. They spoke English. Later I went to Yock Eng, just for a year, there were many activities there. The students were in two groups, one group was pro-China and wanted to return to China, there was then a trend to return and contribute to the homeland; the other group may have been influenced by Malaya, or the Malayan communists as they later said, which advocated that we should stay in Malaya. We were Malayan citizens and should contribute to this place, stay here to build Malaya. So there were two groups. Nonetheless, the arguments basically took place only in theory; all still took part in the activities.

Interviewer: What kind of activities?

Chen: Many, such as picnics, and farewell soirees. At the end of each year, all schools would organise farewell soirees. The graduating classes — Senior Middle Three students and Junior Middle Three students — would organise one. All the schools had their own soiree. I do not know when this trend started and became a tradition. At that time there were class committees and students organised themselves to form a working committee to prepare the programme and perform at the end of the year.

Chai: Each performance would last a week, full house! Ha ha ha!

Chen: Not a week, about five to six days or three to four days. Most of the audience were students from the Junior Middle One and Two. They also had to put up performances in future.

Later, as I recall, many artists in dance, art, drama, many were nurtured here. The most famous was Liu Renxin. I recall a whole group, Zheng Mingwei, Liu Renxin, Gao Jinfeng, Lin Chen, the best drama talents in Singapore were there, so they were very good and the performances were of a high standard.

Interviewer: Were they actually students then?

Chen: They were students then, all over-age because of the Japanese occupation. They were in the same class as my sister Mengwan. My sister did not act but they were classmates and had meal gatherings at times, so I knew them. In the second half of my Senior Middle One, I transferred from Yock Eng to Chinese-medium school, Chung Cheng — I got to know Mdm Cai there when I joined her class. In the afternoon I still attended the Presbyterian school. But I grew to dislike English-medium schools because they were... bland! Hahaha! There were many activities in the Chinese-medium schools. In the English-medium schools, I was only interested in joining a group of students doing body-building, the others were inactive. The Chinese-medium schools were more vibrant.

Interviewer: So what were the English-medium school students doing?

Chen: What they were doing...actually I am not very sure... I only went for lessons, haha.

Later there were more and more activities, so I skipped more lessons and was absent from school more often. In Senior Middle One, during the "Anti-Yellow Culture Campaign",[2] I missed school for almost a month. This Anti-Yellow Culture Campaign was then very well-known. On hindsight, I think the May 13 Movement developed so vibrantly because of the campaign. The latter's coverage was deep and vast, its organisation was well-knit, and supported by schools and the Chinese community, so the campaign was very effective and produced very good results. That gave people a lot of confidence, people felt that as long as we were united in dealing with stuff like pornography, it would be effective. So it bolstered a belief that if something was not right, we could unite and deal with it. There was this belief, and various schools had various organisations and activities like song, dance and drama that developed organisational abilities among the students. Personally, I think that the later May 13 [movement] was of such scale and organisation because of the foundations laid by the Anti-Yellow Culture efforts in the previous year. If not, May 13 would not have been so influential and of such a large scale.

Interviewer: Was the Anti-Yellow Culture Campaign supported by other societal groups?

Chen: Yes. It was supported by groups like the unions and clan associations. But the unions then… they were still sporadic, not as unified as in the later years, it was the individual unions then. I think there was also a farmers' union.

Interviewer: Were they related to the student movements?

Chen: Not directly, but sometimes when there were more significant events… I recall once when there was heavy rain, there were still farms in Toa Payoh then, the students organised relief efforts to raise funds, including a charity performance, the Toa Payoh floods. Later when we were raising funds for Nanyang University (Nantah), because of these earlier activities, when we later held charity performances, basketball matches, they were very supportive too, the unions were supportive. There were charity performances, barbers donating their earnings etc,

---

[2] Not long after World War Two ended, salacious novels published in Hong Kong and Singapore started to pervade the society, novels with American and Japanese prurient films, tabloids and striptease performances of similar nature, such novels are collectively referred to as "yellow culture". In October 1953, a St Anthony Girls' School student, Chong Geok Tin, was robbed, raped and murdered. This was regarded to be the poisonous outcome of yellow culture. Students of Chung Cheng High (Branch) later organised a talk on this, which was covered in the press, sparking off a strong "Anti-Yellow Culture Movement". Through discourses and printed publicity materials, students called for the demise of yellow culture. They also promoted "healthy culture" to the public through theatre and various cultural programs.

they were supportive of students raising funds for Nantah because students had supported their earlier activities.

Students and Bookstores

Interviewer: Did you often bring your classmates to the bookstore?

Chen: No. But it was then very trendy for middle school students to visit bookstores. There was a "self-help society" or something... I cannot remember its name, it helped poor students, there was one in every school. The funds came from students' donations, later they also sold books to make some money. They would buy books from bookstores to sell. The student self-help societies sold books to earn money, this contributed to the learning trend and prompted many people to read books.

Interviewer: Had the British government started banning books then?

Chen: 1955, 1956...I cannot remember. The British government banned all books from 52 publishers in China, suddenly there were no books in the stores, almost all books from China could not be imported. So they came through Hong Kong — many Hong Kong publishers reprinted the China books, changed the cover and title, and they got in again. Based on my observation, the Chinese publishing industry in Hong Kong first gained a foothold because of this opportunity.

Interviewer: What kind of books did students then read?

Chen: Still mainly literary works. There were also a few sets of popular philosophy books written for the masses, especially Li Yi's, he was one of our editors at the Shanghai Bookstore. He wrote a series of books on introduction to philosophy, and sold very well. We students felt that to enrich ourselves, it was not enough to read literary works, we had to read philosophy too. *Da Zhong Zhe Xue* (*Philosophy for the Masses*) was a China publication that was banned then. (**Chai:** Many people were also reading that.) Li Yi had far more readers; I may have kept one or two of his books from the series he published in Singapore and Malaya.

Interviewer: What were the philosophy books like then?

Chen: They were small in size, a series of them. They offered an introduction to philosophy, [on topics like] what is philosophy, what is materialism, what is idealism. They provided fundamental knowledge on philosophy and were considered the best resources for Chinese-medium school students. His series of books sold very well in Singapore and Malaya for a long time, for at least a decade.

Interviewer: What about literature?

Chen: The most popular literary work was *Si Qian Xiang Hou (A Serious Deliberation)*, a love novel that was motivational. The love story narrated a transformation from decadence to a positive and active life, and was deemed an educational novel. I know the Shanghai Bookstore reprinted it over twenty times, two to three thousand copies each time. It was a popular book, it also sold for over a decade.

Interviewer: During which years was the novel sold?

Chen: The 1950s. Later I learnt that the author was a director in Hong Kong. A director at *Chang Feng*,[3] his book was very popular, so we invited him to write another novel but he had no time. (Chai takes out a few books) These were very popular then. These were also popular then — this one is on health, it teaches people how to take care of their health.It is also motivational — teaches one how to develop perseverance and independence. This book *Kerongsang* is also a love novel, with the [lives of] Indonesian Chinese as its backdrop.

Interviewer: Did the students read other books, such as books from the May 4 period?

Chen: I believe so, but after the ban was imposed, it was not easy to find those books in the market. Of course they were still circulated among students, but were bought through non-public channels.

Interviewer: What kind of non-public channels?

Chen: A few were more well-known — one was the Seng Lee Bookstore, this was the biggest; another was the Ipoh Cultural Bookstore; the Students' Bookstore also had some later, but fewer, I heard they got them through sailors. Because the predecessor of the Students' Bookstore was a grocery store, dealing with daily necessities like rice and cooking oil, they had contact with the sailors. The owner's eldest son was entrepreneurial and found that many people wanted these [books]. So he asked the sailors to bring them. Later they made money from selling books and the grocery business became more difficult, so after the old boss retired, they converted the business to a bookstore. (**Interviewers:** Was the Middle School Students' Bookstore beside the Shanghai Bookstore?) It was just beside the Shanghai Bookstore, in the corner, which is the current location of UOB in Bras Basah Complex.

---

[3]A director at *Chang Feng Xin* (short for three film companies; *Chang Cheng* or Great Wall Movie Enterprises Ltd., *Feng Huang* or Phoenix Motion Picture Company and *Xin Lian*).

Interviewer: When was that approximately?

Chen: I cannot remember which period.

Interviewer: Was it around for a long time?

Chen: It was later located with the Shanghai Bookstore. Forced to relocate from Bras Basah Complex, Shanghai Bookstore moved to Victoria Street, in those early days when the Commercial Press was there. It had a small shop there, but closed later when they could not sustain it. It was only there for a few years. At that time it was not called Students' but Middle School Students' Bookstore. Students' Bookstore was another place, it only wound up last year or the year before. (**Interviewer:** Our newspaper reported that.) It was called the Middle School Students' Bookstore, very short period. (**Interviewer:** Was it quite well known for selling banned books?) Yes, it was quite well known for selling banned books. The most famous was Seng Lee of course, Seng Lee was doing it almost openly, selling large quantities, [Students' Bookstore] was doing it on a small scale.

Interviewer: What about your own reading?

Chen: I read many different types of books. I wrote about it in an article published by the Shanghai Bookstore. At that time I did not work hard in school, and was satisfied to just pass and make it to the next grade. As a child I loved playing basketball, and was sent to the immersion programme by Yao Guohua. The rest of the time I spent reading; there were lots of books at the Shanghai Bookstore, various kinds of books from astronomy to geography. As long as I was interested in the book, even if I did not really understand it, I would continue reading. There were plays, poetry, novels, books on geography and history — of course I could not read books that I could not understand, but as long as I understood them I would read. I spent a lot of time in the store then, so I read many different types of books.

The Burgeoning Student Movements

Interviewer: Later you went to Chung Cheng?

Chen: I went to Chung Cheng — Junior Middle Three at Yock Eng, senior middle school at Chung Cheng; I went to Chung Cheng in the second half of 1953. In 1953 there was the "Anti-Yellow Culture Campaign"; in 1954 there was the May 13 Incident, then the boycott against national service. I graduated from senior middle school in 1955, I think there was nothing major that year.

Chai: There was — closure of Chinese schools, reopening of classes.

Chen: No, it was a campaign. What was that? Let me recall. Yes, after the May 13 Incident, students had to re-register for school, it was not called reopening of classes, it was called "Resumption of Studies Campaign". Many families did not go back to register their children, so the [students'] self-help societies started the campaign. They approached all classmates who did not return to school, to find out why they were not back, and tried ways and means to persuade them to resume their studies. I remember that because of this "Resumption of Studies Campaign", I got to know the streets of Singapore very well. We rode bicycles, two or three of us with one name list in each group. Some of those addresses were in little alleys. After school, we would ride around to look for the homes [of students who dropped out], and asked them why they did not return to school. If it was for financial reasons, the self-help societies would help. So there was this campaign in the first half of 1955.

Interviewer: What did you do during the Anti-yellow Culture Campaign?

Chen: I think initially we publish bulletins on notice boards — we wrote articles, did illustrations. Various schools were involved.

Chai: And every school had its own magazine, ours was called *Geng Yun (Cultivation)*.

Chen: But there were several magazines published by the students, there was *Geng Yun (Cultivaton), Huang Di (Wasteland)* and something else... I know that *Geng Yun* was the work of Chung Cheng students; *Huang Di* was from Chinese High.

Chai: I think so. As students we were well organised in helping each other in studies. I was in charge of English and Mathematics, each of us helped a number of the weakest students.

Interviewer: Was that during the period of the Singapore Chinese Middle School Student Union (SCMSSU)?

Chen: It was before that. Self-initiated. Each class had a class committee, with a Learning Sub-committee.

Chai: Because one was afraid that others would say you are too involved in various activities and weak in studies. Your results are poor, that is why you take part in many activities.

Chen: Yes, some did say that these people were not good in studies, that is why you went to organise activities. So these students said no, we can organise activities and we can study, no holding up in both areas. Haha.

Chai: During the final examinations, some said these people boycotted the exams as they could not pass them.

Chen: It was strange, the students' sentiments... I remember, during the "Anti-Yellow Culture Campaign", one night there was a gathering at the Chung Cheng Lake, to celebrate... I cannot remember what activity it was, haha! Chung Cheng has that lake, we did the mass dance around it. Everyone was very excited after the activity and did not want to go home, so we spent the night in the classrooms. Some people paraded along the lake holding torches made from branches, haha, singing and making music.

Chai: "Yellow" books were piled up like a small hill and burnt!

Chen: We collected those pornography works and burnt them, every school did that, not just Chung Cheng.

Interviewer: Weren't parents worried when you did not return home?

Chen: They were used to it. They were also worried initially, but got used to it later. We stayed in school very often then. Many of us in that class...but this is a digression, nothing to do with the student activities. Our classmates got on very well, we still have meal gatherings 50 years after graduation.

Chai: We still met the year before. We looked for a hotel to stay for a night and had a good time till 2 am. We were 68 years old that year, almost 70 years old, reminiscing the past...

Chen: Talking about the past...

Chai: We talked about how we played and scolded each other. We also have a banner that we hang up at gatherings. The hotel is also happy to have that, it attracts business, other customers will ask them what that is. They will say a group of Chung Cheng students are here for a gathering. The other customers will take a look and see that we are so old. That banner is still around. (Goes to look for banner)

Chen: In biology class we made specimens from lizards, pythons, chickens. Originally we should kill the animals through injections and then peel their skin. We asked the Biology teacher not to use injections and drown the animals instead. Why? Because we wanted to eat the meat. There were classmates who could cook and knew how to buy herbs. We were friends with the hawkers in school, so we borrowed their pots. We usually did this in the afternoons — cleaned [the carcasses] after the experiments, cooked with the herbs, and we would stay for dinner that night. There were many such ideas.

Chai: (Carrying banner) "Senior Middle Three Class B Reunion". I had this made and have been keeping it every year, that time we were at Marina Bay? It has been about ten years now, it was 1992 when we [first] used this banner. This is valuable. The herbs cooking, we did not dare to do that later. Once we dissected a monkey, told [the teacher] not to use injections, with injections we could not eat it. We cooked herbs and drowned the monkey in the Chung Cheng Lake. We plucked the monkey's hair and saw that its head resembled a child so much, no one dared to eat it, it was scary. At first we ate even lizards, but after we saw the monkey we did not dare eat [the animals] anymore. Very memorable, it was a lot of fun, those were very happy days. Everyone wanted to excel in studies and we were very united. In the mornings, once you reached school, as I was weak in Mathematics, there would be a "Math teacher" saying to me "Come sit here". Every day I did so many sums, so I made the mark in the final exam. Everyone was good in something, some were good in Chinese or English or Math, the weaker students passed at least three subjects.

Interviewer: Those involved in activities were all outstanding students, were there students who were not involved?

Chai: Very outstanding. There were also those who did not take part, there would be such students in every era. But the difference was the level of participation, these people did take part in the graduation soirees. And the Anti-Yellow Culture Campaign, for example. They were less active in the campaign against national service.

Interviewer: Would they feel pressurised for not participating?

Chen: Almost my entire class was involved, I think no one was absent.

Chai: When we went on tours, it also involved the whole class.

Interviewer: How many were there in your class?

Chai: 38.

Interviewer: Where did you go travelling?

Chen: Malaysia. There was also a trend then, the graduating classes — especially the senior middle school students — would organise the graduating soirees and travels.

Interviewer: It has been fifty years. Half a century. You have a very good memory.

Chen: The memories are very profound. But some things are like that, you can recall while talking about it. If you asked me about it suddenly, I would not be able to tell you. Haha.

Interviewer: When I talked to Mr Lim Chin Joo the other time, he said his involvement in the activities was just for those few years, after which he was arrested. Those few years were enough memories for a lifetime.

Chen: That is right.

Chai: Was Chin Joo older or younger than us?

Chen: About the same age, maybe one or two years younger.

Chai: His brother Chin Siong was one year my senior, Chin Joo was our junior. Chin Joo's wife was in my class, we were in it together, she participated in all these. Later she was also arrested for a period.

Interviewer: In that case, when you were arrested, weren't all the faces you saw familiar?

Chai: We were not [placed] together.

Chen: Different timing. And at different places.

Interviewer: Was it common to be arrested then? Unlike now when it is a major thing to get arrested.

Chen: Yes, it was very common. At that time, it was like... all those who were slightly active were arrested, for longer or shorter periods. I was arrested for a short time, just one month.

Interviewer: Were you locked up in jail?

Chen: Where was I locked up? The previous Central Police Station, is it called South Bridge Centre now? There are many jewellery shops in there after the rebuilding...Pidemco Centre...

Interviewer: I think that building is also gone.

Chen: It used to be a police station.

Interviewer: The Special Branch was there...

Chen: I was locked up in the Special Branch the first night. I was attending the second half of Junior Middle Three at Yock Eng then, when suddenly one day, the military police surrounded the school, surrounded the whole of Yock Eng and called out the students class by class. Those whose names were read had to step out. They went to search our homes and then detained us. They arrested about over 100 people, including teachers and students.

Interviewer: More than 100 people from Yock Eng alone?

Chen: From Yock Eng alone.... because Yock Eng was a rather famous leftist ground then. I was one of those arrested and detained at the Special Branch on the first day — now it is the Capital Tower, the old Special Branch at Cecil Street. The second day I was sent to the Central Police Station I mentioned, [the place which later became] Pidemco Centre. I was interrogated in the day, sometimes at the Special Branch, sometimes in rooms below the Central Police Station. I was allowed to rest at night. This lasted a month.

Interviewer: Why did they arrest you?

Chen: It was still the British government then, they did not give any proper reason. They never told us why. We were just interrogated. Later, I think everyone was released, but I know a few teachers were deported from the country. Two or three teachers were deported, including one of my teachers.

Interviewer: Did teachers take part in those activities?

Chen: No, based on my impression. Some people say that some students went to ask the teachers for guidance in some areas, so the teachers provided guidance. But I do not think they were formally involved. Not in my impression, none through the years. No teachers, not one.

Interviewer: Were you afraid then?

Chen: You mean when I was arrested? I was quite confused then, only in Junior Middle Three, 15 years old, somewhat silly. Because when the police came, it was the whole school, they had guns, the whole school was in chaos, then they called us class by class, there were five or six from our class and we did not know what was going on. Later, we were locked up in a room, a very big room, more than ten students, as well as a teacher who was deported in the end. More than ten students in a room, we did not feel particularly scared.

Chai: It was like just a change of environment.

Chen: And at night we would ask each other "What did they ask you today?" We were confused, and time just passed. Nothing special, just felt confused. So I spent one month in confusion. Haha. It did not leave any special impression on me. Actually now my deepest impression is of the place I slept, it was made of planks and was slanted. The planks and nails were very thick, and there were no pillows. There were nails in the sleeping area, very big nails, they were not nailed very flat, very bumpy, so I could not sleep the first night. Strangely, I got used to it after two nights, the gaps in the planks were so big, it was not flat at all, but I did not mind that and managed to sleep.

Chai: You were a child then…

Chen: Yes, I was a child. My teacher never managed to sleep. I think he kept complaining he could not sleep. We kids did not know anything. The toilet was in the room, a small flush toilet bowl.

Interviewer: Could your family visit you?

Chen: No. No visits throughout the month.

Interviewer: So you did not know how long you would be locked up?

Chen: We did not know.

Interviewer: So there were some families that did not know their child had been arrested?

Chen: They knew, the school informed the families. Another thing that left a deep impression was that there were many such rooms, we were only [in] one of them. Everyday we ate porridge, and it was always *ikan bilis* and *kang kong*, basically every meal was like that. They woke us very early in the morning, and we slept very early. Interrogation was carried out during the day, everyone was asked different questions, sometimes you were interrogated and sometimes not, so you just waited. After a while they would ask you something, then send you out again to wait. Each day passed like that.

About five or six in the morning, actually we did not know the time as there was no clock and it was dark inside, there was always a small yellow lamp on. There was a hole in the wall, with metal bars very high up, you could see the sky. To find out if it was day or night, you could see the sky through that hole. Another thing that left a deep impression on me was that somewhere a few levels away, many rooms away, someone sang *The Singapore River*, and I learnt to sing that song then. [Hums the tune] After I was released, I kept looking for the song. I later found it in a magazine for a graduation performance, at that time there were magazines published with graduation soirees, I found the song in a publication and learnt it.

Interviewer: A local composition?

Chen: Yes, a local composition.

Interviewer: You mentioned earlier that senior students would teach some songs, and there were some printed booklets. Where were these songs from? How did songs from China get in?

Chen: I do not know how they got in, actually later they were published in booklets. (Produces some song booklets)

Interviewer: My generation inherited part of that. Your era is actually quite captivating… we still had the class committees and learning sub-committees when I went to school. Everyone also took part in performances, we still did that when I attended Hwa Chong Junior College, activities day and night, skipped classes. Many. I do not know about the students now, we may have been the last generation. The organisation of activities was not deliberate. (Purely a tradition.)

Chen: (Produces some song books) Copied by hand, handwritten. (**Lee:** It was the same for us in Hwa Chong, though the songs are different. **Zhong:** Should be the tradition passed down from that time.)

In the early days it was sheets, then they collated and compiled them, you can see the handwriting is different. Before it was sheets given out at the picnics, then later I do not know how they compiled them into a booklet. Quite interesting.

Interviewer: Did students print these themselves?

Chen: Not in the later period, they were published. I believe initially it was those students who took these to publish.

Chai: There was a Li Ding who wandered here from China, and taught singing at Nanyang Girls' High School.

Chen: There were actually a group of scholars from China — Zhao Feng, Li Ding and some others. There was someone who later went back to helm the Central Conservatory of Music, very cultured. At that time they ended up in this area of Malaya and Singapore. So there was a Brass Gong Choir and Brass Gong Musical Society then, which nurtured a batch of music talents. Later I learnt that musicians like Lin Zhenzhang and Poh Choon Ann were from the Brass Gong Choir. Poh Choon Ann later studied music in Britain; his first encounters with music were at the Brass Gong Choir.

Interviewer: The cultural scene was so vibrant then, why is it that later it quickly…

Chen: Because a State of Emergency[4] was declared. All activities stopped suddenly.

Chai: There was also a performance that came to Singapore, what...

Chen: It was very early then, we were little during the Japanese Occupation. Lee Howe came then, she followed the Wuhan Choir in support of the national salvation cause and stayed on.

Chai: Tommy Koh's mother too, that was even earlier. We were very young, only in Primary Three or Four.

Chen: So the Chinese dances and activities of Chinese school students were influenced by China, because of the legacies of scholars who had fled to Singapore in the early days.

Interviewer: Culturally, they still identified with China?

Chen: Yes, yes, still China.

Chai: Our first graduation soiree at Chung Cheng, *Meili de Zuguo* (*Beautiful Motherland*) in 1953...

Chen: (Displays photo) This dance was choreographed by the students themselves, using the song from China, *Beautiful Motherland*, I cannot remember whose work it was.

The May 13 Student Movement

Interviewer: What was it like during May 13?

Chen: Actually I cannot remember why, I think there was a notice that students were going to submit a petition to the Governor on May 13. People went there on their own, I do not think we gathered first.

Chai: People first gathered in their various schools that night.

Chen: I went on my own and did not gather first.

---

[4] In 1948, the Malayan Communist Party gave up peaceful resistance and turned to guerilla warfare against the British colonial government, operating from the forests of the entire Malayan Peninsula. To deal with this guerilla warfare, the British colonial government declared a State of Emergency in the entire country. Under the emergency law, the government could arrest anyone suspected to be involved in communist activities at any time. The British troops could also search residences, shift residents to new villages and surround the villages suspected to be assisting communist terrorists. After the emergency law was amended in 1960, it was renamed the "Internal Security Act".

Chai: You were at the sports field, we…

Chen: No, no, I was not at the sports field… There were phone calls that informed students to go on their own. There was an organisation called the "Student Committee Against National Service Exemption", represented in the various schools.

Chai: There was already a communication network following the Anti-Yellow Culture Campaign. Each school had such a network, there were no phones at home then. So students went around informing others house by house.

Chen: It happened to be during the sports meet for all Chinese-medium schools in Singapore. So there was a group at Jalan Besar, I remember after the incident happened, some students were still swimming and several called for lorries and taxis, jumped on board and asked to be sent to the stadium. They went to Jalan Besar Stadium and shouted "*Mata pa hak seng!*" (Police hit students!)

Chai: Later there was a song called *Mata Pa Hak Seng* (*Police Hit Students*): "On May 13, police beat students…", they changed the lyrics of a song from China.

Chen: It was in Hokkien.

Chai: Everyone came to know the song, even hawkers could sing it, because people sympathised with the students who were unarmed. Just sixteen years old, they were beaten up, some were only twelve or thirteen.

Interviewer: Under what circumstances did they hit [students]?

Chai: They probably knew we were going to petition. The whole group, five in a row, many rows of them, the whole pedestrian walk was … suddenly the police came, one or two initially, then the riot police and their red vehicles arrived. We were only kids and did not understand what was going on, we still waited foolishly, wanting to go in, to enter the Governor's residence.

Chen: Queuing up to petition at the Governor's residence. Then the police came up to surround the students and ordered them to disperse.

Chai: There were five or six red vehicles. We heard "ding ding ding ding" above, still looked on foolishly and then saw the whole group of police charged out. They held batons and shields, and charged towards us. Everyone said, let's huddle together quickly, so we hooked our arms together and held on to each other tightly. They charged towards the back, we were in front, there was a large drain at the side, people pulled and kicked, they hit us with batons, regardless of your gender, so we ran! Many fell into the drains, and escaped, ran along that route… we did not know what to do, so we ran to Chung Cheng. Chung Chung High (Branch).

I was really very lost and did not know what to do, and someone said go! Run to Chung Cheng! We had no money too, I had a small bag when we left, dropped my shoes as well, it was really chaotic… really chaotic… it was a moving scene which made many people cry. Some were bleeding from the beating, blood kept dripping… so we said, look! look! See how the police beat up students!

Interviewer: How did it end?

Chai: And then…I think we gathered at Chung Cheng that night, and we talked about what to do next. Some people went home and were scolded or beaten by their parents…

Chen: What happened next…I think we gathered at night and dispersed the next day. After that…

Chai: Oh, the May 22 camp-in. At this camp-in, the police charged in again. The camp-in was at the Chung Cheng High School, we assembled for a night, and [the police] sent in their men early the next morning, even after we gathered, what did we do? Continue protesting? Because the path from Junior Middle Three to senior middle school would be cut off due to conscription. You would not be able to continue with studies in senior middle school after completing your national service, so it would be a pity. Hence we supported the movement and requested for exemption from national service.

Chen: It was called the "Students' National Service Exemption Delegation" i.e. [we campaigned for] students to be exempted from national service. We were disbanded after the May 22 camp-in, we failed.

Chai: At this time, our school announced an emergency closure, classes were stopped indefinitely, because it was already very chaotic. People lost contact and stayed at home. Later, someone suggested that it should still continue, hence there was the June 2 assembly at Chinese High. That was the longest, one month. That time we succeeded.

Interviewer: What was Chung Cheng's position towards the May 13 sit-in?

Chen: The school could not control matters at all. The principal then was Chuang Chu Lin. He was more sympathetic towards the students, of course. On May 13, Chung Cheng's branch campus was the nearest, it was near Fort Canning Hill, we had to find a place to gather, and we did so at Chung Cheng's branch campus. I was not around for this part. Later it seemed people were dismissed. I forgot if they stayed through the night. I think we did not stay for the night on May 13. After the dismissal, the May 22 camp-in was organised, we gathered at Chung Cheng (main) and spent the night there, but dispersed the next morning once the police charged in.

Interviewer: Were there conflicts?

Chen: I do not think so…

Chai: That time it was more peaceful. They kept broadcasting at the entrance, our metal gate was locked. They got the parents to bring their children home, so the parents did, and we were dismissed. It was very peaceful.

Interviewer: During May 13, was it Lee Kong Chian who went to Chinese High to persuade the students?

Chen: Lee Kong Chian? ……I cannot remember many of the details, I need to read the materials again. Based on our memory, there was something like that, we failed after the May 22 camp-in. Then it was June 2, after a few similar incidents, we gathered at Chinese High on June 2, that was organised, so there were pickets, I was one of them, we did shifts from midnight till dawn, 24-hour shifts. The police were on the roads and we were behind the fences. To avoid being photographed, we tied handkerchiefs, and did not allow them to enter. We would inform the rest if they did. Inside the school, we were very organised, lessons went on, performances at night. Lessons in the day, Chinese, English, Mathematics, we organised the lessons and taught each other.

Interviewer: What about the teachers?

Chai: There were no teachers. It was the school holidays then, we went in and conducted lessons ourselves. Chinese High has a clock tower, right? It is still there. We lived below the clock tower, and that bell, the students were resourceful, they moved the whole bell down to where we stayed. At six in the morning, they would ring the bell for morning exercises, life was very orderly, as good as [imposed order by] the school.

Chen: We cooked our own meals; there were students in charge of cooking and students who washed bowls. There was the learning group, recreation group, practices for performances every night. It was great!

Chai: Girls and boys had separate living quarters. Then for bathing, there were so many of us, so timeslots were allocated for each room [of students] to take turns. Very good management!

Chen: The leaders were also elected by the students.

Chai: There was one leader for a certain number of students.

Chen: So I say it was the Anti-Yellow Culture Campaign, the organisation, the core was still there, it was this group of people.

Chai: Our legal consultant should be Lee Kuan Yew then. Initially it was someone called Xu Chunfeng, he did not perform well. Later, we did not want him and turned to Lee Kuan Yew.

Chen: At that time Rajaratnam was writing the editorial at *The Straits Times*... no, not *The Straits Times*, it was *The Standard*. And Lee Kuan Yew was our legal consultant.

Interviewer: So your families...

Chen: Our families could not control us and did not interfere, they let us be. Because my family members were involved in many of such things, they were more receptive, perhaps many people... actually many parents then wanted to take their children home, so we got a group to persuade the parents. When parents came, we would receive them in a place like a visitors' room, reasoned with them and let them observe our lives.

Chai: There were unfavourable things that people said, so we showed them that boys and girls lived separately, how the canteen worked, it was like a school tour! Haha! Some parents were thus convinced by us and went back.

Chen: Some parents even supported us, gave us things and money.

Chai: Some parents — because the first night was the most chaotic — came to bring their children home the next day. Then their children sneaked back again. So we persuaded them that their children were alright, they were behaving well, let them stay. We also did home visits then.

Interviewer: Was it organised by the SCMSSU?

Chen: No, the union was set up later. These people came forward to set up the union.

Interviewer: How did you choose... you have been mentioning "organisation", how did you organise yourselves?

Chen: Frankly, it was a bit chaotic. My impression — I was not in the organising team, not at the top, I was a participant — was that initially there was an organisation that led the Anti-Yellow Culture Campaign. Then there were nation-wide activities for student exemption from national service, I think the assembly was organised and led by this group.

Interviewer: Who was the leader?

Chen: It was Soon Loh Boon and his peers. Many of them. Later, some of them were repatriated. Fu Sunmin was also one of them. He was Chung Cheng's representative, Chinese High's representative was Soon Loh Boon, none for Yock Eng, Li Shuhui for Nan Chiau, Feng Yihua for Nanyang Girls'.

Interviewer: These people were influenced by leftist thought? (**Chen:** That is for sure.) Or were they… because I read the government's White Paper on the closure of the SCMSSU, they think the communist party was controlling behind the scene…

Chen: This issue…I recently read the memoirs of the Plen, Fang Chuang Pi[5], and found that the Malayan Communist Party (MCP) then had a group in Singapore called the Student Movement Group. Maybe these people were involved in the activities, or they may have been leading the activities. But as participants, we did not see or feel it, and they were self-initiated. Because those incidents were related to students' benefits and the issues had an impact on students, so the sense of self-motivation was strong. The MCP's activities in Singapore had already been disrupted, the only group that could remain active was what they called the Student Movement Group.

Chai: It was also written that this group also could not function in the later part.

Interviewer: It seemed like there were not many of them.

Chen: This is a digression of course. Because of my recent interest in these memoirs, I read Fang Chuang Pi's and then Chin Peng's. I also read *Dialogues with*

---

[5] Fang Chuang Pi was born in 1924. After graduating from the Chinese High School, he worked as a journalist with the Nan Chiau Jit Pao and later became the editor of *The Freedom News*, the key mouthpiece of the Singapore branch of the Malayan Communist Party (MCP). In 1950, through the recommendation of Eu Chooi Yip, Fang officially joined MCP. In the early 1950s, the Municipal Committee of the MCP was arrested, dealing a huge blow to the Student Movement Committee, Labour Movement Committee and the armed forces. Nevertheless, after the June 20 event, the units under the leadership of these various committees managed to survive by avoiding face-to-face meetings and maintaining contact with correspondents through secret underground networks. Fang and Eu assumed leadership after they re-established contact with the correspondent of *The Freedom News*. In 1953, Eu moved to Indonesia and Fang later became the de facto leader of the MCP in Singapore. During the late 1950s, Fang met up secretly for several times with Lee Kuan Yew, the then Secretary-General of the People's Action Party, to request for collaboration. Lee called him the authoritative MCP representative. Fang later escaped to Indonesia for 10 years and participated in guerilla warfare at the Thai-Malaysian bordering forests in the late 1970s. Ending his guerilla lifestyle of over a decade, he settled down in southern Thailand in 1991 and passed away in Hat Yai in 2003.

Chin Peng[6]. After reading these, my sense was that the MCP was weak then, the leadership organisation was very weak. And the Student Movement Group seemed somewhat independent; it developed in reaction to the social environment and incidents. So although there was this organisation, there were obviously no policies or a systematic and strategic leadership. This was also why the MCP could not succeed.

Interviewer: Had the MCP gone into guerilla warfare?

Chen: They had gone into guerilla warfare.

Chai: But to us — for example those students who had to join the army, for example Fu Sunmin from our class — we felt that our classmates were going to become cannon fodder, and especially when the army belonged to the British, that feeling… And after these people left and came back a few years later, they would not be able to join senior middle school, their education will end at Junior Middle Three. Everyone wanted to study. For me, this was my motivation to join the movement. Most people who joined the army would not return, and if they returned, they would have to start work, they would not have a chance to go to senior middle school.

Interviewer: Joining the army after Junior Middle Three, so they would not have reached 18 years old?

Chai: Should be after senior middle school. But you must know that many people then were still in junior middle school, many were still in Junior Middle Three when they became of age [to be enlisted]. All in all, we felt that the senior middle schools may have to close down because there were too few people, because at that time students in English-medium schools could graduate at 18 years old and enter university, but we could not enter university yet. Because for a long time after the war, students were already eight or nine years old when they entered school.

Interviewer: Students then were more mature, older, and quite strong in organisational skills.

Chen: Correct. I know many students then were already working before they came back to study. Something that left a deep impression on me was once when we wanted to organise a charity performance for a flood, we were at the Happy World Stadium to set up a stage. Those students were very skilful, and put up the stage themselves. Aiyah, I saw them climbing up like monkeys, binding together the

---

[6]*Dialogues with Chin Peng: New Light on the Malayan Communist Party*, edited by C.C. Chin and Karl Hack, was published in 2004 by the National University of Singapore Press.

beams with rattan, they set up the stage just like that. Later I asked around and they said these students performed such tasks at work originally, they put up racks for people. There were students like that. So when it came to cooking, many students were hawkers, and were good at cooking. During the camp-in, many hawkers supported us by giving us vegetables. In the mornings, they came in lorries, and they also sent us rice. There were about a hundred students at the camp-in, food was given to us through the month. During that time, many students already had experiences in life and society. No matter what we did, someone could rise to the occasion.

Interviewer: Did the alumni come back to join the student movement? For instance, those who graduated from Chung Cheng…

Chen: There were no alumni then, hahaha! The school had just started classes, very few! The war had only just ended. We were the first batch of students after the war ended.

Chai: I was in Primary One or Two when I returned.

Chen: I was in Primary Three.

Interviewer: What happened after the month-long camp-in?

Chen: What happened was this — many social groups like the Chinese Chamber of Commerce, as well as distinguished individuals came to persuade the students. So the students made some requests and negotiated with the government. You should be able to read from the old newspapers that some kind of agreement was achieved, then we dispersed peacefully.

The Impact of Student Movements

Interviewer: Were the student leaders on good terms with one another? Or were there also factions…

Chen: That I do not know, because I was not participating at that level, I was lower in the hierarchy. If there were [factions], it would be Chung Cheng and Chinese High, different schools would have different preferences, but I cannot tell if they formed factions.

Interviewer: Student activism was very popular then, were the bookstores in any way linked to this?

Chen: Yes. Amidst the tides of student activism, students were very passionate about pursuing knowledge and ideals, so business at the bookstores was very good.

New books on new knowledge sold particularly well, the reading atmosphere was very good. At that time, comparing students from Chinese-medium schools and English-medium schools, frankly there was a large gap in various areas of knowledge and cognitive depth. This situation carried on till later when the group from the Socialist Club at University of Malaya, they felt that, aiyah, Chinese schools... it was this batch. Another batch returned from studies in England then, the batch that included Lee Kuan Yew, they felt that there had to be deeper concern and participation in society. So it was the Chinese-medium schools that started the trend, the English schools caught on, and later with the change of the entire education system, there were no more Chinese-medium schools. So it became...

Interviewer: So students then had a strong desire for knowledge and books sold well. Did the management of a bookstore have to import many books in order to meet demand?

Chen: Yes, that is right. If my impression is correct, the Shanghai Bookstore experienced several peaks in sales. The first was when the primary school textbooks were published. The second was after the liberation of China, China exported a lot of books, that was the second peak which lasted till the ban on books from China. Then it was Hong Kong publications that filled the void, and then the peak ignited by the student movements. Nantah was established in 1956 — in 1956, 1957, 1958, the Nantah students gathered every Saturday at bookstores, the bookstores at North Bridge Road and South Bridge Road. We stayed in hostels then, and would go downtown every Saturday, most of the time we met at the bookstores.

Interviewer: Students in bookstores, even if they did not buy books ...

Chen: They were also there to read, meet friends; the contact point for other activities was also at bookstores. Business was very good, students then brought Singapore's Chinese book industry to a small peak, especially with the establishment of Nantah. There was no more after that, it was the last peak.

Active Older Siblings

Interviewer: The first time I met you and Chen Mong Sing, we spoke of your elder sister, Chen Mong Hock[7], the participation of your family...what was the whole situation like?

---

[7]Linda Chen Mong Hock was born in 1929 in Zhejiang Province, China. She came to Singapore with her mother at three. A graduate of the Department of History, University of Malaya, in 1953, she was a member of the Socialist Club and was active in anti-colonial activities. In 1956, Chen Mong Hock

Chen: It was quite different in my family. I was the youngest and Mong Hock was in the University of Malaya then.

Interviewer: Was she from Chung Hwa Girls' School?

Chen: She was from Chung Cheng. After three years of Junior Middle School, she went to an English-medium school.

Interviewer: Why did she go to St. Margaret's?

Chen: Why? Because the activities were all amongst Chinese-medium school students, so there was also a call then for us to influence English-medium school students. So a group of people joined the English-medium schools. But it was not very successful, many people came out after a while like myself, we left as we were not used to it. She was more successful. She joined the school and also boarded there, so she came home only once a week and had less contact with us brothers. As for her friends, we only knew those whom she brought home.

Interviewer: How many years older was she?

Chen: She was much older than me. Mong Sing was born in 1932, she was born in 1929, me in 1937.

Interviewer: Did your father agree to let her attend an English-medium school?

Chen: My father agreed. One good point about my family is that we are very liberal. So after something happened to Mong Chow, our family never stopped us from doing anything. As long as we did not break the law and do things like gamble, cheat, joining secret societies, there were strict rules in that area. But apart from that, they were very liberal and never deterred us from doing anything. This gave us great convenience. Mong Chow also boarded at Chinese High, so I did not have much contact with him. It was very early on when he got into trouble and left home. Actually I have the most contact with Mong Sing.

Interviewer: Mong Hock was in the women's federation.

Chen: Yes, she was.

---

was heavily involved in establishing the Singapore Women's Federation, becoming its President. However, the Federation was banned by the government within half a year. Chen Mong Hock was arrested in 1956 and 1963. Her academic work in English, *The Early Chinese Newspapers of Singapore 1881–1912*, an important work in the field of local Chinese history, has been translated into Chinese. She passed away in 2002.

Chai: She was in that Socialist Club.

Chen: No, she had left. The Singapore's Women's Federation, let me think…was she working…she also taught for a while but was disallowed and she stopped.

Interviewer: Was she involved in underground work?

Chen: Maybe…what they called the peripheral organisations, yes, I believe so. There were many peripheral organisations then, I do not know which one she was with. I believe it was one of the peripheral organisations.

Interviewer: The relationship between the women's federation and the students was…

Chen: The women's federation had a very short history, it was shut down after barely a year, it was shut down and she was arrested. The women's federation did not have much activity. Its history was too short, you could say that it was nipped in the bud. It was formed at the Happy World, its history was brief.

OBSERVATION AS HISTORICAL PARTICIPATION
AN INTERVIEW WITH LEE LEONG SENG

Lee Leong Seng

Interviewed by Chan Cheow Thia and Teng Siao See

Transcribed by Lee Hui Jun, Ding Lee Yong and Chan Cheow Thia

Translated by Teng Siao See

Date: 27 December 2006

Family Background

Interviewer: Mr Lee, where were you born?

Mr. Lee: Born in Singapore.

Interviewer: Which year?

Mr. Lee: 1940.

Interviewer: How many siblings do you have?

Mr. Lee: I have an elder sister, two younger brothers, one younger sister. There are altogether five of us.

Interviewer: Were you all born in Singapore?

Mr. Lee: Yes, all in Singapore. We were the first generation to be born in Singapore.

Interviewer: Then...where did your parents come from?

Mr. Lee: From Fujian, China. They were natives of Fujian. My father came rather early, through the coolie trade to Singapore, later he went around Nanyang, including Sumatra and Penang, to earn a living. He only returned to China when he was thirty to get married. After marriage...he came over first, then my mother and grandmother followed suit.

Interviewer: What work were your parents engaged in?

Mr. Lee: The area of work my father was in when he was younger — I don't know as I was not yet born. But I heard that he was making the spicy stuffed sausages that the Hokkiens eat.

Interviewer: Oh, stuffed sausages.

Mr. Lee: Yes, stuffed sausages. Spicy stuffed sausages. He had a small business in that, and was also doing distribution. But he did not continue with it. If I am not wrong, he went on to become a seaman. I am not sure what happened afterwards. They never told us about the past. We only heard about it indirectly sometimes. Later he became a seaman, collaborating with a ship owner. He invested in that ship. He then went to Indonesia to transport those timber. At that time, Indonesia exported a large quantity of timber to Singapore. He earned a profit this way. After earning a profit, he was engaged in the development of lumbering in Sumatra, he had a few lumbering sites. Unfortunately, later, his ship carrying the timber sank, and a number of such accidents followed. His career collapsed. At that time, the money (he lost) should be an entire million; in contemporary terms, it would be even more. It was an irrecoverable blow.

Interviewer: How old were you then?

Mr. Lee: I remember I was probably in Primary Five. I entered school in 1948, around 11 years old.

Interviewer: Did your parents go to school?

Mr. Lee: No. My father knew only how to sign his name. He used Chinese characters for book-keeping. He was illiterate, so was Mother. They were considered very poor during those days.

Interviewer: What language did you use at home?

Mr. Lee: It was Hokkien at that time.

Interviewer: Among siblings?

Mr. Lee: The siblings used Hokkien when we were young. Later, we studied till about Primary Five or Six. Before Primary Five, we were still using Hokkien with classmates in school. From Primary Five onwards, the teacher wanted us to speak in Mandarin. Only then did we begin speaking in Mandarin. Later on, we siblings would use both Hokkien and Mandarin, mixing them together.

Interviewer: Did your mother work?

Mr. Lee: My mother was not a career woman, she did not receive any education. But her contribution to the family was greater than my father's. She is the most unforgettable person in my life. At that time, after my father's business failed, he stayed in Indonesia and couldn't come back. We had many siblings then, five altogether. On her own, she had to go to work and take care of us, you can imagine how hard it was. Because of this, my elder sister had to stop schooling at that time. As she is the oldest sister, she had to take care of us. I am number two, boys were given preferential treatment and priority in education, it wasn't necessary for girls to receive education, thus I had the chance to go to school. Later, my younger brothers and sisters also had the opportunity to receive education. But my oldest sister didn't, she was sacrificed. The situation was like that then. My mother was a housewife, she was also a domestic helper. There were no Filipino maids or Indonesian maids at that time. I remember it was the year when I graduated from primary school and wanted to embark on middle school education. My grades in Primary Five and Six were not bad, but due to declining family circumstances — my father's failed business caused the family's financial situation to fall below the poverty line — I seemed to work very hard. I don't know how I survived before Primary Five, I was naive, didn't know how to self-study. But I met a very good teacher when I was in Primary Five. I have always regarded him as a teacher I am deeply indebted to. I kept trying to locate him but couldn't. When I was in Primary Six, I met another great teacher. If not for this teacher, when I graduated, I wouldn't have the opportunity to go to middle school. But he came to my home, talked to my mother and said your son is good at his studies, you should let him continue his education. After she heard those words, my mother decided to ignore the neighbours' sarcastic remarks. They would comment that there's no money at home but the son is still going to middle school. It did not bother her. She went on with her work as a domestic helper. After she worked for a month, she requested for an advancement of salary so that I could pay the school fees. Ten dollars per month at Chinese High. Ten dollars at that time, 1945, was a huge amount. It's now a hundred dollars? (More — two hundred) Two hundred? (Laughs) So many of my Primary Six classmates did not get the chance to further their studies. But I went on as I was encouraged by this teacher and had my mother's support.

Interviewer: Why did you choose Chinese High?

Mr. Lee: Chinese High? Why choose Chinese High? It seemed to be renowned at that time, and I chose it because I had heard only of this middle school. For the girls, it's Nanyang and Nan Chiau. I don't think I had heard of Chung Cheng then. Perhaps Chinese High was more famous then. Also, I think I also asked my teacher who said, go to Chinese High, the one who taught me. Later, I secured a scholarship at Chinese High during my first year there, a hundred and twenty dollars. Wow, I was very happy. Gave the money to my mother. As for my own living expenses, I often worked part-time. While studying at Chinese High, I would take on part-time work after school.

Interviewer: Where did you live then?

Mr. Lee: I lived in Beach Road at "Wa Diam Kao". In Hokkien, it is called *pa di gui wa diam kao*. "Pa Di Gui" was most famous in *Xiaopo* (the city area north of the Singapore River). There was a street which specialised in blacksmithing with various blacksmiths creating household metal products. "Wa Diam Kao" was somewhere there. There were many shops selling electronic products and bowls, it was in that area, that's why it was called "Wa Diam Kao". You can't locate it now. At four in the morning at the market, the fish distributing centre would begin operations. I had a classmate at that time who lived near the area, he asked me to go with him. We went there to work, from four to six. What did we do? When the fishmongers obtained a basket of fish through a bid, we would assist him to carry the baskets to his lorry and load them onto the lorry. From four o'clock to six o'clock. At that time, we were paid only fifty cents for the work. Sometimes there were leftover fish and he would give them to us to bring home. We would be very happy then. We would give the fifty cents to our families. We would then have something for breakfast before we would go to school. This was the life then…

Interviewer: How did you go to school? Walk?

Mr. Lee: Of course I took the public bus at first. Later, I was unable to take the bus as I didn't even have money for the bus fare and had to stop going to school. I stopped schooling for three days. My classmates came to look for me suddenly and asked why I did not go to school. I said I did not have money, had no money to take the bus, no money to have meals. So I had to stop schooling. They returned home after that. A few days later, they came to see me again and brought a bicycle along. I asked them, what is the matter? He replied, you don't have money to take the bus, right? We went back to class and asked for donations and bought you this second-hand bicycle. He said, you can cycle to school. I was so touched then. So I could ride the bicycle and once again returned to my middle school, Chinese High. But I had no money for meals. Sometimes I would eat only after cycling back home. Returning home at two or three, I was hungry and would eat rice, at that time we were very poor. Sometimes Mother needed to go out and work. We would have plain cold porridge with soy sauce. The Hokkiens says *or dao you* — black soy sauce, it was very tasty, we would eat like that. But my classmate found out. One of my classmates was very nice, he lived somewhere behind Chinese High. He said you could come to my place to have lunch. Because he knew I would go on with extra-curricular activities on an empty stomach. He would ask me to have lunch at his place. Thus I would just go.

Interviewer: Was his family better off?

Mr. Lee: His family was not exactly very rich, they did alright. His mother reared chickens and ducks. He wasn't the eldest, he had older sisters and brothers. Thus, at that time, he fared better than us. (Laughs) He asked me to have lunch at his place. For two years, I did that. Fortunately I was lucky to have these classmates helping out… ties among classmates at that time were very good. There was this spirit of camaraderie amongst us. I was moved by it and later also liked to help others a lot, including my own siblings, some other people and my classmates. We would not be jealous of those classmates who performed better in school. We wouldn't. Those who were better at their studies would often help those who did less well. We would have tuition sometimes, after class, tuition before extra-curricular activities. Those who were good at their studies helped those who were weak. At that time, our class consisted of students who did well in their studies and those who did poorly. Now the good ones are clustered in a group, the bad ones in another. During our time, the good and bad ones were together. I think this is good. As the bad (students) can be influenced by the good (students).

Interviewer: And you had classmates of different ages?

Mr. Lee: Different ages. At that time, there was the Japanese occupation which lasted three years and eight months. School was closed during that period. Thus, my class … mainly at that time when I was 13, just graduated from primary school, entered Chinese High at 14 in 1954. But in the class, there might be students aged 17 and 18. They were already 10 and 11-year-olds entering primary school. In class, there were students aged 15 and 16. There was one student who was very tall, we were all small and short. Due to the war, we had greater age differences.

Interviewer: Apart from tuition, what other activities do you think built up the spirit of camaraderie?

Mr. Lee: Let me see ... in my opinion, at that time, there was the student movement, that was very vital. As the student movement brought together and united people of varied ages and family backgrounds. Like now, let's not talk about the present, even during my children's time, I could sense that there was an absence of unity among their classmates, there was no such unity already. Now, there's certainly none. During their time, it was already *jigei gu jigei* (Cantonese, meaning "everyone for themselves"). During our time, I think it was because at that time, under such circumstances, the student movement was formed, creating unity among students, it had something to do with this.

The May 13 Incident and the SCMSSU thereafter

Interviewer: What kind of circumstances, can you elaborate?

Mr. Lee: It was the British colonial era then. Chinese schools and Chinese school students were neglected, they were marginalised. In those days, there was an air of discontentment among Chinese school students, plus at that time, 80 or 90 percent of them were very poor. They went to school hoping to improve their chances for the future. But they could only work hard individually, they did not come together as a group. However when I went in that year, 1954, there was one issue, the British wanted to recruit for the military. We were not sure then, but later learnt that Malaya had entered a State of Emergency in 1948, the emergency was declared by Britain. You couldn't have a gathering of more than five persons. So, we were "newborn lambs unafraid of the tiger". As Britain wanted to implement military service, those older classmates would be affected, we were not affected as we had not reached the age.

They were against the enlistment, they were unwilling to serve in the army. Once, there was an All-Singapore Chinese Schools' Sports Day at Jalan Besar. We were there watching the sports meet, I think it was the 13th of May. Suddenly, some students arrived and shouted, our classmates are being beaten up, let's go and help them! His appeal moved some people, and some present (at the sports meet) went with him. I was one of them. Along Jalan Besar, Bencoolen Street, we kept running till we reached what is it now called Oxley Lane, that Fort Canning. It turned out that they were beaten by the police there. Thus, we, many people ran over there. There were tens of thousands of people at the sports meet at Jalan Besar. Of course, not everyone went, but at least a few thousands did go. So, that day, a conflict occurred between students and policemen — they clashed.

We didn't know what was going on at that time. We only felt that students were beaten up by policemen, we went to help them out of a sense of injustice. It was only later that we discovered it was such a serious matter. They later seemed to have gathered at a place, I think they were dispersed because they were surrounded by the policemen, not sure if they ran to Chinese High or Chung Cheng High before dispersion. I think it was Chinese High or Chung Cheng High, maybe I didn't know the way then, a senior led me along, I think it was Chung Cheng, because I remember there was a lake, there is no lake in Chinese High. So it was at Chung Cheng. Afterwards, I couldn't stay on because my mother was doing other people's laundry, I was responsible for delivering the clothes to them, that was our source of income. I told him I couldn't stay, I needed to go because I needed to deliver the clothes.

I didn't know how to get back at that time. I cannot recall now and only remember they told me where to take the bus. Because it was my first time to travel so far. I reached home ultimately. Later, this matter subsided, was resolved, it seemed to have gained the attention of the public. The Chinese Chamber of Commerce also stepped out to resolve this problem, but after the incident, when I returned to school, I felt that interactions among classmates were unlike before, they interacted more closely and were caring towards one another, it's like ties became closer, right. I think this was the starting point. Later, this became a Chinese school tradition. Up to the 1960s and the 1970s, this Chinese school tradition was preserved, until the schools disappeared, became history, then it changed.

Interviewer: Did you hear from your seniors about the entire process, what actually happened on the 13th of May, 1954?

Mr. Lee: I learnt more details only afterwards, that they were resisting against military conscription. We unintentionally supported their resistance against military conscription. Later on, the British government gave way, allowing them to postpone the draft. As we were still in senior middle school, postponing meant that many students who were older than us, those over the age of 18, were permitted to finish junior middle school and senior middle school before serving. As the British had their pride too, the service cannot just be withdrawn because you opposed, the students were permitted to postpone it for two years, they accepted postponement and the matter was settled. Developments after that, whether or not they actually did the military service, we don't know. But when we reached 18 — I was 19 when I graduated in 1959 — the situation then was different. Singapore was embarking on self-governance, it began in 1959, thus, the (school) publication mentioned self-governance. It appeared that we had high hopes for self-governance, we had hoped that we would have internal autonomy with it, but national defence and army affairs, national defence and foreign diplomacy still remained under British control, the government could have internal autonomy. We were full of hope as we entered the working world then. (Smiled)

Interviewer: Did you participate in the aftermath of the May 13 Incident? Or was it only a coincidence that day?

Mr. Lee: It was a coincidence that day, but later, I was involved in some events. There was a gathering at Chinese High. I don't know which part of the Chinese schools' structure Britain wanted to alter, this I am not sure, but I went to the gathering at Chinese High. That gathering at Chinese High, many Chinese school students went, I also joined in.

Interviewer: Why did you want to join in?

Mr. Lee: Because the purpose was to defend Chinese education. Because at that time, it appeared that the British colonial authorities had the intention to alter the structure of Chinese schools and switched to a predominantly English teaching medium. We couldn't accept that. For instance, English would be used to teach the subjects of History and Geography. Also, there was an official report on education which aimed to change the character of Chinese schools. Chinese schools were not under governmental control prior to this, they were managed by the schools' board of directors. But the report appeared to be interventionist, so it was strongly opposed by us, students. There was already a Singapore Chinese Middle Schools' Student Union (SCMSSU)… a union for middle school students. Students were very well organised in those days. Lee Kuan Yew was our legal adviser. Thus, at that time ... later on, we supported the People's Action Party, they seemed to have represented us in court, defended us in court regarding some matters. Some students were arrested then or something. So, Chinese school students therefore supported him, right? This was inter-related.

Interviewer: So were you yourself part of the SCMSSU?

Mr. Lee: Yes, I think almost a hundred percent joined. Students at that time … I think only very few did not. Take my class, for instance, I think almost the entire class joined, all participated. But among those who participated, they responded differently. Some were very active, some in comparison, merely joined in lah, yeah, more passive. There were also some who were detached, yes, but most people were enthusiastic.

Interviewer: Who took the initiative to urge you to join the SCMSSU?

Mr. Lee: Firstly, because of the senior students, they were the organisers. They went to register with the government, you needed to register. They registered a SCMSSU, set it up legally, then they of course had a branch at Chinese High. They called their branches the Chinese High branch, the Chung Cheng High branch and so on. At the Chinese High branch, there were 6 levels, Senior Middle Three, Senior Middle Two, Senior Middle One, Junior Middle Three, Junior Middle Two, Junior Middle One. Each grade had its level unit and class unit. In each class unit, everybody chose a class monitor, this class monitor headed the class unit. These class monitors were the leaders of that level unit, responsible for the activities of that level.

Interviewer: When you were a member of SCMSSU, what kind of activities did it organise outside class?

Mr. Lee: There were many activities during that time. For instance, the class would organise learning classes, meaning tuition, helping those students who did not do well academically. Closer to the school vacations or during the vacations, picnics or group activities such as autumn camps or summer camps would be organised. Sometimes these activities were for the entire level, sometimes other schools such as Nanyang Girls' or Nan Chiau or Chung Cheng were involved too. It depended on the district. Chinese High was closer to Nan Chiau and Nanyang. For Chung Cheng High, it would be Chung Hwa, they were in the same area.

Interviewer: Was this organised by the class or by the SCMSSU branches in school?

Mr. Lee: Basically, the SCMUSU had what was called guiding principles. But it would come up with a mission each year, for instance, saying this year we would do this. They were like slogans. It had been so long that I had forgotten them, but they would be implemented throughout all levels. So, every level would decide what each would do based on this directive.

Interviewer: So was this type of social networking activity, for instance, a collaboration between grade one and the grade one of another school?

Mr. Lee: Oh yes, yes, of course it would be the same level. If we from junior middle school went to work with the senior middle school students, we wouldn't be able to fit in. So honestly, the organisational abilities of Chinese schools students were very strong. This was praised by Lee Kuan Yew many times, and he often said that this was also the strength of Chinese school students. At that time, apart from school work, these activities were very vibrant. Thus, we were very poor in life, but very happy in spirit. We wouldn't feel, as some from my children's generation or current students would, they would say, "it's boring, boring", right? "Boring boring" became a pet phrase, as some young people feel bored, we at that time felt fulfilled and lived quite happily. Now you wouldn't be as happy as back then even if you had money. That is true.

Interviewer: Was your family aware that you were involved in the activities of the SCMSSU?

Mr. Lee: They knew.

Interviewer: What did they think?

Mr. Lee: They were not against it. My parents, you see, when I participated in the campus sit-in that year, they even went to watch.

Interviewer: Which year?

Mr. Lee: That year at Chinese High, after the May 13 Incident, there was another occupation movement at Chinese High. They went to see me, expressed support, no opposition. At that time, the Chinese Chamber of Commerce and various organisations within the Chinese community supported us, we had around a thousand people. What did we eat? At that time, we led a communal life, living out of a huge rice pot. We had a classmate who used to be a cook, he was older than us. In those days, although the food was no delicacy, it was delicious to me. Especially for us from poor families, the food was very delicious. Of course, there were some students who came from affluent families and found the food unsavoury. Their parents would sometimes buy food and deliver it to them. We ate with great appetite and relish. I ate seven or eight bowls of porridge in a row, I had a good appetite then. I was rather slim, wouldn't grow fat no matter how I ate, right. Then where did these come from? These vegetables and rice came from external donations, we didn't have the means. Thus, parents at that time were supportive, so was the public. Later, I think the report, the official education report was retracted, not implemented. We won. Thus, at that time, it was mainly to protect Chinese education, protect vernacular education.

Interviewer: So when you were studying at Chinese High, apart from studies and SCMSSU activities, did you participate in other activities outside class?

Mr. Lee: Personally, I couldn't participate, as my family was comparatively poorer. Apart from these, I had to earn a living, meaning I had to take on part-time work. At first, I had mentioned that I went to deliver fish, but I would be too tired for other activities. In the afternoon, I still had work. It was the selling of noodles, the Teochew fishball noodles. If was done using a stall, a little cart being pushed along the street peddling noodles. Usually it would be a child who would make a sound "kok kok kok kok kok kok" along the street, and he would strike a bamboo pole as he walked along, creating the "kok kok kok kok kok kok" sounds. I assumed this role. I did this then, from afternoon to night, after which the stall owner provided a bowl of noodles, *aiya*, how delicious it was. Afterwards, he gave me one dollar. Once, it was very good, I could bring food home. So I didn't have time to participate in other activities. I think it was not long after the May 13 Incident that the People's Action Party was formed, it was around 1955 or 1956...

Interviewer: 1954.

Mr. Lee: I think it was not long after. I still had interest then. I wanted to go, to participate in the inauguration meeting. But at that time, Lim Chin Siong, Devan Nair, Lee Kuan Yew, Rajaratnam, they were very youthful on stage. I think I was the youngest who went to participate. I didn't care. But after attending the meeting, I thought to myself that I wanted to join the party. But I couldn't find the application form despite searching for it. So I went back. If I had joined, maybe my history would have been altered. (Laughed)

Interviewer: So after that ...

Mr. Lee: After that, no more. After that I did not join any political party. I only went home to do some work after class. At first it was to deliver clothes, then when I was older, I took on some part-time work outside. Then after I started Junior Middle Three, I had acquired more knowledge, so I went to give tuition classes, teaching primary school kids. When I reached senior middle school, I went to some schools, I think they were commerce schools, there were bookkeeping and English classes. So I worked in the day and managed a second job at night. There was no choice then because I had three children. After graduation, I married around 1966, at the age of 26 and came to have family responsibilities. Although I didn't complete university studies, I hoped that all my children could complete university education. I set my heart on that single desire then. So I went all out to work, went all out to earn money. My wife was a teacher, teaching primary school, we worked hard together.

Interviewer: Apart from the establishing of the PAP, do you remember the dissolution of the SCMSSU?

Mr. Lee: The SCMSSU was banned in the end, it seemed...

Interviewer: Was it in 1956?

Mr. Lee: It was, the British government. The British noticed the growing strength of the SCMSSU. Because in reality, SCMSSU at that time was very well-organised. Honestly, it gained the support of most Chinese school students. Of course not a hundred percent of Chinese school students supported them, it couldn't be. Of course no organisation could gain 100 percent support, I don't think so. Thus, it was true that it won the support of an overwhelming majority. But, after it was banned, of course Britain had its reason, right? When the SCMSSU was banned, we were very discontented, very dissatisfied in our hearts, but we had no choice. Anyway, we accepted this reality. There was no choice, we couldn't change it. But when it was banned at that time in 1956, which grade was I in? I was 16. I think it was senior middle school that year. Or 1956, 57, 58, Senior Middle Three.

Interviewer: Yes, Senior Middle Three. After the SCMSSU was banned, did student activities stop?

Mr. Lee: Although it was banned, student activities did not cease due to this. We would go for picnics on Sundays or some days as usual. During Senior Middle Three, Chinese middle schools had a tradition of putting together a farewell party for the Junior Middle Three students. The Senior Middle Three students also had a farewell party. Junior Middle Three, Senior Middle Three, two graduating classes came together to organise a farewell party. Thus this farewell party became a tradition, an activity we would participate in despite the dissolution of SCMSSU. There would be a farewell activity every year, since every year there would be Junior Middle Three and Senior Middle Three students. So there were all kinds of activities outside of class–dance, choir and others, and there was also what was it called, a Drama Club, and there was also a Study Assistance Society. That Study Assistance Society became history along with the SCMSSU. Because that was organised under the SCMSSU specifically to help poor students. I had served as a surveyor for this society. Someone needed to check the applicants' financial status and then recommend whether or not to financially support him. After the SCMSSU was banned, we still had activities. Although farewell parties were for the Junior Middle Three and Senior Middle Three students, the activities could involve other levels, like the Junior Middle Two, the Junior Middle Three or the Senior Middle Two. As they themselves were too busy in their graduating year, the graduands could not have much time to organise these activities, so they recruited others to be involved.

Interviewer: After the SCMSSU was shut down, how did students express their views towards the developments of some current affairs?

Mr. Lee: After SCMSSU was banned, I don't think we had any, no such channel to express students' views. No such channel. Only after we graduated, students joined individual organisations or political parties. Some also joined political parties, there were also various organisations. There was another kind of activity, that was the alumni. With the SCMSSU gone, some students went to their individual school alumni. For instance, I was from Chung Cheng Primary School, I joined the Chung Cheng alumni association. There was the Yang Zheng Alumni for Yang Zheng Primary School. Alumni associations were very active in those days. Apart from gathering professional youths, alumni associations also attracted students. As long as they were alumni, they could join.

Interviewer: Did you switch to, for example, writing articles in publications to express your views on the current situation? Because we noticed some articles contained responses towards current affairs. There was the Anti-Yellow Culture Movement and some others ... And some views on politics, or even encouraging everyone to learn Malay, this sort of ... For instance there is this article, "Discussing Yellow Culture", and some like "Prospects of Self-government in Singapore". These are on some current affairs developments and events then.

Mr. Lee: We didn't seem to have any opportunities to publish these later.

Perception of Current Affairs

Interviewer: What about previously?

Mr. Lee: This was after 1959, when self-government was implemented. But before this, Chinese school students participated in many societal activities, such as during the serious Potong Pasir floods, Chinese school students went to help with the rescue operations as well as fund-raising. I think we organised a large-scale performance. I still remember it was at the (Singapore) Badminton Hall, a large-scale performance to raise funds for the flood victims. I think there was also a huge fire at Bukit Ho Swee, which we also helped out.

Interviewer: In 1960?

Mr. Lee: 1960, Chinese Schools also participated. I had graduated by that time. But my juniors, they were concerned about society, they even acted upon their beliefs, actual action. So honestly, the Chinese School students in those days, they weren't nerds. They did not only study. They were concerned about society, concerned with state affairs.

Interviewer: May I ask if you yourself wrote some articles?

Mr. Lee: Here? (Smiles)

Interviewer: Here. (Pointing to the publications) Can you tell us which ones?

Mr. Lee: I think I only have two. One is "Thoughts on Self-government".

Interviewer: So, that was written by you.

Mr. Lee: This was written by me. And another on Indonesian history.

Interviewer: Oh yes, yes, development.

Mr. Lee: "500 Years of Indonesian History of Struggle for Independence", this is a book review. 500 years of the struggle for independence. I only have these two. Because of these two articles, I can't bear to throw this publication away. Even when I moved, I treated it like a treasure and kept it. So you have the opportunity to come today. If it weren't for these two articles, I may have thrown it away.

Interviewer: Articles like these touching on self-government, there seem to be several of them. I have seen (them in) these Chinese school publications.

Mr. Lee: Yes. We had very high expectations for self-government then. Because we had hoped, at that time people said that self-government was the first step towards Singapore and Malaysia's independence. At that time, Malaya seemed not to have obtained independence, 1959, it had not achieved independence. Not sure which year ...

Interviewer: 1957.

Mr. Lee: Independence in 1957? They were already independent, we were not. Britain separated Malaya and Singapore then. Actually at that time we thought that our homeland was Malaya, this Malaya included Singapore. Many people then sometimes vilified us, saying that we were inclined towards China. That was inaccurate. I myself had never thought of returning to China. But there were some students, they went back to China. They went to China as the government here wanted to arrest them, they called it "seeking refuge", right. Under such circumstance, they had nowhere else to go, they could only escape to China. After they arrived in China, this is beyond our topic, I won't go further. Later, their predicament in China was terrible. But I never said I wanted to return to China. I had always thought that I was local.

Interviewer: So, in your opinion, what would self-government bring?

Mr. Lee: Self-government, I believe, meant that we could govern ourselves, Chinese school students would be looked after by the government. In the past, the British did not care about us, those who graduated from Chinese schools. They only cared for those from English schools, those who graduated from English schools. Chinese schools were neglected. Although we were all citizens, we did not have equal treatment. They were the favoured, we had no one to take care of us. So, we had very high expectations for self-government. We hoped that with self-government, we would be able to gain recognition in society. Then our job prospects would be better. Then, we also hoped that self-government was the first step towards merger with Malaya, right. In fact we never thought of Singapore as independent. Even Lee Kuan Yew had never thought of it. So when he received news that day, he was in absolute shock, he even cried, right. We never thought Singapore could be independent.

Interviewer: I don't know if you and your classmates were as optimistic and happy about the partial self-government in 1955?

Mr. Lee: The partial self-government in 1955?

Interviewer: Yes.

Mr. Lee: No. 1959 self-government.

Interviewer: Yes. Like how our present textbooks would describe 1955 under the Marshall government — it seemed to be portrayed as partial self-government, isn't it?

Mr. Lee: We didn't see that as complete self-government. At that time, the British still governed, because of that Constitution. It was like a city council, a municipal administration in a city. It managed various administrative tasks of the city and (oversees) people's daily needs, hygiene and all these. It had no internal self-autonomy. In 1959, it was different. In 1959, Britain wanted to let the local government have control over the police force, at least the police would be under the government's control. And national defence was under Britain ... as well as foreign diplomacy.... we thought that only with that did we have powers of self-governance. During Marshall and Lim Yew Hock times, there were elections nevertheless. But there wasn't an autonomous government, they did not have this power. It was just managing some internal city affairs...

Interviewer: Do you remember a movement, a "Malayan movement" between late 1950s and early 1960s? ... Because just now you ...

Mr. Lee: Malaysia, Merger with Malaysia ...

Interviewer: Yes, yes.

Mr. Lee: Around 1959, as suggested by Tunku Abdul Rahman. Once he mentioned during a lunch meeting, Malaya, Singapore, Brunei, Sarawak, North Borneo, later called Sabah, right? These five places to form one Malaysia, one country. Yes, I seemed to have graduated by then.

Interviewer: Probably...

Mr. Lee: Should have graduated. Working in society.

Interviewer: But we meant, earlier on, in terms of culture, everyone had this awareness, "I am Malayan", and this phenomenon of "I want to promote Malayan culture". It seemed ...

Mr. Lee: Culture of patriotism.

Interviewer: Yes, for instance. ..

Mr. Lee: Culture of patriotism. I remember when I was in middle school, that year, they came up with a Anti-Yellow Culture Movement, that was to resist yellow culture. Anti-Yellow Culture Movement is local. There was a switch in cultural flavour to the local, not China. As the new generation was born here, born here just like me. The concept of China became more fuzzy, we only knew we originated from China. But my feelings for China differed from my parents'. Like my son, my children, their feelings towards China are different from mine, even more different for my grandchildren. Feelings become diluted from generation to generation. Thus, a culture of patriotism emerged at that time, this meant promoting writings on local society, reflecting the realities of this country.

Interviewer: Did this country refer to Singapore?

Mr. Lee: At that time, it referred to Malaya. Malaya included Singapore. Peninsula Malaya, Singapore, including Penang, formed Malaya. In our conception then, the country of Malaya included Singapore, the Federation of Malaya had a number of states, nine states, plus Penang. We never thought Singapore was an independent nation.

Interviewer: Do you still remember what activities were organised to promote such a culture of patriotism and national consciousness in the society, including schools?

Mr. Lee: Organised what activities? The SCMSSU might have been shut down already then, banned. So, there was no activity in public. No public activity. Maybe there were some classmates, who wrote some articles published within the literary circle. There were many Singaporean and Malaysian writers. I remember at that time there was a rather famous poet, called Du Hong. Ah, Du Hong. He published a book called *The Month of May*, a collection of his poems. I believe I bought a copy to read, but I don't know where it is now. Maybe it is still around. He was a student of Chung Cheng High. I read many of his poems eulogising Singapore and Malaysia which included Malaya and Singapore. His poems had a strong local flavour. There were also some novels, I think there was one called *Ye Feng Jiào Ying*.

Interviewer: Were there similar literary works or artistic performances that also advocated patriotism at Chinese High?

Mr. Lee: At that time … I graduated in 1959. In 1959, there wasn't this issue. Even in 1960, I think it was close to Singapore's independence, 1965 or something. I am not sure of the situation in school at that time.

Interviewer: In your impression of your time in middle school, the Anti-yellow Culture Movement was not that vibrant?

Mr. Lee: The Anti-Yellow Culture Movement seemed to have taken place while I was still in school ..

Interviewer: Right, it seemed to have started.

Mr. Lee: The Anti-Yellow Culture Movement arose due to the rape-cum-murder case at Pearl's Hill. The movement started thus. We had posters, at that time, we had posters, some used paper to copy, some used chalk to write, some just wrote there. But whether these articles are kept till now, I don't know. Maybe they are gone. But the literary circle at that time seemed to have started a movement against yellow culture too. Honestly, few students in schools can really write. Because of school work — workload was heavy. Those involved in writing were the ones who had more interest in literature.

Interviewer: What significance did the Anti-Yellow Culture Movement of that era hold for you personally?

Mr. Lee: In those times, the main thing was, we rejected yellow culture, meaning we opposed the reading of obscene publications. Due to this movement, we recognised the poisonous effect of yellow culture.

Interviewer: How would you define Yellow Culture?

Mr. Lee: Yellow culture of that time refers to representations that were more obscene or engaged in excessive exposure, especially in the depiction of women. At that time, our thinking was less sophisticated. Now, attitudes are different. For instance, portraits of nude bodies at that time appeared to be very "yellow". But now, it is not the same. If it is decent, then it is not "yellow". During student days, our thinking was unlike now. In those days, in our imagination, the over-exposure of women's bodies and novels with descriptions on so-called sexiness and sexual satisfaction were all "yellow", including those "yellow" comics. There was a book entitled *Lan Pi Shu* (*Blue Paper*). *Lan Pi Shu* was a famous "yellow" publication. It was from Hong Kong. The impact of Anti-Yellow Culture Movement on us was like how we ask youths now not to take drugs, to recognise the ill effects of drugs and not to come into contact with it. I see it as having such an influence.

Interviewer: Concepts of those days, like this Anti-Yellow Culture, if you recall now, who passed them on to you? Was it through reading? Exchanges with classmates, or your teachers sharing their ideas with you?

Mr. Lee: Teachers then were very fearful. They would not promote these. You know there was something called the white terror at that time. After the SCMSSU was banned, there was a climate of white terror, you could face arrest or be stripped of your position at any moment. We had a history teacher called Chen Yangcheng at Chinese High. He and his brother were famous in the music circles. He appeared to have been stripped of his job by the Ministry of Education, stirring up our (students') reactions. We went to help him ... resisted against the Ministry of Education's action. Later the government retracted its decision, he was alright. Students supported him. In the past, Chinese schools students were vilified as disrespectful to the elders. In reality, we weren't. Perhaps a minority was, even now it is the same. Now, it is worse than before, isn't it? Actually we would respect good teachers. The respect for teachers could still be found in us.

The Establishment of Nanyang University

Interviewer: How did you all feel about the establishment of Nanyang University (Nantah) then?

Mr. Lee: Because for most of us, this was the opportunity to embark on university. But this did not mean a lot to me as I knew I didn't have the chance to study at the university. When we were in senior middle school that year, some did not need to go to Nantah. If one had money, he could pursue his studies overseas. Of course, those with less money could only enter local university. I did not dare to harbour this university dream. I knew if I could complete three years of junior middle school and three years of senior middle school, that would already be precious. I was already forever indebted to my father, mother and teachers. I wouldn't dare think of studying at the university.

Interviewer: But do you remember students' reactions then (toward the establishment of Nantah)? Was there any reaction?

Mr. Lee: We supported the founding of Nantah and we also expressed our support through actions. We also went to raise funds for Nantah by selling stuff on the streets. I think we raised funds for Nantah by holding a performance, it was very successful as well. We did those things voluntarily. No (payment), at most we had some tea and beverage. But we mostly contributed our labour, the monetary contribution had to come from the rich, like Tan Lark Sye, the Chinese Chamber of Commerce. They contributed money, we offered labour. But the establishing of Nantah ultimately gave us a way out. Because Chinese school students in those days really did not have much prospects. After graduating from senior middle school, one could only go to China or overseas English-medium universities for higher education. Only those who were comparatively rich could do this. The average person was unable to do so. Therefore, Nantah gained the support of the students.

Interviewer: About the mood within the Chinese community, do you remember what it was like? Because we heard that the trishaw pullers and hostesses also went to donate ...

Mr. Lee: At that time, every strata of the society supported it. The rickshaw pullers offered rides for donation, the hostesses also contributed their earnings for a night, and there were barbers who offered cuts to raise funds, right, and we raised funds on the streets. We students contributed our efforts, there were these. Actually the establishment of Nantah was supported by the entire Chinese population in Singapore, and even the entire Malaya. That was why it could be established successfully. Later, it also absorbed many students from Malaysia, and even from Sarawak. So the ceremony of Nantah's establishment was very grand and unforgettable. I heard that the crowd spanned the whole of Jurong, stretching 11 kilometres. That scenario, you would not see it today, can never see it now. Now, even if you want to establish a university, you ask people to raise funds, you would not be able to see that grandeur. Because the government could do it on our behalf, there is no need. (Laughs).

Interviewer: Then, do you remember that the Chinese Chamber of Commerce led a citizenship campaign...

Mr. Lee: The Citizenship Rights Committee?

Interviewer: Yes, did you students notice this event?

Mr. Lee: At that time, I might have been about to graduate.

Interviewer: 1957 ... It was before, (it) began in the 1950s, but 1957 ...

Mr. Lee: Yes. It was to fight for ...

Interviewer: Citizenship rights.

Mr. Lee: Fight for citizenship rights.

Interviewer: Yes.

Mr. Lee: To ask this government to allow those who had lived here for a very long time to be able to apply for Singapore citizenship, to register their citizenship rights. In those days, I think we even got the students to persuade people to accept Singapore citizenship. Because at that time, the older generation, our parents, their concept is still that of China. They didn't know, and many of them did not receive an education, they did not know what citizenship rights were. Thus, this needed publicity. We also went to do publicity.

Interviewer: Do you remember which year it was when you went to help out with the publicity?

Mr. Lee: I think it was 1956, 1957? I myself went back home, I kept persuading my parents to go. In the end, they went, they went to register. I also urged people around me to persuade their parents to go. If you want to continue to live here, your children to grow roots here, you have to obtain citizenship rights, otherwise you would be thinking of returning to China. But my parents didn't want to return.

Interviewer: Is this part of SCMSSU activities?

Mr. Lee: The SCMSSU was probably banned by then. We Chinese school students still cared about society, only that it did not have a legal status. Depending on how people tried to galvanise, he could only participate in one's personal capacity. Just like that. Including the election events, participation was also done in one's personal capacity. Of course, not everyone was interested. Those interested could all go.

Interviewer: So, before 1957, some people could not obtain citizenship easily. Because of those regulations, for instance, one needed to know English or Malay, regulations akin to this, or you were required to have lived in Singapore and Malaya for a particular number of years.

Mr. Lee: Later, later, because of this campaign to struggle for citizenship rights, we got rid of some restrictions. My mother was illiterate and could not speak Malay, she knew only Hokkien. She was only required to provide evidence of the time she arrived in Singapore, when she came over and how long she had lived here. Because you would have a record when you came over. She only needed to prove that and present her children's birth certificates. Like my birth certificate. I was born in 1940, my older sister in 1939. This would prove that she had been living here till then and didn't go away. So it was more acceptable at that time, no restriction. At that time, due to this campaign, many who would think of themselves as "China people" applied for this citizenship.

Interviewer: But in your impression, students in those days would participate in such a campaign or ....

Mr. Lee: I had graduated by then. But I believe students then would have supported this campaign, and individually, they could only individually attempt to persuade their parents, persuade them to apply for citizenship. I believe they would. I personally took the initiative to persuade my parents and some relatives. So this Citizenship Rights Campaign was successful. It changed many people's opinion and they accepted this citizenship. You don't have citizenship rights, you wouldn't, say, be qualified to apply for a government flat, right? Actually it had practical significance, the practical significance made it attractive. So I think students at that time did not have a public organisation, they couldn't express their views. The government at that time thought that students only needed to attend to their studies. Subsequently, students only cared about their studies. Later, I remember Ong Teng Cheong encouraging students to participate in social activities, to care more about national affairs, because they no longer cared for national affairs the way we did back then, right?

Interviewer: Do you talk about these topics with your children?

Mr. Lee: What?

Interviewer: Have you mentioned the content of this conversation to your children?

Mr. Lee: Some, when they were young. But not the entire thing. For instance, I would talk about how our classmates got along with one another, were united and helped one another out. They would say this did not occur amongst their classmates. Now, you are jealous of me, I am jealous of you. Some are very selfish. I only knew about this when they told me. This may be due to the changing times, and the macro situation of the times did not encourage such a spirit any more. Frankly, it was not conducive. Actually we were very self-disciplined then. Our classmates were independent, got things done independently, didn't rely on the teachers. Teachers at that time were afraid, didn't dare to participate in our activities. Like that Chen Yangcheng, that teacher. He was more concerned about us, but he was wrongfully accused and stripped of his job.

Concern for One's Future

Interviewer: Just now Siao See mentioned you all were concerned with other labour movements?

Mr. Lee: Honestly, we wouldn't think of these when we were in school studying. For example, when I was graduating from senior middle high school in 1959, I felt that we were concerned with our learning and our future more so than these labour movements. Because they were not our business. Of course, some students might have joined labour unions after graduation, they might have participated in some labour union activities. Or he might have gone to become a full-time clerk at a labour union. This was possible.

Interviewer: Like the 1955 Hock Lee Bus incident. Because students and workers did come together, so ...

Mr. Lee: Perhaps. Because there were many types of students. I myself had absolutely no connection with workers and labour unions. But in 1955, there appeared to be some labour movement like the Hock Lee Bus protests. They went to support, this was possible, there would be some. But I did not participate in the labour movement. I only read about it on the newspapers, wow, such a serious conflict occurred.

Interviewer: Would the SCMSSU encourage students to interact with the workers?

Mr. Lee: No, we did not have such a mission. I feel ...

Interviewer: From your personal experience ...

Mr. Lee: From my experience, nobody said to go where, no. Because that didn't seem to have any direct connection to us. Because maybe some students of the higher levels, I think they might have gone to lend support.

Interviewer: Did your classmates like to read the papers? How would they know about other realms of society ...

Mr. Lee: Most read newspapers. Even now, I would read everyday. It would be like forgoing some meals if I didn't read.

Interviewer: A habit acquired during your student days?

Mr. Lee: Acquired indeed in the past. Also, I insist on reading Chinese newspapers. Although I can read English, I am more accustomed to reading Chinese newspapers. In terms of earning a living, I had to use English to earn money. But in terms of the cultural aspect of life, I gain satisfaction through Chinese. I can understand the meaning in English, but it has no cultural hold over me.

Interviewer: Do you remember if there was anyone among your classmates who did volunteer work?

Mr. Lee: In those days, there didn't seem to be much volunteer work around. What volunteer work was there?

Interviewer: For instance, a woman we interviewed previously–she took literacy classes organised by the Itinerant Hawkers and Stall Holders Association, and the teachers were students of Chung Cheng. Lessons were free.

Mr. Lee: Held at the trade unions.

Interviewer: Literacy classes organised by the trade unions.

Interviewer: Their teachers were students of Chung Cheng High.

Mr. Lee: I think so. I remember that year, I mean after graduation, initially, I wanted ... later I think I became a teacher for six months, in the Sembawang area. At that time, some classmates approached me asking me to teach at some place. They have the farmers' union then, right? It's the farmers' union in the village. Ah, "Rural Village Farmers' Network." I was asked to teach classes there. I think I wasn't interested in going then. I told him I had no time to go. I later taught for half a year, then quitted. I went to study at the University of Singapore. I think those people only had time after they graduated. Went only after working upon graduation. Did they participate (in volunteer work) during their student days? I don't know ...

Interviewer: The woman we interviewed, their teachers were senior middle school students.

Mr. Lee: Senior middle school students, maybe the work was the near where he lives. He...maybe there were some. But I think this was no longer a movement.

Interviewer: Right. You are not sure whether this was a popular phenomenon?

Mr. Lee: I am not sure. But I think it was possible. After I graduated, I taught adult literacy classes. Government-run.

Interviewer: You were paid?

Mr. Lee: I was paid. By the hour. I was living below the poverty line then. So I went to teach adult literacy classes. There was the Adult Education Board then. The office was at Fort Canning. The school I taught at was the Cantonment School. The school at Cantonment Street, it is still there. I taught them Chinese. Most of the students were English-educated. I think there were more girls than boys. The girls were more eager to learn, the boys were lazier. (Laughs)

Interviewer: Did you have time and money to watch movies in those days?

Mr. Lee: Hardly. You can say that I hardly watch a film each year. During student days, I basically had nothing for three meals, how could I ... rarely caught a movie.

Interviewer: So apart from learning and the SCMSSU activities, you said the SCMSSU also organised some recreational activities, right? Like picnics, and some dances. Did you yourself participate?

Mr. Lee: Picnics, yes.

Interviewer: Picnics. How were these picnics organised, where did you go?

Mr. Lee: In those days, we often went to areas around Pasir Ris and Bugis. At that time, the beaches were not bad. Or we would go to Pulau Ubin, and a chalet in Pasir Ris area, not sure of its name, I had forgotten now. We stayed there for a week, summer camp, during the vacation. It was there that we recruited many students. We were on our own there, we had to cook for ourselves three meals a day. We had a general affairs committee and a culinary committee, the culinary committee was responsible for food and beverage, and there was this cultural activities committee, right. I think it was such an arrangement. We experienced communal living, in the morning, there would be a broadcast, which woke us up to exercise. After the exercise, we had breakfast, studied, and then took a break. After the break, it was studying again, and then dinner. There would be some entertainment in the night.

Interviewer: Would you get students of other schools to join in ?

Mr. Lee: Both boys and girls.

Interviewer: What did you learn?

Mr. Lee: Such as telling stories, or some historical knowledge. Let me think of some examples, like we talked about the riddles on television or something like that. Sometimes we would learn from the newspapers, including current affairs, knowledge learnt outside the classroom. We had more entertaining literary activities. At that time, these were highly popular. Many people would ... because we were young.

Interviewer: You all have wonderful memories.

Mr. Lee: We have wonderful memories. Thus, in those days, the government did not need to worry about us and matchmake us. (Laughs) Because everybody was interacting frequently, right? No problem. Because everyone, like my wife, we met during student activities. Most of my friends around me were also the same. We had frequent contact in our student life, had the chance to interact. We had the occasion to befriend one another. Our purpose in making friends was not to seek a partner, it was through interacting that bonds were slowly built up. So in our times, we did not have social problems of this kind. In contrast, it is different now. In this area, the government is anxious on your behalf. (Laughs)

Interviewer: Which school was your wife from?

Mr. Lee: Nan Chiau Girls' High School. People were surprised, didn't you look for a Nanyang Girl? I said, it wasn't meant to be. I actually knew students from Nanyang Girls, some of whom I knew very well. I ... anyway, this depends on affinity. First, it's the affinity of the eyes, right? (Smiles) First comes the affinity of the eyes. Then it's dating after that.

Interviewer: Affinity of the eyes.

Mr. Lee: Yes, it has to be mutual.

Interviewer: Did you meet your wife during student days?

Mr. Lee: Yes, we met as students. During these student activies.

Interviewer: Do you remember during which special occasion or activity?

Mr. Lee: I was active in my school activities while she was active in hers. Once we had a meeting across school for the same level, it was to discuss some collaboration. She came for the meeting. I then realized that she was an active member of her school. It was then that she knew about me and that I was from this school. This left the deepest impression — we were travellers of the same path. (Laughs) At that time relationships were quite pure, they didn't change much….. whether they were between classmates or friends. After we graduated from senior middle school, we met up more frequently. In those days, although some students pursued romantic relationships, I did not agree with it. I thought, firstly, there was no financial stability. If I were to pursue a romantic relationship, I should have a career and financial stability. So, having a romantic relationship was not on my mind during my students days. But we could make friends, right? There were many friends, males and females.

Interviewer: I guess it was not easy to keep in touch after graduation?

Mr. Lee: After graduation, some kept in touch. Contact would continue if it was meant to be. For some, it wasn't meant to be, right? Being too contrived is no good, right? There would be a mutual understanding naturally after interacting with one another for a long time. At that time, we would place importance on mutual understanding, we care less about the form. Interaction with one another, heart to heart. No, unlike now, we do not need to go for a ride, or have a big meal or something. When did we have that?

Interviewer: Do you remember what other recreational activities outside school did your classmates engage in?

Mr. Lee: During our student days?

Interviewer: Yes, outside school, not necessary organised by schools …

Mr. Lee: Outside school, I think there wasn't anything special …In my impression, during our student days, we didn't go to nightclubs, listen to songs or something, I think we didn't. At that time, we lived simply. After classes, we went home. After school activities, we went home. Of course we had our own individual activities at home. Like me, after returning home, I had to work, had to earn some money and help the family. Some students might have more time, maybe they had time for their studies. I rarely went out at night, I was usually studying at night at home. Chinese middle school students were basically rather poor. But a few were rich. But these people were in the minority right. What other questions do you have?

Interviewer: That's about it. Thank you Mr Lee.

Interviewer: Thank you for agreeing to our interview.

Mr. Lee: Thank you for giving me this opportunity. (Smiles)

Interviewer: Do you still keep in touch with your former Chinese High classmates?

Mr. Lee: Yes, a few, there are very few of them now. We have a gathering every week. We just chat, like in the past, it seems that we don't change much. It is hard for the leopard to change its spots, we are still concerned about current affairs, we would talk about local affairs, international affairs, we often make these our topics of discussions.

Interviewer: To have kept in touch till now, they must be your bosom buddies.

Mr. Lee: It has been over 50 years, half a century.

Interviewer: Would you chat about the past? Like what you've chatted with us today?

Mr. Lee: Sometimes, we would, but not much. Because each of us has his individual life course. Some had a smooth sailing life, some had a hard life, but whether it is a hard life or a smooth sailing one, we had a particular memory of the past, so we do not feel regretful. We feel rather proud, we were privileged to have this chance to live through such an era, we are big-hearted people and will not bear grudges against heaven and other people just because we had met setbacks in life. We feel that we had fulfiled our historical mission, we have no regrets. Although some people may have faced some setbacks, they are still very optimistic. I think if I sum it up, I would use a line from Su Dongpo's poem. He said, "Looking back at the desolate place from which I come, there is no wind, no rain, and no clear sky." When we look back over these 50 years, although there were rain and storms, but now we are like Su Dongpo, those experiences actually were neither storms nor sunshine. We feel composed and even feel proud. People now do not get the same chance to have a taste of the fast and fury days of our era. We can never forget this part of our lives.

GROWING UP WITH LITERACY CLASSES
AN INTERVIEW WITH TAN TECK KENG

Interviewed by Chan Cheow Thia, Teng Siao See

Transcribed by Ku Ka Tsai, Lim Woan Fei, Chan Cheow Thia

Translated by Ho Sheo Be

Date: 7 December 2006

Family Background

Interviewer: When were you born?

Tan: I was born in 1945, in Johor State's Muar.

Interviewer: What were your parents doing then?

Tan: Then in Muar, my father owned a goldsmith shop. I had four siblings then, after I was born in 1945, my mother gave birth to three more.

Interviewer: So you are the eldest (among your siblings)?

Tan: Yes, I am the eldest.

Interviewer: Are the rest sisters?

Tan: Then in Muar, I had a younger sister and two younger brothers. In 1955, I still remember that it was Christmas Day, my whole family moved to Singapore, as our business failed. We also moved many times in Muar — living in a place for three months, and then another for a few months. My entire family subsequently moved to Singapore in 1955. Although we were very poor, my father actually valued our education. When school term started in January 1956, we went to school just like the rest.

Interviewer: So you went to primary school when the term started?

Tan: As I was in Primary 4 back in Muar, I went to Primary 5 when we came to Singapore, but that only lasted for half a year.

Interviewer: Why was that so?

Tan: Because we could not afford books, textbooks, so my younger sister and I stopped our education. Back then, my younger sister was in Primary 3, my mother gave birth to another younger sister in Singapore in 1956. Our teacher kept telling us to go back to school, so my second younger sister returned to school, but she also stopped after half a year as we could not afford it. My two younger brothers subsequently went to school. There were four children in Malaysia; my mother gave birth to four more in Singapore. Altogether, I have three younger brothers and four younger sisters.

Interviewer: What are your age gaps?

Tan: ...in the likes of four years, two years, three years.

Interviewer: So the age difference between you and your younger sister is two years?

Tan: Right, one of my brothers is five years younger, another is seven years younger, then my next younger sister is 11 years my junior — 11, 13, 15, the age difference between my youngest brother and I is 17 years. So, when my brother helped to man my business, many thought he was my son. We actually have elder brothers in China, my mother didn't give birth to them.

Night School

Interviewer: So how did you get to know your husband?

Tan: When we met, I had stopped schooling for two years, it was 1959, I was about 14 years old.

Interviewer: Right, one is 11 or 12 years old when one is in Primary 5.

Tan: 11 is the exact age, you are 12 years old when you are in Primary 6.

Interviewer: I see.

Tan: Right, then we started school at the age of 7, that was formal education, after which I dropped out and started working at the age of 12. I worked in the Khong

Guan biscuit factory, I was handling that small biscuit topped with icing in the shape of a flower.[1]

Interviewer: Oh, I see.

Tan: Later I went in to ask if they were taking in students. They said yes, so I started to study there. It was a hawkers' association called the Singapore Itinerant Hawkers and Stall Holders Association (SIHSHA). Their objective was to ensure that children of hawkers also had a chance to be educated, as many of these children were not going to school since they could not afford it. I think the year was 1959 when I commenced my study there.

Interviewer: Were you then at the age appropriate for Primary 5 or 6?

Tan: Are you referring to night school? I went to Primary 5, that was the highest level in night school. There were three Primary 3 classes, they were held either on Tuesdays, Thursdays and Saturdays or Mondays, Wednesdays and Fridays. I felt alienated when I first went. My class was not taught by my husband, there was another teacher, but my husband was one of the main persons in charge. In 1959, he was then attending senior middle school and had been in charge of the night school for some years.

Interviewer: You said he was a person-in-charge ...

Tan: That meant being in charge of what we called literacy classes[2] then. They were our *"Xiao Xiansheng,"*[3] we didn't address them as teachers but *Xiao Xiansheng*. We also just addressed them by their surnames: some were *"Xiao Li"* (Young Li). My husband's surname is Huang, so some called him *"Lao Huang"* (Old Huang), there were *"Lao Lin"* (Old Lin) too.

Interviewer: Your actual age difference was just a few years, yet you addressed them as *"Lao Huang"*?

Tan: Right. Some were called *"Lao Li"*, people then loved to address others using the term *"lao"* (old), so there was *"Lao Li"*, *"Lao Chen"*, etc.

Interviewer: So, your husband was then in middle school ...

---

[1] Interviewee was referring to the colourful little icing heads on the "Iced Gem Biscuits".
[2] The interviewee later added that the literacy classes were also known as "night school" by outsiders.
[3] Literally meaning "little teacher," better understood as "young mentor," alternatively called *"Xiao Laoshi"*.

Tan: senior middle school!

Interviewer: Were other teachers also in the senior middle years?

Tan: Right, right, several were in senior middle years, one of them, *"Lao Lin"*, taught my class.

Interviewer: How many *Xiao Xiansheng* were there?

Tan: At that time, the main ones were the few of them, when they were not free, they would get other classmates to stand in for them. We gradually got to know those relief teachers too. Some stood in for a few weeks, others for a few months, but the bulk of them were there for a year or half a year. I remember there were quite a few (relief teachers), some have since passed on. There were Nanyang University (Nantah) students among them too.

Interviewer: Were they in Nantah then or subsequently?

Tan: Subsequently. At that time, many teachers were students from Chung Cheng High School, maybe it was because it was easier to mobilise students from the same school. My husband told me that he was a class monitor in middle school and that the class monitor was the person-in-charge, that was what he said, so probably the relationship amongst students from different classes was quite good.

Interviewer: You mentioned they were the main persons-in-charge, what were they in charge of then?

Tan: For example, there were so many students, other than our studies, they were also teaching us how to sing and dance, organising extra-curricular activities, as well as visiting students at times…

Interviewer: This is to say, in the literacy classes, apart from learning to recognise some words and read some essays…

Tan: There were also song and dance, reading and posters.

Interviewer: Were these all part of the literacy classes?

Tan: Right, right, all part of literacy classes, and they visited parents…this was done almost weekly, to understand their situation, to stay in touch with the parents. In 1962, subsequently, a pre-school class began.

Interviewer: So what were the teaching materials?

Tan: I recall that there was a Geography textbook and another called *Treating Oneself and Others* which was a self-enrichment book.

Interviewer: Where was it published?

Tan: I forgot. Sometimes, we went to the movies, after which, teachers would casually talk about the movies, such as their contents and themes, then we would work on our compositions. It's very funny; a friend borrowed an essay book and has not returned it to this day.

Interviewer: So there was homework?

Tan: Yes, we had to make sentences too. These sentences could be very long, thought-provoking, and could potentially become essays.

Interviewer: How were the literacy classes conducted, was it to read a book and then …

Tan: We read too. We had a book on Malaya's geography and there was that *Treating Oneself and Others*, the teachers seemed to have a lot of teaching materials to use.

Interviewer: You said there were a lot of teaching materials, does that mean there were many textbooks, or did the teachers prepare other teaching materials themselves?

Tan: As I was in a different class, I don't know what went on in the class that my husband taught. The teachers were very good. When they discussed a topic or a subject, they could relate it to many things, we listened to them attentively and enjoyed it very much. (Laughs)

Interviewer: Did you have to take notes or to copy texts?

Tan: No, we didn't really take notes, we didn't really have examinations, maybe there were examinations for Geography, but for the other subjects they probably asked about problems in the society or some issues that we already knew. After watching movies, for those who were interested and willing, we could write essays, the teachers would not force us. For instance, it was like I wrote an essay after watching a film and someone helped me to vet it.

Collective Recreational Activities

Interviewer: Was watching movies a main activity of the literacy classes?

Tan: Not really, usually when there were good movies, the teachers would recommend them to us, many of us would then go to the movies together.

Interviewer: Would the teachers take you to the movies?

Tan: We usually went to the movies together, quite a few of us went to the movies together, and usually it was after our classes.

Interviewer: Where did you usually go? To the Cinemas?

Tan: We used to go to the Majestic Theatre. Some cinemas specialised in showing movies from China. We watched *Cheng Feng Po Lang (Riding the Wind and the Waves), Bing Shang Jie Mei (Girls of the Ice Track), Nü Lan Wu Hao (Female Basketball Player Number 5)*, there were quite a lot, and we wrote our essays after watching.

Interviewer: In other words, apart from attending classes, there was contact among classmates and teachers when classes were over, and watching movies was one of the activities?

Tan: We only watched when there were good films, like we did not watch movies from Shaw and Cathay in the past, as we felt that these movies did not have healthy themes.[4]

Interviewer: How was that so?

Tan: Like those …I don't know. Anyway, we would not watch those movies, what we watched were those with distinctive themes, and we knew exactly what the movies were about. China movies in the past were really interesting, but perhaps if we watch them now, we might find the pace too slow.

---

[4] These were two competitive film-making companies in the 1950s and the 1960s. They were targeted at Chinese movie-goers in Singapore and Malaysia and followed the styles of Europe-American and Hollywood movies. They groomed popular film stars such as Lin Dai, You Min, Ge Lan and Lin Cui, among others. Made shortly after the People's Republic of China was established in 1949, they were different from those films which emphasised educational and thought-provoking messages. They reached out to a different crowd too.

Interviewer: You caught movies which had distinctive themes, what would they usually include?

Tan: Usually they were about collective living, like in *Nü Lan Wu Hao*; *Bing Shang Jie Mei* also had a similar theme, these were movies made in the 1960s.

Interviewer: Apart from watching movies, what were other extra-curricular activities?

Tan: Sometimes, we went on picnics, these were usually held in Punggol and Pasir Ris. When the weather was good, we would climb the Bukit Timah Hill. We visited Kota Tinggi too and the Botanical Gardens in Johor Bahru. These activities were sometimes for older students, not for those who were too young, the younger ones went on picnics, as we could not take so many students along with us. So, partly because the teachers had also wanted to group the older ones who were more mature together. Besides studying, I was also assigned to teach a class at the same time. It started with more than 10 students, then the number grew and there were two classes on Mondays, Wednesdays and Fridays, as well as Tuesdays, Thursdays and Saturdays — I can't really recall, but there were five classes in all, five classes of students.

Interviewer: When you were attending the literacy classes, what was the background of your classmates, were they the poorer folks?

Tan: We were all very poor (Laughs). But a few male students in my class were better off. They went to English schools in the morning and attended the literacy classes at night, perhaps because their parents thought they should learn Chinese.

Interviewer: Did you have to pay a fee for the literacy classes?

Tan: Yes, about 50 cents a month, but it was free for some.

Interviewer: Was that very different from normal, mainstream schools?

Tan: I think so, it must have been very different.

Interviewer: Did those who attended school in the morning go on the outings as well?

Tan: Yes, we went together. There was one who didn't go to English school, I think he is now a fishmonger in Tampines, I have seen him there. Then there was one whom I understand used to work in Khong Guan. I am not sure if he is still working there, he must be holding quite a high position now if he is still there. I saw him at Khong Guan in 1994. But I have yet to run into those who went to English schools. My husband told me subsequently that one of them held quite a high post in the Tat Lee Bank,[5] that was what he told me.

Interviewer: For those organised outings, did a few classes go together or was each teacher in charge of a particular class?

Tan: If there were picnics, then we would have gone together, and the older ones were expected to take care of the younger ones.

Interviewer: For instance, would students in a particular class know those from another class?

Tan: Yes, yes. And if it was to watch movies, then it would be older students from two classes, there were more than 10 of us.

Interviewer: What about those who went to Malaysia's Botanical Gardens? You mentioned earlier that most of the students were from very humble backgrounds, then how did they make it to these places of interest?

Tan: Ha ha ha, we often went for a day or two, there were 11 or 12 of us, ha ha ha. There were many of us, there seemed to be a photograph. Our car broke down half way, then a British man helped us.

Interviewer: Did you stay overnight when you went on such outings?

Tan: No, we returned the same day, not overnight.

Interviewer: What jobs did they take up subsequently?

Tan: Subsequently ... a few were then packaging tea leaves, but not now. Now most are not working. Some are now already grandmothers and don't work anymore.

---

[5]Tat Lee Bank was established by Singapore Chinese businessman, Goh Tjoei Kok in 1973. The bank merged with the Keppel Bank in 1998 and was acquired by the overseas Chinese Banking Corporation in 2001.

Interviewer: Were they working when they were attending the literacy classes?

Tan: Yes, yes. Some were picking coffee seeds.[6]

Interviewer: These students, including you, when you attended the literacy classes, how often did you have to attend a week or could you choose freely?

Tan: No, We couldn't, it was thrice a week. Mondays, Wednesdays, Fridays or Tuesdays, Thursdays and Saturdays.

Interviewer: Within the three days, how long was each class?

Tan: It was about two hours or so.

Interviewer: Was it in the morning, afternoon or …

Tan: At night, because most had to work, so it was known as "night school". The *Xiao Xiansheng* also had to study in the day.

Interviewer: How did you usually go to class, did you travel from your workplace?

Tan: Oh, fortunately my workplace was very near home, as well as the literacy classes.

Interviewer: Did you go on foot?

Tan: As I used to knock off quite early, at about 4 plus, I got home at about 5 pm. At night I attended the classes — not too far. It wasn't far to travel from the workplace to home too.

Interviewer: Where did you live?

Tan: Lorong Tai Seng.

Interviewer: Oh, you stayed in Lorong Tai Seng?

Tan: Right.

---

[6] According to additional information provided by the interviewee, the coffee seeds underwent a process of selection, during which the damaged ones were taken out, leaving the remainder to be packed in gunny sacks. Wages was calculated based on the number of sacks packed. Female workers in those days were all very young, most were only twelve or thirteen years old. There were even mothers who brought along her children and a pot of lunch, looking after the kids while they worked.

Interviewer: Were the literacy classes held there too?

Tan: No, they were not, they were at Paya Lebar Road, that was the road. Do you know Tai Seng Garden, where a Malaysian bakery was? It's still around. It was Lorong Koo Chye, it is now an industrial park. Even Lorong Tai Seng is now an industrial park.

Interviewer: Was the Hawkers' Union or the Singapore Itinerant Hawkers and Stall Holders Association (SIHSHA) also nearby?

Tan: Are you referring to now or in the past? Back then it was on this main road, but we had to walk a distance to get to this main road, it was not in Lorong Tai Seng.

Interviewer: From your home, how long did you have to walk?

Tan: Approximately the distance of more than one bus-stop, took me about 20 minutes. A market was also nearby, as the association was also responsible for matters pertaining to the market. As the Tai Seng market caught fire previously, the hawkers first looked for a place to settle down, then the main persons–in–charge of the association and the market owners — markets were privately owned previously — negotiated. In other words, these hawkers handed over an amount of money each day as a form of savings, someone was responsible for the collection, then a stall was reserved for each of them in the market upon completion.

Interviewer: Were the classrooms of the literacy classes at Paya Lebar Road located in the same premises as the SIHSHA?

Tan: They were located under one roof: SIHSHA and classrooms of the literacy classes. The association had its own premises, it would not be an association without its own premises. On those premises, business pertaining to the association was conducted there in the day, while literacy classes were held at night, since the objective of the association was to make available night classes for children of the hawkers. But it didn't mean that you had to be a member to attend classes. As long as you were willing to study, it didn't matter who you were, they would take you in, the majority were girls.

Interviewer: Since the association's premises was for holding meetings and other uses during the day, were the classrooms properly equipped?

Tan: Yes, there were tables and chairs — the long ones. I knew the class that I taught had two square tables and two long benches. That's all ...

Interviewer: Oh, was there a blackboard?

Tan: Yes, of course there was. As there was another class subsequently, a board was used as a divider...My husband knew carpentry work, a lot of things were made by him, he was good at construction.

Interviewer: So there was only a class when you went and then there were two classes?

Tan: No, there were three classes when I first went and then the number increased to five.

Interviewer: How many students were there in each class?

Tan: My husband was responsible for two classes — one class took place on Mondays, Wednesdays and Fridays, the other on Tuesdays, Thursdays and Saturdays; one was of a higher level, the other was lower. The class I taught had more than 10 students, my husband's had more than 20. Then the other class also had quite a number of students, probably around 20. The class my husband taught had students who were younger, there were also some who were older, the age gap was big. As they were older but were not educated previously, their command of the language was a consideration. So, we couldn't have a blanket rule that the older ones had to go to classes of a higher level.

Interviewer: What was the age of the oldest student?

Tan: For each class ...like the class I am referring to now, some were rather old, some should be around my husband's age and some could even be older than he was.

Interviewer: But the majority were girls?

Tan: Right, there were more girls.

Interviewer: So what was the percentage of girls?

Tan: Percentage ... I think at least 80% or so. Ha, if you were to look at my husband's graduation photographs, you could see how many girls there were. I learnt recently that some mothers had stopped some from going to school in the morning. Their parents would not even allow them to attend night schools, they were worried that their daughters would be led astray.

Interviewer: What about your parents' opinion (on your attendance at night school)?

Tan: Quite alright, my parents were quite ok ...

Interviewer: Your parents did not object to your attendance at night school?

Tan: No.

Interviewer: Was there encouragement?

Tan: I can't say there was encouragement, I often took my friends home, for instance my husband, those *Xiao Xiansheng* often went to my house. As my parents thought they were good boys, especially since they were all senior middle school students, they were fine with it. However, a friend's parents were mistaken, thought others were interested in their daughter, so they went to pick a quarrel at the teacher's house. Oh, there was this person who still maintains close contact with me, her brother knew my husband and asked his sister to come along to study, so her mother went to my husband's place to create a scene. It was very funny.

Interviewer: So did you join the association later?

Tan: No.

Interviewer: What about other students?

Tan: Apart from attending the literacy classes, we did not care about other matters, we didn't pay attention to matters pertaining to the association. However, if it was the association's anniversary, etc., and we were required to perform, sing and so on, then we would just oblige. Yes, we would participate in those activities. There were more than one branch, I remember there was a branch in Lorong 25 Geylang, and another at a location I cannot recall, there were three branches altogether.

Interviewer: This is to say that the one at Paya Lebar Road was one of the branches?

Tan: Right, we even had a headquarters, which was located at the Lee Federation along Jalan Besar. I think it was leased from the Lee Federation. At the same place, there was another organisation engaging in cultural and recreational activities called "*kang le*". We knew people from there too. They had a lot of students, the group was located in the same building, I think the Lee Federation at Jalan

Besar was a three-storey building. I can still spot it now when I pass by while on board a bus, sometimes I would still steal a glance. I still feel for it, it's very strange. We used to go in and out of the building, although we were not involved in matters pertaining to the association. My husband and the rest, they sometimes ... they were involved in some kind of publicity and educational activities, perhaps they had to write reports, so they must be around whenever a meeting was called.

Interviewer: So performances took place at the headquarters or were there activities at the branches too?

Tan: A particular branch would celebrate its anniversary at one time or the other, we would then go to render support, we would also have to perform. Once, we went somewhere to perform, it was a stage performance and we took a lorry there. We clapped as we sang.

Interviewer: What songs did you sing?

Tan: We sang quite a lot of songs. I remember singing in 1963 or 1964 this number in Singapore that goes "Golden flowers bloom, silver flowers bloom, self-governance does not fall from the sky…" As for what then follows, I have to sing it to recall the lyrics.

Interviewer: Perhaps you can sing a little, how does the tune go?

Tan: (Sings) "Golden flowers bloom, silver flowers bloom, self-governance does not fall from the sky, it materialises through the people's struggles…" I think that's what it's like.

Interviewer: So you sang such songs when you went on outings?

Tan: Yes, we would sing once we got on the lorry. We also sang *Little White Sail*, etc., quite a lot.

Interviewer: Did someone take the lead in these?

Tan: Yes, my husband could sing quite well, he was good at teaching (us) how to sing. We watched *Female Basketball Player Number 5*, there was a song entitled … youth, something about youth.[7] Kim Leong just published a book

---

[7] The theme song of the movie is called "Sparkles of Youth."

recently. I heard that the book mentioned this song. I think we watched *Hua Zhong Ren* (*Man in the Painting*) and we also learnt its songs.

Interviewer: So the lorry that ferried you to the performance, did you have to hire it?

Tan: Oh yes, we had to hire it.

Interviewer: Did you hire it yourself or did the association rent it on your behalf?

Tan: This I am not sure.

Interviewer: However, did you get to interact with people from SIHSHA through such activities?

Tan: We knew some from the literacy classes.

Interviewer: What about apart from the literacy classes?

Tan: There was little interaction with people beyond the literacy classes ... we usually got to know more of the people through the classes. Many of them were actually students around my husband's age. Some could have thought that joining the association meant the possibility of organising some activities from within, some taught dancing, among others.

Interviewer: So such activities helped you to know people from literacy classes held in other branches of the association?

Tan: Right. Sometimes it was perhaps because of some interactions that we got to know people from the groups in the villages, particularly during the General Elections, we saw them coming out to visit the electorate.

Interviewer: Did you also participate in raising awareness for the elections?

Tan: For us who were older, we did.

Interviewer: How was that done?

Tan: That primarily meant visiting parents of our own students, informing them what the situation then was like, so that they could better understand. We also went to homes of citizens who resided in the villages. They were usually very happy to see us. In the early years, people were generally friendlier, they did not turn down our visits.

Activities and Current Affairs

Interviewer: What did you talk about when you visited the students' parents or villagers?

Tan: That included current situation, for instance current political parties, etc., as it was a time for the national voting exercise then.

Interviewer: How did you obtain the knowledge on current situation? Were you told by the *Xiao Xiansheng*?

Tan: Yes, the *Xiao Xiansheng* would tell us, they often told us about the contemporary political situation. But, they only did that to students like us who could understand. I attended classes for committee members of the association Sundays, although strictly speaking I was not a committee member, they allowed us to attend since we were willing to listen.

Interviewer: So what was the content of such classes?

Tan: I also don't quite remember, that was so long ago… it was also about the situation then and the association's mission …

Interviewer: Did you enjoy participating in these activities, be they literacy classes or …

Tan: I really loved them, I really loved doing so then.

Interviewer: Why?

Tan: I don't know too, I just loved them then and it was as though I was so energetic. I have a friend, sometimes I would tell him … he would also talk about those days … At that time I lived nearby, my friend came all the way from Lorong Ah Soo. He cycled all the way to "*Hong Chang*", near the current location of Geylang Police Centre. I still remember a trade union there, think it is now a place for making roasted meat. The trade union was known as the Singapore General Employees' Union, that was a rather big trade union of Singapore, our factory also joined the union. However, as we had sub-contractors, it was more problematic, I was also severely reprimanded by my supervisor for joining the union.

Interviewer: Why?

Tan: This supervisor was my father's friend, I got the job because of the ties with him. After which … actually, I didn't quite understand at that time, my other friend was better at this. The factory had many departments — packaging, "*che jiao*"[8], etc. Our department had only more than 10 workers, those who were in charge of packaging the biscuits were those with strong ideology. Apart from playing the role of committee members in the factory, since every factory had committee members which included posts such as secretary, chairman, etc., they also held positions in the union and had duties to fulfil. Actually, many female workers were from the literacy classes. Female workers might not have much education then but they had strong ideological awareness.

Interviewer: So how big were the classes for committee members?

Tan: Oh, they were fairly big. That was held once a week and involved committee members of the factories. They assembled and held meetings at night. These classes were rather profound to me.

Interviewer: So were other classmates of the literacy classes with you?

Tan: No, just me alone as I was a union member.

Interviewer: Which union did you join?

Tan: The Singapore General Employees' Union.

Interviewer: What kind of union was that?

Tan: A union that allowed people from different trades to join. There was a union for seamstresses and only employees from garment factories could join. There were some unions for the automobile industry...

Interviewer: What were the prerequisites to join?

Tan: No prerequisite.

Interviewer: Did you have to pay a fee?

Tan: Yes. But I can't remember how much it was. At that time the fee was known as monthly donation. It was then quite difficult to get employees to join unions, we had to tell them the benefits of joining.

Interviewer: So were there many staff who were as enthusiastic as you were?

---

[8]According to the interviewee, the term referred to the bakery department.

Tan: There were quite a lot at certain places, for example, more than 10 staff in our department joined the union. A friend of mine was a committee member, of course he was enthusiastic, then there was me, but then again there was also a friend who didn't take part in any activity but was supportive of our activities. There were also such employees.

Interviewer: You earlier mentioned that SIHSHA had three branches, so did those who attended the literacy classes choose a venue which was closer to their home?

Tan: I am not too sure of this point too. This was not always the case, I had a classmate who was living some distance away. They usually walked to school, but there were also colleagues who accompanied one another to the association's night classes, they lived in different places.

Interviewer: So they did prefer to go to classes nearer home?

Tan: Some lived nearby, others some distance away, some students lived as far as Paya Lebar. One of them lived near the current Paya Lebar airport, it was called "*Chai Shan*" then, think the airport was not operational at that time, it was not built yet. It was very dark, so the *Xiao Xiansheng* usually accompanied the students back. It wasn't easy for the *Xiao Xiansheng*, they had to take the students back on bicycles.

Interviewer: Did you ever discuss with your friends from the literacy classes on how they came to know about the classes, were there advertisements?

Tan: No, no advertisements.

Interviewer: Did you learn of it at Khong Guan?

Tan: No, I saw it while walking around. I also heard people talking about it.

Interviewer: Did you see a small notice?

Tan: There wasn't any notice. There were quite a few night schools then, but I had thought that place was nearer to where I lived, so I went to check it out. I was then very young, only 14 or 15 years old.

Interviewer: So you heard people talking about a night school nearby?

Tan: Right. After which I went to check it out, think I stood outside and started looking around.

Interviewer: You were quite brave. Did you then find out from friends how they knew about the literacy classes?

Tan: I think it was the same for another friend, her brother introduced her to it, as he knew my husband was involved in organising it, just like organising activities.

Interviewer: So it was through word of mouth...

Tan: Ah, ya. I think that was the case.

Interviewer: For the literacy classes, were there people who joined mid-way?

Tan: Yes, yes. There were also people who left, some got married, they were quite old. I remember when we were still studying, a student one year my junior got married during her teens. We even went to her house to check out her dowry. Ya, think she was one year my junior, she got married at a tender age, I was then still in the association, 1960s and she was already married.

Interviewer: At that time, when did most of you get married? Wasn't it too early?

Tan: Getting married at 25 or 26 was not considered young then. People in the past got married at a young age, for males to get married past 30 years old was considered late. But now, it is not too late to be married in the 30s, things are different now.

Interviewer: So when you were teaching, what other materials did you use?

Tan: Taught Chinese and civic education, these are the two books.

Interviewer: Civic education ...

Tan: The main purpose was to recognise words.

Interviewer: Was that done through writing?

Tan: Yes, through writing practices, one has to write to recognise a word. There was copying of text too, and examinations. Examinations were based on textbooks. I didn't really know, but I drafted examination questions, I was then in charge of everything. Looking back now, it's really funny.

Interviewer: The examination content ...

Tan: That was according to the textbooks.

Interviewer: Were the textbooks you used to teach the same ones that you used earlier to learn?

Tan: No, not the same.

Interviewer: So what materials did you select?

Tan: I didn't select the teaching materials; they did.

Interviewer: Who were they?

Tan: My husband, etc., those *Xiao Xiansheng*. They were responsible for the selection, I was only responsible for the teaching.

Interviewer: When you taught, did you make the students read aloud after you had read once?

Tan: That should have been part of it, there was writing on the board too, to help them recognise the words.

Interviewer: Were there other teaching methods?

Tan: I think methods then were very simple. It was easier with children, they were obedient, but some were older, even older than I was.

Interviewer: At what age did you start to teach?

Tan: During my teens.

Interviewer: You attended the literacy classes when you were 14 or 15 years old, so when did you begin to teach?

Tan: In a pretty short time…I was already teaching one or two years later.

Interviewer: Do you think that students at the literacy classes were interested in learning? What were their attitudes like?

Tan: Fine. Not bad, but some loved to joke around with us.

Interviewer: Were there naughty ones?

Tan: Many were quite old, the younger ones were naughtier.

Interviewer: How old were the older ones?

Tan: For those that I taught, some were past 20, I was still a teenager then.

Interviewer: Through activities organised by the literacy classes, both when you were a student or subsequently when you became *Xiao Xiansheng*, did you have an opportunity to hear about school activities in universities or senior middle school?

Tan: No. Kim Leong saw that my results were quite good, so he said he could help to enrol me in the Chung Hwa High School, a girls' school. But I said no as I was then working. My family needed my income, so I told him I didn't want to.

Interviewer: So did you at least find out from your husband what had happened at Chung Cheng?

Tan: No.

Interviewer: They hardly mentioned it?

Tan: It was quite quiet during my husband's era — there were more happenings in the 1950s. When I started attending the classes, it was 1959, everything was over. In 1959, the PAP was already governing, before that, it was the colonial government.

Interviewer: But many of your pictures seemed to have been taken in schools, like Pei Hwa and Nantah?

Tan: Oh , that was Malacca — Pei Feng, I think? At that time I went with my classmate and my husband's sister, as his aunt was living in Malacca. We went to visit her, he had classmates living in Malacca too. We did go to Nantah quite frequently.

Interviewer: Why?

Tan: Because at that time a teacher was studying in Nantah, his surname was Lee. Subsequently, there was someone whose surname was Zhang. They lived in the hostels in the early years but rented residences outside subsequently.

Interviewer: Why did they become *Xiao Xiansheng*?

Tan: They became *Xiao Xiansheng* when they were studying in Chung Cheng. They went to Nantah only after graduating from Chung Cheng.

Interviewer: Did you hear of the Anti-Yellow Culture Campaign or anti-colonialism activities when you were attending literacy classes?

Tan: I did, that was during the Lim Yew Hock government. When PAP started to govern, we had not attained independence. At that time there were talks of merger, that was the referendum. Think there were such discussions; I read about them in the newspapers too.

Interviewer: For you and your classmates of the literacy classes, were you interested in such campaigns and slogans?

Tan: I suppose we were, yes, we were concerned. The union held some activities then, I remember there was a member working at a steel factory, his palm was chopped off by his boss or for some other reasons. Think it was because of some strikes, that triggered some clashes.

Interviewer: When was that?

Tan: I forgot the specific year. I still remember his name, this "Tang Songli" then organised a delegates conference to support the union in getting compensation from the boss. The matter was blown up, I can still recall. Moreover, the person whose palm was chopped off, his brother was a committee member of the SIHSHA.

Another event occurred on May 1st, Labour Day, this I have a deeper impression. Then, a union rallied some tens of thousands of people — the number of people in Singapore then could not be compared to what we have now — there were some 50 or 60 thousand people... Wow, it was raining so heavily, everyone refused to leave. I was in the rain for an entire day and was ill the next day.

Interviewer: Was that a demonstration?

Tan: No demonstration, it was just a meeting, listening to what the unionists had to say.

Interviewer: Where were these 50 or 60 thousand people?

Tan: Think it was the Jalan Besar stadium, as far as I can recall. The stadium was quite big. There were 50 or 60 thousand people, Singapore's population was not big then. In the 1960s, that was a lot of people, all of us went.

Interviewer: You meant all of you from the literacy classes?

Tan: I think we went with them, those who were older.

Interviewer: Why did you decide to go? Was it out of your own will?

Tan: It was partly to support the union's activities, I think that was the case, I cannot remember a lot of things now.

Interviewer: Were those classmates of yours from the literacy class union members as well?

Tan: Some were, some were not.

Interviewer: Although you didn't hear your husband talk about life in Chung Cheng, did you hear him recalling memories of the student movements?

Tan: The student movements took place in the 1950s. I heard him mention before that he didn't dare to return home at night. Students were then braver, not afraid. If you were to talk about some students who were sympathetic towards China's plight, etc., then Kim Leong did mention that, there was a student who subsequently went to China, they all felt that was not right.

Interviewer: They felt he didn't fight for Malaya?

Tan: Right, they thought since you were here, you should identify with your own country. Actually, many people went to China then, I remember that my husband's elder brother also went to China during that time. His elder brother went to China in the 1950s. As for my two elder brothers, the second one went, that was around 1952, he went from Malaya to China.

Interviewer: You meant your half-brothers?

Tan: Yes, the other went a few years later. It was to some extent also due to difficulties in getting along with my father. So they went to China subsequently. Quite a lot of people went to China. Some parents were funnier, they wanted to send their children — one or two of them — to China. What happened to my brother-in-law was funnier. His father had decided to send him there, but his younger brother cried and wanted to go, so the father did a swap, the elder brother was brought back. His younger brother had a difficult time in China, at that time (Laughs), I think he went from Malaysia. Some parents had wanted to send one or two children there, and these things always happened. My brother-in-law's father had wanted to send him to China, but his younger brother cried, wanting to board the ferry, so he was swapped at the last minute.

Interviewer: When you started to attend the literacy classes in 1959, did you know how long the classes had been held?

Tan: I didn't pay attention to this.

Teaching Literacy Classes

Interviewer: So how long did you teach there?

Tan: Think it was 1963, a kindergarten was started then, I taught that too, so did my husband. That year, we were forced to close, together with three other groups, namely: the Singapore Hawkers' Union, the Singapore Itinerant Hawkers and Stall Holders Association, the Singapore Rural Residents' Association and the Singapore Country People's Association, the four organisations often issued statements, joint statements. I think there was then a "February 2 Arrest", many were detained.

Interviewer: February 2 Arrest?

Tan: Yes, February 2, the association was forced to close some time in September or October.

Interviewer: This took place in 1963?

Tan: Yes, 1963. They said that at that time ... but I am not too sure ... not sure if it had to do with the arrest of the Members of Parliament from the Barisan Sosialis, it appeared to have been during the same period. It was then quite chaotic, they said many who demonstrated in the street were arrested. I remember that previously SIHSHA had a committee member ...actually he was quite all right, was very timid ... but he was jailed for a few years due to unknown reasons.

Interviewer: Were any of your union members in contact with the Barisan Sosialis?

Tan: I doubt there was much contact.

Interviewer: What happened during the forced closure? For instance, did the government claim the premises?

Tan: Think it had to do with some statement, seemed to have been one that criticised the government or something along that line.

Interviewer: Right. So did the government claim the premises? Did closure mean that all activities had to stop?

Tan: Probably the registration was revoked, all groups had to be registered, right? If we were not forced to close, we might not have disbanded; we then had no choice but to disband. ... It seemed that the forced closure came about suddenly without much warning...Singapore has an Internal Security Department, it can carry out arrests without reason, right? Think it had to do with such problems. So as a result, many could not continue to study. After we separated our ways, there were students who lived closer to villages, I remember that two village groups subsequently continued their activities under the name of the Barisan Socialis. So, a few students of the classes organised by SIHSHA went there to study, but I did not.

Interviewer: Oh, so some who studied at classes held by SIHSHA or by other unions were transferred to village organisations affiliated to the Barisan Sosialis?

Tan: It was originally the premises of the Singapore Rural Residents' Association, but they were subsequently transformed into the Barisan Sosialis'. They died a natural death later. I don't know what led to the change, but some of the students continued their studies there, as they did not want to stop schooling.

Interviewer: How did you feel then?

Tan: Then, I was actually quite sad and helpless. As for me, I had not harboured the hope of studying with the Barisan Sosialis. So, I stopped schooling thereafter.

Interviewer: So you meant that as you taught the literacy classes, you continued to study, there wasn't any break?

Tan: (Speaking animatedly again) No break, I taught for three days, learnt for three and attended committee members' class, that was the life I led.

Interviewer: Were you not tired?

Tan: Hahaha, yes, I don't even know why I was so energetic then. Hahahaha ... We often visited fellow workers on Sundays too, these were workers from the department where we worked. You had to stay in touch with them, had to go to their residences, had to visit students, and had to visit young students etc.

Interviewer: Were the outings held on weekends too?

Tan: Sundays, so students had to prepare for them and rope in other students. Think we then had roasted pork rice, and we often brought our own water along.

Interviewer: Who was in charge of the roasted pork rice?

Tan: I have forgotten who, it was after all only a few cents....

Interviewer: The value of money was quite high then, right?

Tan: Yes.

Interviewer: So even a few cents could be quite expensive.

Tan: I think each cost 30 cents.

Interviewer: 30 cents each, that was quite a lot.

Tan: We had to pay for the lorry too, I don't know how much it cost. If my husband is still around, he would know, as he was responsible for many things. We didn't ask about these then. Perhaps I have heard about the cost before, but I have forgotten. We used the lorry for several occasions, we often used it; wherever we went, we used lorries.

Interviewer: What about other students who attended the literacy classes? You mentioned earlier that some of them had perhaps gone to study at classes run by the Barisan Sosialis, what about the rest?

Tan: All of the younger ones did not pursue their studies. Those who went to join classes at the Barisan Sosialis were the older ones, but actually there wasn't a lot of them. For my class … think there were only three, a classmate joined the automobile industry, but those Barisan Sosialis' literacy classes were also stopped subsequently.

Interviewer: Why?

Tan: The classes were stopped not too long after they (interviewee's classmates) went over, but the Barisan Sosialis then had kindergarten classes. Many who are now in their forties had studied in the kindergarten of the Barisan Sosialis, so did my younger brothers and sisters.

Interviewer: Why did they study there?

Tan: Well, it was because the kindergarten classes at the Barisan Sosialis were well-organised, the People's Action Party also started kindergarten classes subsequently. (Laughs) Their kindergarten classes seemed to have been quite successful, but the Barisan Sosialis ones were cheap. I remember that even my younger sisters went to the classes at the Barisan Sosialis, it was also because they were close to where we lived, they were located at Lorong Tai Seng.

Interviewer: They seemed to have a few branches …

Tan: Actually they were located at a few places. If we are referring to their party branches, then they (the kindergarten classes) were actually located at many places.

Interviewer: Most students of the literacy classes were females, right?

Tan: Yes.

Interviewer: Most of the teachers were probably males.

Tan: Yes.

Interviewer: Were there female teachers?

Tan: There didn't appear to have any. Female teachers only came once or twice as relief teachers.

Interviewer: Where were the relief teachers from? They were …

Tan: They were also students, but there were very few of them. If they come, it was only for a couple of days; it was usually when the male teachers could not make it, usually because of exams, etc. … I think it was when they were held up elsewhere. If it was because of exams, I remember that my husband and some of his classmates stayed in this small room in the badminton hall, many of them squeezed into that room. My husband went there just two weeks before the exams to prepare, it was then that he stopped his work at the association to concentrate on his studies. He seemed to be always running out of time, it was then the senior middle school national exams.

Interviewer: So your classmates at the literacy class, how many of them were from the villages?

Tan: Most were from the villages at that time, almost everyone lived in attap houses.

Interviewer: So they went to work at the factories in the morning?

Tan: That's right.

Interviewer: Lived in the villages, went to the factories in the morning to work and then studied at night?

Tan: That's right. I have a friend who lived where the current Maris Stella High is. It was then a remote area, his residence was right inside, I loved to go to his place then. I went to his place when I was out of work, his residence was close to where the Gurhkas were.

Interviewer: So were the majority of those whom you taught from the villages too?

Tan: They were from the villages and lived close-by.

Interviewer: Is it fair to say that boys had a better chance to study in schools then and as for girls, they perhaps went to night schools or attended literacy classes?

Tan: I remember when I first moved to Singapore, I was studying at Chiao Nan School, it was also at Paya Lebar. I remember there weren't many students when we were in Primary 5, as Primary 5 and 6 classes were taught together. For the Primary 5 class, there were 20 students, four girls, I am still in contact with one of them; she got in touch with me. I run into another at times. Actually, there was no deliberate effort to stay in touch with all four, we run into one another on and off and still remember one another, that's all. I still remember, when I first went to school, the teacher was also the school's principal, his name was Lin Jinxiong, he later became a Nantah student. There was also another teacher, they stopped teaching after they went to study at Nantah. There was another called Liang Guanfei, think I read about him in the newspaper. The two of them became quite famous in some fields, I still remember their names. After perhaps less than half a year, think we couldn't afford the books, we previously had to purchase books every half a year. We didn't have any pocket money when we went to school, we were very poor, our parents could not afford to give us money, so we went straight home after attending the classes...

That was not too long after we came to Singapore, my father said we would soon run out of money. My father started a stall at the Lorong Tai Seng Market; a licence was not necessary to start a small business then. He sold the incense papers for praying purposes. It was about time for him to call it a day when we went home after school, so my younger sister and I would help him pack up. My younger sister was so hungry that she passed out, we didn't have money for food. Things were really bad for a period of time — having to move in and out of three businesses in a week, how pitiful was that!

Marriage

Interviewer: After enrolling for the literacy class, when were you married?

Tan: I joined the literacy classes in 1959, I got married in 1969.

Interviewer: 1969. That was after independence. You and your husband knew each other for some time before deciding to get married?

Tan: Ya, we knew each other for 10 years, we were engaged in 1965.

Interviewer: That was the year when Singapore gained its independence. Was the engagement held before or after independence?

Tan: Engagement should have occurred at the end of the year.

Interviewer: What was engagement like? He bought you a ring?

Tan: Engagement in the earlier years involved rings, some chose to distribute cakes … at that time, we were … you know parents at that time were still feudalistic, you can't be together with your boyfriend without a confirmed status. But if you were engaged, then it is alright to get married later. Still, there were many who skipped the engagement.

Interviewer: What was your husband doing when you got married in 1969?

Tan: When we got married in 1969, my husband was still selling fruits. He became a fruit seller when he could not find a job upon graduation. The association was then no longer in existence. So he started to sell fruits with a couple of his classmates, we said in jest that their certificates bearing their qualifications should have been displayed.

Interviewer: (Laughs) By doing so, the fruits might have been more fragrant …

Tan: After my child was born, he went to work at this place called *"Li Da"* … that should have been started by a Hongkonger and the former boss of the Emporium Holdings in Singapore. The company shifted to Malacca later, my husband didn't go, he became a taxi driver.

Interviewer: When did he graduate from the senior middle high school?

Tan: 1960.

Interviewer: So he continued to teach at the literacy classes upon his graduation?

Tan: Yes, he did.

Interviewer: Did he teach full-time at the literacy classes after 1960?

Tan: That was when he started to sell some fruits.

Interviewer: Did he join the union?

Tan: No, he didn't.

Interviewer: So he devoted his time to the literacy classes?

Tan: That's why we were very poor. (Laughs)

Interviewer: That's quite special. Then at the literacy classes, the students were mainly females and the teachers were males, so were there many girls who admired the *Xiao Xiansheng*?

Tan: Yes, yes, that should have been the case. There was another teacher who was livelier, many girls liked him. There was one by the surname Lee, frankly, he was very good in his teaching too. He could be quite funny too, at times, he and my husband would have rather heated debates over some topics.

Interviewer: So you were not taught by your husband, did you then attend the classes taught by this Mr. Popular?

Tan: Yes, many girls liked him, and he got very scared at a later stage, scared that a particular girl was interested in him. I would tease him, pointing out that while he was very willing to help, he forgot there were differences between boys and girls. I said, "You forget that there are differences between boys and girls when you rendered assistance, that's why they misunderstood!" I would say that to him! (Laughs)

Interviewer: So did he get married later?

Tan: Yes.

Interviewer: Was he married to someone from the literacy classes?

Tan: Ah … yes. (Laughs)

Interviewer: Apart from him and your husband and you, were there any more such instances?

Tan: Not after that.

Interviewer: Just two couples?

Tan: Actually there was another person with the surname Chen from the literacy classes. He had expressed his interest in me, he was also a teacher.

Interviewer: Were there many couples?

Tan: No, no, not many. Because there weren't many teachers. There was then a teacher, I am not sure why he came to the literacy classes, think he was a Malaysian, and also with the surname Chen. He told me he liked me and bad-mouthed some other teachers. So I said, "Why did you do that? Were there misunderstandings? You should be frank about it." He then said that the other teachers were lazier. Although I was young at that time, I knew how to distinguish right and wrong, so I told him, "There could be problems among you all, you all should sit down and talk about them."

Interviewer: You said there weren't many teachers, so how many were there in a year?

Tan: Usually they were there only as relief teachers. Some two or three of them, one has the surname Lin, he taught for quite long, think he left upon graduation. The one with surname Li also taught but went to Nantah subsequently.

Interviewer: So, there were five of them. Were there mainly five persons responsible for the classes?

Tan: No, there were only two or three main persons-in-charge, the rest came and left mobile, the turnover was rather high.

Interviewer: So was your husband in contact with other Chung Cheng classmates after graduating from the senior middle school?

Tan: I think so. Quite a few passed away over the last few years. They were not very old, most were in their sixties... two attended Nantah, one had the surname ... he had heart problem all these years. The other was also ill. Yet another with surname ... owned a shop selling electrical appliances, heard that he passed away two years ago. One who was a Chinese physician also had heart problem.

Interviewer: When did your husband pass away?

Tan: 1993, 13 years ago.

Actually Kim Leong ... you look at the earlier section of this book, he was quite vocal, see the way he spoke about students' strikes, etc., how could he remember such things so vividly? Perhaps because he had the habit of collecting old newspapers ...(sighs) Kim Leong collected so many newspapers! Chinese newspapers! Wherever he went for tours, he would look for the local Chinese newspapers. Didn't he donate his collection just recently? Yes, he donated the newspapers![9]

Interviewer: Would you know where they were donated to?

Tan: I have forgotten.

Interviewer: When Singapore gained independence, were you and classmates of the literacy classes …

Tan: Quite happy, but that was already 1965. When we attained self-governance, we were already very happy. We were then aware, we were very happy.

Interviewer: So, in 1963, SIHSHA …

Tan: Because we attained self-governance in 1963, I think.

Interviewer: No we merged with Malaysia in 1963, self-governance was attained in 1959. You were enrolled in the literacy classes at about the same time when Singapore started self-governing?

Tan: Yes.

Interviewer: So, when the Hawkers' Union and SIHSHA were forced to close, had Singapore been merged with Malaysia?

Tan: Ah, yes, oh, not sure, probably so, because we participated in the referendum … think the merger had taken place.

Interviewer: How did you feel then?

Tan: Frankly speaking, we were quite young then, just teenagers, actually we didn't quite understand …

Interviewer: What about your husband and the previous generation, did they have special feelings? From those people you observed…

---

[9] For the "World Chinese Newspaper Exhibition" held in 22 December 2000, Lee Kim Leong contributed his personal collection of over 700 titles of Chinese newspapers published in different parts of the world. After the event, he donated part of his collection to the Chinese Heritage Centre at Nanyang Technological University, the Chinese library at the National University of Singapore and the National Library Board. For more details, see "Chinese Heritage Center and NUS share Lee Kim Leong Collection of Chinese Newspapers" (*Lianhe Zaobao*, 23 December 2000) and "Lee Kim Leong Entrusts Collection of Chinese Newspapers to National Library Board" (*Lianhe Zaobao*, 3 January 2001).

Tan: Perhaps already so ... not sure. At that time, there were changes ... think once the literacy classes were shut down, my husband was not too interested in other matters of the association. He wasn't too interested about political parties. But now that you talk about it, that might not be the case. I think he was involved in quite a few elections in which the Barisan Sosialis participated ... I remember he was responsible for overseeing the voting once or twice, he did.

Interviewer: Did someone get him to go?

Tan: I think so, I am not sure if he was doing the same during the referendum, but he went during the elections.

Inspired by Literacy Classes

Interviewer: So, Madam Tan, how has the literacy classes impacted your entire life?

Tan: It was very important... very important...

Interviewer: In what sense would you say it's very important?

Tan: Very important, because if I didn't attend the literacy classes and just led my life aimlessly, perhaps I could have been led astray, perhaps I would not have made good friends. I could have been led astray, some girls were quite bad at that time.

Interviewer: What do you mean by "bad"?

Tan: We used to refer to bad as "gangsterly", aimless in life and didn't seem to be able to differentiate good and bad, perhaps it had to do with the clothes ... At that time, if one's clothes was too outlandish, it wasn't a good thing. We were then very innocent, very plain, the friends we made then were really quite good, we knew how to behave, at least we knew what's good and what's bad, at least we knew how to make distinctions. Now if you were to speak to some people, they don't know a thing. We were quite lucky then, we did not have much education, we could actually have been led astray very easily.

Interviewer: So you have been inspired by the literacy classes?

Tan: Yes, quite so...

Interviewer: What do you mean?

Tan: Actually, I feel ... when I was someone's daughter-in-law and now I am someone else's mother-in-law, I cannot treat my daughter-in-law based on how I felt when I was a daughter-in-law in the past. They are different. You have to change many things to get along well ... really, this is not easy, one must communicate with others. When I was someone's daughter-in-law, when I just got married, I had to wash the clothes and prepare the meals for 15 persons. I didn't know how to cook then, so I learnt earnestly, but I didn't feel bad, I thought that could be done. I didn't think it was too hard, there wasn't much quarrelling.

I got along quite well with my mother-in-law and her family, my mother-in-law saw that I was worldly wise and knew the importance of respecting elders, at that time she also lived in Lorong Tai Seng and invited some neighbours over, she felt she had a good daughter-in-law. People then told my mother about it, they said, "Aiyah auntie, you know how to educate your daughter, her mother-in-law has been praising her!" Is this not filial piety towards my mother too?

Interviewer: So you think that you learnt the way to behave appropriately at the literacy classes?

Tan : I have learnt a lot, a lot. Attending the literacy classes ensured that I would not lose my culture. If I didn't go to the literacy classes, perhaps I would not have the ability to recognise so many words, when I knew more words, I could read books and newspapers, and my knowledge grew.

Interviewer: So do you think that the beneficial experience at the literacy classes has affected the way you lead your life?

Tan: I think so.

Interviewer: What about your views on life?

Tan: I think so, I think so. Because that book we read about *Treating Oneself and Others* was very good.

Interviewer: Were there stories, or..?

Tan: No, just how to treat oneself and others. When talking about life, even when it was just a small issue, they could make many connections and discuss it with much depth.

Interviewer: Were the teachers very enthusiastic when they talked?

Tan: Yes, yes. Very enthusiastic.

Interviewer: Did the teachers discuss such points with you?

Tan: Yes, sometimes, after the teacher had taught us, we would ask why, and he would also question us again.

Interviewer: That meant there were opportunities for discussion.

Tan: Yes, yes. Our teachers were not the very serious type, I think at that time there were quite a lot in the literacy classes.

Interviewer: Are you referring to people?

Tan: A lot of places had them, what was called night school then. For those of us who were plain in what we wore, you know what they used to call us? They called us *"shi bu shi"* ("yes or no").

Interviewer: Which *"shi bu shi"*, how do you write that?

Tan: I don't know, it was very weird, we wore simple clothes, you look at the photographs, look at everyone of us. Moreover, our hair was either plaited or cut in a particular style...

Interviewer: Did you wear the same kind of clothes to your excursions and to class?

Tan: We were dressed like that all the while, wherever we went, not flowery and in very light colours.

Interviewer: When you went on excursions and took photographs, was everyone in charge of a different task; one was responsible for the roasted pork rice, another for the photograph-taking, was it like that?

Tan: I think so.

Interviewer: Did you develop the photographs yourselves?

Tan: At that time ... my husband was usually the photographer ... he would number the photographs after the excursions and then asked us to make our selection before developing them. It cost about 10 cents to develop a photograph at that time.

Interviewer: Thank you Madam Tan, let's call it a day. Thank you very much for your time.

The Sojourns of a Village Youth
An Interview with Chua Hiang Yong

Interviewed by Chan Cheow Thia

Transcribed by Chan Cheow Thia, Chan Cheow Pong

Translated by Lim Meow Nar

Date: 23 June 2007

Interviewer: Which year did you enter Sin Min[1]?

Chua: I was born in 1947; delayed entry to school by a year, later I skipped a grade. When I was eight, which was in 1955, I entered Sin Min studying in Primary One. I graduated from junior middle school in 1963.

Raising Funds

Interviewer: During the March alumni gathering, what left the deepest impression on me was when ex-principal Mr. Chew Peng Leng mentioned that a funfair would be organised every year and he would bring students out to raise funds after class.

Chua: Yes, we did that too, I can recall going with the senior students to raise funds around South Bridge Road, to all kinds of shops, including those that sold rice, seafood, mostly around Pickering Street. We raised funds by inviting them to advertise for our funfair. I remember better those years in junior middle school, around Junior Middle Two and Three.

Interviewer: Did you go after school?

Chua: After school. Sometimes, we ran into difficulties, but the shop owners then were rather supportive, they were all very supportive of Chinese medium schools,

---

[1] The interviewee had attended Sin Min High School, which is now known as Xinmin Secondary School.

so we generally would not encounter major problems. Especially when it came to private schools like ours, they were quite enthusiastic to offer help, most were willing to place advertisements.

Interviewer: So in terms of how you were organised, did the principal and several teachers lead different groups of students?

Chua: No. Some might have gone with the teachers. I went with the seniors. For instance, when I was in Junior Middle Two, students from the senior middle section would bring us along to participate in this activity and organised the funfair. Generally, the seniors would take the lead and work on the graduation book. When donations were needed, they would bring us along. I was the class monitor, so I was asked to go. At that time, it was quite common for schools to organise funfairs to raise building or expansion funds, and hence the need to solicit for donations.

Interviewer: How long would the fund-raising usually take?

Chua: It usually took a few weeks. It was mainly to ask businesses to place advertisements, be it during the funfair or in the graduation yearbook.

Interviewer: How would the seniors normally go about raising funds? What did the work entail?

Chua: Most of the times it was about getting businesses to place advertisements; the school would collect the money from them later, according to the size of the advertisements published.

Interviewer: There must be many other after-school activities in preparation for the funfair. What I heard at the tea session was, besides donations, there were also rehearsals for activities such as dance performance.

Chua: I did not participate (in those), because I did not have the aptitude in this aspect. However, my eldest brother (he was a teacher in Sin Min) worked very hard, it was in his character to do so. That was my late brother Chua Theng Tong, he used the pen name Sha Jia for his poetry. I have deep respect for him. It was in fact under his influence that I developed my passion for writing.[2] He would teach dance, he taught the primary school students a dance called "Catching Butterflies". At that time, many teachers did everything by themselves. In contrast to how things are now, the performances then were put together by teachers and students, there was no way the school could afford to hire instructors, there weren't any

---

[2]The interviewee later added that his secondary four Chinese language teacher Liu Yu, who writes under the pen name Fu Te, had an immense influence on him in this aspect as well.

external dance instructors either. Usually, if there were students or teachers who were talented in this area, they would do it themselves. My deepest impression was of a teacher called Lin Zhongqing. He later left the school and became a businessman. His family was involved in local performing arts; I think it was a Hokkien opera troupe. He was very capable, he even taught some students how to wave the big flags, perform acrobatics, and the performance was truly exciting.

Joining Small Learning Groups

Interviewer: Looking back, what was the relationship between the middle school you attended and the society at large? What happened in the society may affect certain aspects of students' life, and in fact, students were involved in a wide variety of activities, not necessarily only those related to student movements.

Chua: Indeed it was not necessary so. This was because the society as a whole was still relatively poor. The trade unions were very influential and there were many alumni associations at that time. The alumni associations were left-leaning, for example, the Kong Yiong Alumni Association. However, the irony was that of the two schools in Hougang; one was extremely left, the other extremely right. The extreme left school was Sin Min, started by the first principal Yap Fun Fong; Fong Chong Pik, also known as the "The Plen" (Plenipotentiary) of the Malayan Communist Party, who subsequently became a wanted man, taught in Sin Min in its early days. From what I heard from seniors, Sin Min even flew the five-star red flag of the People's Republic of China (ruled by the Chinese Communist Party) during its initial days. The extreme right school was Kong Yiong School which pledged its allegiance to the Kuomintang (KMT, the Nationalist Party), apparently they used to fly the KMT flag. However, the Kong Yiong Alumni Association was an extreme leftist organisation. In the early days, those alumni associations conducted their activities vigorously. As for civic organisations, the more active ones were mainly the labour unions. When I was in primary school, anti-colonial sentiments and the fight for independence united the alumni associations and labour unions, and this very strongly affected us. That was a time when events such as the struggle against the colonial government, protests and events such as the Hock Lee Bus Incident occurred. I had an old neighbour who was the leader of the bus union. He had represented the union and visited Lee Kuan Yew at his home to seek legal assistance, and Lee was very willing to help them. At that time Lee Kuan Yew was the legal consultant of the student and labour movement. During my secondary school days, even though Singapore had already achieved self-governance, the civic organisations were still very strong, and it was primarily because the alumni associations and labour unions were still around. Besides, there were also organisations in the countryside, for example, the Singapore Country People's Association and Singapore Rural Residents' Association, also known as SCPA and SRRA, these were two different leftist organisations well established in many villages. All these inevitably affected us. Even when I went into middle school, even though Singapore was already autonomous, these organisations were still very influential. In our school, we had a learning group; it was basically influenced by these organisations. I participated in the group's activities, even though at that time I did not understand what was going on.

Interviewer: What did you learn in the learning group?

Chua: The learning group was supposed to be a tuition class, but in fact, politics was taught. The group talked about Asian, African and Latin American politics, for example, Lumumba of Congo, Ahmed Ben Bella of Algeria… These political topics were brought into the learning group, so on the surface it was a tuition class, but that was just a front.

Interviewer: Did the learning group conduct its activities after school hours?

Chua: After school. I remember sometimes they were conducted at my home, sometimes at other classmates' homes. The seniors from senior middle school would take the lead and explain the school work, but often, politics became the focus, politics always became the main topic. Many classmates from the junior classes did not understand much. In short, these organisations were still very powerful at that time.

Interviewer: How did the content of the learning group affect your classmates? How can we categorise the students at that time?

Chua: The funny thing was the learning group had an impact on students like me, those who loved studying, but failed to influence Goh Tong Pak. We liked studying and were rather bookish, and more curious in this aspect, plus we were more introverted and inclined to contemplate, this made us more likely to be influenced. Simplistically speaking, we can divide the students in those days into three categories.[3] One category was like me, our results were above

---

[3] The interviewee clarified (in an email dated 24 May 2007): Firstly it is with regard to your question on "how the students in the 1960s can be categorised". I had answered three categories, namely one, those who only focused on their studies; two, those who would only care about play and three, focused on studies and concerned with politics (I classify myself under this group). However, this is still an oversimplification, especially since there were many overlaps between the first and third category. Upon reflection, was I not also a "bookworm"? Apart from a few occasions, I rarely participated in

average, we loved reading and were introverted bookworms; the second type was the direct opposite, they were extroverted, loved sports and were playful, Tong Pak belonged to this category, he was very good at basketball, but could not care less about campus politics. Then there was the academically inclined group, they generally also did not bother with politics. Chng Teow Hua, who later became the first Commissioner of the Civil Defence Force was my monitor in Junior Middle Four, he belonged to this group. He was focused and motivated. He was very good in English since his secondary school days, and of course he would not get involved in student riots. He did not belong to my category, but was not mischievous as well. So to put it simply, there were three categories of students. For those like Teow Hua, they focused on academic pursuits and results; I must say they were the most sober of the lot. Looking back now, we were a bit duped to the other side. But I did sense something amiss eventually and hence never got too deeply involved in politics. In senior middle school, the undercurrents were still quite strong. I had transferred to The Chinese High School, you know that Chinese High was the base camp, I recalled the year before we gained independence, because of involvement in these activities, I think it had something to do with anti-Malaysia sentiments. Even though I only cared about my studies at that time, my suspicions were already aroused. The undercurrents were really turbulent then, if you were not careful, you would be done for. For example, some students appeared to be very left-leaning and encouraged everyone to take part in demonstrations, but some participating classmates came back and told me that those fellows did not even show up.

---

school activities (except for the joint exhibition I organised with a few avid classmates interested in art when I was in Junior Middle Two); In contrast, for people like Chng Teow Hua who eventually became Singapore's first Civil Defence Commissioner (he was the monitor of our Junior Middle Four class, we transferred to The Chinese High School and attended senior middle school together, he was in the science stream, while I was in the humanities), besides focusing on studies, he was also active in school activities, a truly "all-round student". As for the second type, I said they "only wanted to play", this is not a fair statement as among some of these students, many of them were athletes (Goh Tong Pak was an excellent basketball player). Perhaps, let me try and recategorise: First, good and upright students who excelled in academic performance, they were also active in school activities (may or may not be concerned with politics); second, students who focused on studies and were concerned with politics at the same time (may or may not be actively involved in school events, for example I belong to the latter group), third, those who whole-heartedly got involved in politics (they might also excel in studies, or simply could not care less about "examination and diploma"); fourth, students who were playful (many of whom were athletes) and fifth, those who cannot be easily categorised. (The first four categories would usually see some overlaps, but this is how one is just able to categorise them.)

Interviewer: Did you know why? Have you thought about why it was so?

Chua: We all knew, we began to see light. There were many "professional students" at that time, from middle school to university. Was that fellow one of those "professional students"? We discussed about it privately and became suspicious. Luckily the majority of us did not show up. There were many underlying threats like this at that time, it was very hard for you to tell, it was very dangerous.

Interviewer: How long did you participate in the learning group?

Chua: I remember it probably lasted till the year I was in Junior Middle Two, after that the activity just fizzled away. However, the school was still riotous at that time, and this made me very averse to the leftist students. How can they be so unruly? For example, when rallying students for a meeting, the student leader simply snatched the microphone away from our principal Tung Sey Yew. Although we referred to the principal as "old fogey" and disliked him, but I thought to myself, he was the principal after all. If I remember correctly, it had to do with boycotting the examinations, opposing the institution of national exams at Junior Middle Four; that was a time when the system was about to change, from a three-three structure (three years of junior middle school education and three years of senior middle school education) to a four-two structure (four years of junior middle school education and two years of senior middle school education). The student leaders gathered all the students in the hall. Sin Min High School then built a new campus after seeking donations. The three classrooms on the ground floor could be merged into one, by pushing the doors to the sides. The leftist student leaders suddenly gathered everyone there. We were curious and so we went. The student leaders were giving speeches on stage, the principal arrived to stop him and asked everyone to return to the classrooms and resume lessons. The student leader snatched the microphone from principal Tung Sey Yew in front of all of us. I thought to myself then: How did it come to this stage? Honestly speaking, I found it detestable. How can their behavior be so indecorous? I became averse to them. A second thing was becoming averse towards the extreme left. Come the 1960s and the 1970s, the activities developed into violent street riots. Personally, I was against them.

Organising Art Exhibitions

Interviewer: During your middle school days in Sin Min, what was the atmosphere of the school like after class?

Chua: Some schoolmates were involved in preparation of the funfair, some leftist students organised learning groups, we once organised an art exhibition, that also took place after school.

Interviewer: Right, you mentioned that at the alumni tea session. Tell us more about the art exhibition you organised.

Chua: I did mention it that day. The only person who really became an artist was Hua Chai Yong. He specialised in water colour painting. He was the one who led us to organise the exhibition. If I remember correctly, he was in Junior Middle Four that year, we were in Junior Middle Two. Of the schoolmates who participated in the joint exhibition, my classmate Liu Deyuan was the most gifted. But later on, he stopped painting and became a businessman instead, and he made it big.

Interviewer: How did the idea come about in the first place?

Chua: Because we all loved to paint. I remember in the cohort-based art competition, Deyuan came in first. Cai Wensheng was runner-up and I took the second runner-up; there was a Liu Deliang, he had also taken the third position. We frequently shared our experiences of painting and enjoyed coming together to discuss. What we did at that time was, whoever had some art books would bring to the school for all to read and we would exchange notes, we liked to do that. As for the art competition, Deyuan would always be the champion. Deyuan told Deliang and I that he knew Chai Yong who was thinking of organising an art exhibition and asked if we would like to make it a joint effort. This was how it began. There was Chen Changyi who loves to write as well as paint. This was how the few of us gathered and organised the art exhibition. Hua Chai Yong later moved on to become the organising secretary in a community centre and held art exhibitions, he became a real artist. I did not continue my pursuit along this path, however out of passion, I taught art, apart from Chinese language and Chinese literature in secondary schools. I started teaching in Thomson Secondary and Yishun Secondary School, after which I went to Kong Yiong High School. As the number of arts classes grew, I switched to teaching art exclusively and became head of the arts department. I fell in love with art in junior middle school partly because of my eldest brother Chua Theng Tong's influence, he was highly skilled at sketching; the other reason had to do with the old artist Mr Lim Tze Peng. Mr Lim Tze Peng was then the principal of Sin Min Primary School at Pasir Ris. Under his guidance, many students became pretty good at art, and Deyuan had graduated from Sin Min Primary School to attend Sin Min High School. Fortunately, we had a teacher called Sim Kwang Teck in Sin Min High School at Hougang. Mr. Sim was a very good watercolour artist. Highly skilled, he was also the first president of the Singapore Watercolour Society and engaged in paintings of still life. He also influenced my brother Theng Tong. Even though Mr. Sim Kwang Teck never taught me, he was on very good terms with my brother and often came to our place. Occasionally, when he came over and saw me painting, he would give some pointers for which I am very grateful. At that time, I think he was teaching art at Chinese High School or the Chung Cheng High School. However, he and his wife Chen Huiqing, who was our English teacher, lived in the school (the school had lodging for a few teachers); coupled with the fact that he was on good terms with the principal, we decided to ask Mr. Sim to help us organise an art exhibition. He readily agreed and said he would take care of everything. And he really went to discuss with our principal Tung Sey Yew and borrowed a "Mongolian yurt"[4]. The art exhibition actually came true and was held in the "yurt". It was really audacious.

Interviewer: In which middle school year did that event take place?

Chua: I remember Deyuan, Deliang and I were in the same class, we were in Junior Middle Two; Wensheng was also in Junior Middle Two but in a different class. Chen Changyi was in Junior Middle Three, Hua Chai Yong Junior Middle Four.

Interviewer: After the principal agreed, how long did the preparation take? How long was the exhibition?

Chua: The exhibition was only for one day. The preparation did not take too long. We all stayed back after school, Chai Yong would instruct us on how to cut out border frames out of cardboard and that was how we got things going. At that time, I even made a resolution to become an artist! I started loving art very early, due to the influence of my eldest brother Theng Tong. My brother was very good and talented in art. I fell in love with calligraphy and writing mainly as a result of his influence as well. At the end of the lunar year, our grandfather would stick couplets on both sides of every door and he would be the one writing them. When he wrote, I helped to "pull the paper" and tagged along. I learnt many things from him, including charcoal sketching and plaster relief sculpture. He could draw, carve wood and handicraft, he could do anything. He was deeply influenced by Mr. Sim Kwang Teck. Mr. Sim was also adept at watercolour painting, oil painting, handicraft and many other things. Mr. Sim could also play the *dong xiao* (vertical flute)!

Interviewer: How many afternoons did you spend working on the art exhibition?

Chua: Not very long, we stayed back after school for at most two weeks. At that time, we did not have stipulated extra-curricular activities; we did this out of our own free will. There were no mandatory extra-curricular activities, none at all. If you had the interest, you just got things going. It was very enjoyable; I thought

---

[4]The interviewee explained that the "Mongolian yurt" was so called because there were two detached bungalows which looked like yurts in the old school compound.

about it later on and wrote an article on it, we were simply young and fearless to hold a joint exhibition! Within the group, only Hua Chai Yong became an artist, Liu Deyuan became a businessman; Liu Deliang joined the army and served as an officer until retirement. I can still be considered as one making a living out of art as I subsequently taught the subject at secondary schools.

Interviewer: Do you remember how many pieces of work were on display? What different types of work were there?

Chua: There were about sixty or seventy pieces, of which at most ten were mine; that was about it. Hua Chai Yong loved charcoal painting then; Deyuan used watercolour and pencil; as for me, I just started painting with watercolour and charcoal drawing. These were the main media. We were not yet good enough to do oil painting. Only when I took classes at the Nanyang Academy of Fine Arts because I was teaching the subject in schools did I pick up oil painting.

Interviewer: Did you invite your family to attend the exhibition?

Chua: No, but my eldest brother might have attended, he had always encouraged me to paint. We did not open it to outsiders, it was only for fellow students.

Interviewer: Your seniors and teachers should have attended as well, I guess?

Chua: Some seniors and teachers did. Mr. Sim Kwang Teck was extremely supportive and full of praises. He was the teacher who influenced me most. When I was taking classes at the Nanyang Academy of Fine Arts, he also taught there after his retirement and we had many opportunities to talk. Mr. Sim was the first president of Singapore Watercolour Society, his style was realist and he was extremely talented. It is a pity he remained unknown.

Interviewer: At that time, did you learn woodcut printing during art lessons?

Chua: No, the junior middle school art curriculum focused on still life. We did not really approve of our art teacher then, we felt he was not as good as some of our classmates. But, he was a very responsible teacher.

Interviewer: Wasn't Mr. Sim Kwang Teck your art teacher?

Chua: He had taught in Sin Min too, but he was not my teacher. When I was in primary school, he lived in Sin Min, Sin Min then had a teacher's hostel. His wife taught us English. At that time, several teachers lived in the school compound. There was a Ms. Chen Wenbin, she also lived in campus. I came under her influence in primary school. She drew beautifully, the pencil lines she drew flowed and inspired. Surprisingly she did not become an artist. In the early days, many art teachers had a real solid foundation, many of them had graduated from specialised art schools in China.

Senior Middle School Classmates

Interviewer: What activities did you participate in middle school?

Chua: At Chinese High, I did not participate in any activities as I was a bookworm and would stay in the library after school. Also because I was poor, I could not afford to eat at the canteen with others during recess. The money I saved would be all used on buying books. My father had found work by that time, but we were still poor, so I would go to the library immediately after class. The Chinese High library was different from others. There was an art museum too. That was where I first saw an authentic piece of work by the Ming Dynasty calligraphist Wen Zhengming. That left me with a very deep impression. It was Wen Zhengming's *xing shu* (running script) written in small characters. I veritably admired the work in adoration. Besides that, the teachers at Chinese High had a great influence on me too, especially my Chinese teacher in my second year, Mr. Zhao Manyuan. Mr. Zhao could write beautifully, he "forced" us to write *da xiao kai* (standard regular script in large and small characters) and also to use the brush to write essays, it was unbearably painful, however, this was also how our calligraphy foundation was forcefully laid. Mr Zhao spoke perfect Mandarin and loved to recite the textbook passages out loud. When I started teaching, I also emphasised reading aloud, all because of Mr. Zhao's influence. That weekend when we had the tea reunion at Xinmin Secondary School, didn't Goh Tong Pak tease us for transferring schools as our results were good, and he could only stay behind because his were bad? It was indeed true that the better students all transferred. Chng Teow Hua transferred to the science stream in Chinese High (I transferred to the arts stream). Our homes were very near each other, hence we would go to school together in the morning. Teow Hua's family was better off and they lived in a semi-detached house, he would help us in mathematics. When he took part in Chinese High's oratorical contest, he asked me to help him write his speech and came in second! Some day after graduation, Teow Hua cycled to my place and asked me to help him write a speech. I asked him what he was up to and what kind of speech he needed. Lee Khoon Choy had just won over the Hong Lim constituency from Ong Eng Guan, Teow Hua was thinking of participating in the oratorical the contest in the Hong Lim constituency. I told him I received a letter from the Ministry of Defence, asking me to go for junior officer training. I had just graduated and was spending the entire holidays at home. That should be around the end of 1965. I did not like it at all, as I was, firstly, thin and frail, and couldn't have met the requirements for that NCO (Non-Commissioned

Officer) Course, whatever that was. That was the very first cohort for NCO Course and I simply had no interest in becoming a soldier. Besides, my English was lousy, I knew I would be asking for trouble by going into the army if my English was not good. Furthermore, I always took the literary path and only enjoyed the company of books, at that time I had even started writing some poetry. Teow Hua panicked upon hearing about the letter and asked why he had not received the letter but I did. He was so anxious that he went to look for Hong Lim's Member of Parliament Lee Khoon Choy, asking why his classmate had received the letter but he did not. When we were in Junior Middle Four in Sin Min, Teow Hua was our class monitor; his robust physique made him a good officer candidate. Eventually, he also received the letter and immediately joined the army. He was very motivated in this aspect and worked very hard, and indeed he rose through the ranks and became a lieutenant colonel. After that, he was transferred to the Civil Defence Force and became its deputy commissioner. When the New World Hotel collapsed, he was on site to lead and command rescue works, after which he was promoted to the rank of colonel and took up the inaugural appointment of Commissioner of the Singapore Civil Defence Force. This is really quite a story. When Teow Hua was in Sin Min High School, he belonged to the group of students who focused on academic achievements. Unlike the rest of us who were somewhat still involved in some activities and came under left-wing influence, he stayed away and this naturally had to do with his family circumstances.

Interviewer: For this group of students, what did they do after school?

Chua: They generally did not participate in political activities. They put in a lot of effort into their school work and would always top the class. I am not aware of other activities. The third type of schoolmates was more playful, a few of my old friends, take for example Goh Tong Pak, they belonged to this group... after I left Sin Min, Goh Tong Pak's results made phenomenal progress and was top student every year. Actually, he is very intelligent. Tong Pak eventually became our alma mater's principal and led Sin Min to become the best school in Hougang. His achievements were not incidental. This man is smart and has both ideas and creativity. He was a cheeky troublemaker, a "bad student" whom teachers did not enjoy meeting, but he went on to become a renowned educator,[5] who could have imagined that? However, this is precisely the interesting part of education in that era. I often think to myself, fortunately there wasn't any "primary four streaming",

---

[5]Goh Tong Pak was a deputy director at the Schools Division of the Ministry of Education before he retired in 2007, after which he became the group chief executive officer of local food company BreadTalk.

otherwise Goh, Tong Pak would long have been assigned into the "Normal" or even "Normal-Tech" stream and never made a comeback.

Interviewer: How did someone as introverted as you become good friends with an extrovert like Goh Tong Pak?

Chua: Tong Pak was on very good terms with us because he lived near us, he was taught by my eldest brother too. Frankly speaking, those who had been taught by my brother were all very good to him. The people of Sin Min were all very grateful to him. Mention Chua Theng Tong and every alumnus would express gratitude. He was a very good teacher who taught very well and deeply influenced his students. Tong Pak was my brother's student and often came to visit us at home. Although I was not a prankster like him, I was quite playful in school too, but I did not dare to behave similarly outside of school. Outside of school and at home, I dare not hang out with them as my family upbringing was very strict and deterred me from making trouble outside, but when in school, we had so much fun together.

The World Beyond the School Campus

Interviewer: Over the four years you were in junior middle school, Singapore saw several major events, including attaining self-government in 1959 and a referendum voting in 1962. Were you aware of these events when you were in school? Amongst fellow schoolmates, or let's talk about you, did you feel anything special?

Chua: Honestly speaking, we were against the merger with Malaysia. We felt aggrieved and very reluctant. We wondered why we had to depend on others for a living. But there was no alternative and there was a feeling of helplessness at that time. We were basically not supportive and were very against it, even though we did not participate in the protests. Those who participated took to the streets and protested, they were against the national voting exercise (we didn't call it a "referendum" at that time) or something like that. I remembered in my last year at Sin Min, we even had to sing the Malaysia national anthem. We were very reluctant (hummed a segment of the anthem) and thought what a lifeless and dull song it was. At the flag-raising ceremony, we had to sing "Negara Ku"… I had very deep impression of that. During my second year at Chinese High, we became independent, we really felt as if we were liberated and were overjoyed. Actually, the people of my time had a strong sense of nationhood: aha independence at long last! That was really gratifying news. We had finally broke away from Malaysia. Of course, this had to do with the strong oppression we experienced during the merger period with Malaysia. Did Lee Kuan Yew not shed tears then? Although we did not shed tears, we were not that noble, but we were also... I remembered I only wanted to run home quickly, in short, I was very excited upon hearing the radio broadcast. I remembered there were the racial riots the year before independence (the clash between the Chinese and the Malays), we were having classes in Chinese High when a State of Emergency was suddenly announced. A few classmates who lived in Hougang and I wanted to go home, but there were no buses because of the emergency order, so we had to hitch a ride from a lorry driving past. The lorry driver heard that we wanted to go to Hougang and very kindly sent us home. The society at that time frequently tugged at your heartstrings, making it impossible for you to be unconcerned. Even if you were a student, you would also care about it naturally. Our village was also affected during the Chinese-Malay clashes, because there was a neighbouring Malay village, a Malay kampong, basically all were affected. Fortunately, our village was unscathed, although at times things felt very strained, disasters were headed off eventually. I recalled there was a grocery shop between our village and the Malay kampong, next to it was a man selling coffee and we addressed him as "Uncle Yong Lim". Even though his coffee tasted really horrible, he was a very righteous man. There were a few occasions when the Chinese and Malays almost broke into a fight and Uncle Yong Lim would always step forward. I remembered he would hold a carrying pole or hoe or something as "weapon", patiently dissuade the Chinese who were raring to run into the Malay kampong and finally got the trouble-makers to turn back. A plain-looking elderly person, just another villager, yet he understood what it meant to be racially harmonious and averted a bloodshed. Looking back now, he still evokes a lot of respect. Actually, be it Chinese or Malay, most of the people were kind-hearted and could live harmoniously together, the despicable ones were the opportunists who stirred up unrest. We all knew that the racial riots were incited.

Interviewer: Comparatively speaking, when you were in Junior Middle One and that was also in 1959 when we gained self-governance, how did you feel?

Chua: When we gained self-governance, the feeling was very strong and happy. After all, we got rid of colonialism, got rid of the British. But frankly speaking, the feeling under PAP's rule then was very different as we were still inclined towards the other side. The entire political climate in the 1960s was very tense (primarily against leftist organisations), we did not agree with it; but in my opinion, the political organisations to the extreme left in Singapore did not choose the correct path either, especially that of the Barisan Sosialis. We lived in a village where the left had immense influence. The main political groups at that time were the SCPA and SRRA, i.e. the Singapore Country People's Association and the Singapore Rural

Residents' Association. Many of the villagers supported the Barisan Sosialis. If you think about it, the people voted them into parliament, yet they backed out! They basically ruined their own chances. Many people were very upset, in fact they were furious! And because of this, people lost all confidence in the opposition.

Interviewer: Do you think they acted impetuously?

Chua: I do not think so. I just felt it was all a political whirlpool even though I still could not make sense of what had happened. I just felt that it was wrong for the Barisan Sosialis to resign from parliament and encouraged people to take to the streets. If they had retained those ten over seats, it would have prevented a one-party dominance situation, which was after all unhealthy for politics. As for what exactly was in the "political whirlpool", it remains a mystery even until today.

Interviewer: In February 1963, there was a massive arrest operation codenamed "Cold Store", Lim Chin Siong and an ex-editor of the Malay newspaper vanished overnight. Did this incident have any effect in schools?

Chua: If I remember correctly, I was in Junior Middle Four then. SCPA and SRRA were also closed that year. Alumni associations subsequently closed down one by one too. I felt whoever was in charge and decided to close off the alumni associations made a very smart move, this was because majority of the associations were left-leaning, especially the associations of the Chinese medium schools... many people either could not help it or were implicated into political activities without understanding. I was lucky and did not get involved. Even though I was involved in a learning group for a short while, I kept questioning some issues and began to feel something was amiss. Especially when the Barisan Sosialis resigned from parliament and rallied people to take to the streets and turn destructive, I really disagreed with them in my heart. What kind of politics were they playing?

Interviewer: Regarding the social incidents that took place when you were in primary school, including the setting up and closure of the Singapore Chinese Middle School Student Union (SCMSSU), how did you know about it?

Chua: I came to hear about it mainly from my family, that was from my brother. I think my elder sister was involved too. They would gather at Chung Cheng, they were all involved in the early days. We even had a neighbour who was a unionist. Through the contact with other family friends, this was how we became influenced — being in this kind of environment since young. I was only a primary school student then, but the newspapers reported on the strikes and rebellion against the Lim Yew Hock administration, I read that and was influenced. For example when they used water hoses to spray at the workers, I felt very angry, after all, man is born to be compassionate. I actually felt that these people had made a tremendous contribution to Singapore — Singapore was built by the participation of these unsung heroes. Although some were exploited by the extremist movements of the leftists later on and took the wrong path, but when the union and student movements first started, they were born out of a sincere motive — to seek independence and decolonisation. Wasn't Lee Kuan Yew their legal advisor? I felt these people made great contributions and should not be effaced. Lee Kuan Yew too had to admit later that the students in Chinese medium schools had great organising capacity; he had all along thought of them as remarkable, in regard to their mobilisation ability. He also said that Lim Chin Siong was very talented in this respect and used this strength of Chinese medium school students. In the early days, the elites in English schools did not have much grassroots support, and so they had relied on Chinese school students to mobilise the masses. But in the end, partly as a result of the leftist taking the wrong path and crossing over to the extreme, we see the situation we are facing today.

Interviewer: So in your opinion, is the image of Chinese medium school students still negative in some of the documentation out there? I am asking this because there exists a view that Chinese medium school students have been "demonised" in many narratives.

Chua: Of course, the image as a whole is still rather negative; however, Chinese medium students are responsible for creating this impression too. To put it more objectively, they had gone overboard and did not clearly think of the path they were taking, either that or they were blindly following the extreme leftist from China. The path they took was in fact an incorrect one; which is to say it was unrealistic. When organising a movement, you cannot afford to do that, especially when you are organizing a political movement, you cannot afford to be so immature, unrealistic and reckless. Hence, that was why people coined the term *zuoqing youzhi bing* ("the leftist infantile syndrome"), this was similar to what the Hong Kongers refer to as *gaokong zuoye* ("unfounded operation") of China's Great Cultural Revolution. Chinese medium school students have to undertake partial responsibility. The Nantah incident was another case in point, and it gave Lee Kuan Yew a very good excuse. Back in my junior middle school days for example, my senior, the leftist student leader who snatched the microphone away from our principal Tung Sey Yew, and also the subsequent furore over attacking the principal all made me feel that the actions were infantile and immature. Hence, we must shoulder some responsibility for being "demonised" to some extent. This was because we made a mistake, or were misguided right from the start. Many people working in the literature and the arts were also conducting "unfounded operations". My friends from the literary field and I were joking at that time about how so many people were learning from Lu Xun, but what did they learn from him? Did they learn his true spirit? I am afraid not, what they learnt was very little and superficial; they did not grasp Lu Xun's essence. They could not even master his sharp and pugnacious style. What is the source of Lu Xun's style? It was the prose from the Wei-Jin period[1]! Lu Xun especially valued the Wei-Jin prose, only when one had studied to great depths the Wei-Jin prose can one write with that kind of style and vigor. If they cannot master that style, what did they learn then? The only thing left to learn was a politicised Lu Xun, cast in the familiar lines of his saying "with slanting brows I cast a cold glance at the thousand pointing fingers; but bowing my head, I gladly be an ox for the children", which had been interpreted by Mao Zedong to have extended meanings.

Interviewer: Many people at that time were talking about the idea of "Malaya"...

Chua: Yes, my eldest brother (Sha Jia) wrote this in a poem, "Motherland, still groping for the way forward in the dark..." The "motherland" referred to Malaya, as when Mr Fang Xiu talked about *mahua wenxue* (Malayan Chinese Literature), he was also referring to the whole of Malaya (which included Singapore).

Interviewer: In other words, at that time, there were already people thinking how not to follow China blindly and to introduce some local flavour. If it were these people who took charge, instead of the People's Action Party or those with "the infantile syndrome", do you think the situation would had been more hopeful?

Chua: It would be, but I think these people lack the power, perhaps there were too few of them. Those who were pro-Malaya were the extreme leftists, and in the end they did not even recognise Singapore's independence and insisted it was bogus independence.

Interviewer: But were they agreeable to joining Malaysia?

Chua: Not agreeable and they were against the referendum and joining Malaysia. They wanted a Malaya, the Malay peninsula that included Singapore as part of Malaya. They felt the whole of Malaya should be a single entity. Let me give an example, in the poet Yuan Dian's *Our Hometown is a Mountain of Ten Thousand Treasures*, that was a famous poem and the hometown in it referred to Malaya and not Singapore. Many people in the early days shared the same sentiment.

---

[1] The Wei and Jin Period (AD 265–420) is a historical period in China that existed in between the two glorious dynasties of Han and Tang. Lu Xun was known to write in the Wei-Jin clear and succint prosaic style, common in that period.

Ethnic Chinese Students Learn Malay

Interviewer: We also found that the cultural performances in schools saw Chinese students actively participating in Malay dance and plays translated from Malay language; also, many of them were learning Malay language. Can we say that the idea of Malaya was better received amongst the students?

Chua: It was indeed better received (by the students). Take me, for example, I was not a good performer, so funfairs were not for me. My younger brother was more active and participated in the Malay dance performances. I have a very lasting memory of that. It was very natural for us to talk about racial harmony and there weren't any signs of racial discord, nothing at all. The subsequent Chinese-Malay clashes were incited, especially in Malaysia; the clashes were incited by the Muslim fundamentalists in UMNO. The relationship between the Chinese and the Malays in the early days was very intimate. My grandfather was a businessman, when his business failed, he moved back to the kampong. The Malays there respected him and hailed him as the village chief. I really admire his spirit, after his business had failed, he began repairing roads and building bridges in the kampong. When we were young, we all helped with work like reclaiming the earth after school or during the holidays. This was how he mobilised the people and built several bridges. In front of our house, there was a huge drain and only a crude wooden bridge over it, my grandfather later changed that into a cement one; he couldn't stop flaunting the fact that it was a steel and cement bridge built from aircraft metal. There was another place called *san tiao ye duan* ("three strips of coconut trunk") where the "bridge" was roughly put together by combining three sections of coconut tree trunks, and even that was replaced with a cement bridge by him. I wondered if the Malays developed great respect for him because of his contributions to road and bridge building. The Chinese kampong we were living in then was called *ye jiao di* ("below the coconut tree") and was right next to the Malay kampong. When the Malays ran into problems, they would even engage him to help resolve and refer to him as the "Penghulu"[6]. They would look to him for mediation and consultation. "Below the coconut tree" and the Malay kampong were opposite the old Sin Min High School (where the Helping-Hands Centre currently is), that was in the Charlton Road area where the Lorong Ah Soo HDB estate stands today. That place was originally known as Lorong Ah Soo, after which it was changed to Aroozoo Lane. There were two schools then, namely Aroozoo and Charlton School. The two Chinese and Malay villages were both there. In short, the Chinese and the Malays did not have any problems with each other in the early days. Because of my grandfather,

---

[6]Penghulu is a title equivalent of Malay village chief.

whenever there was a Malay wedding ceremony, we would be invited too. Come to think about it now, I still feel very touched by the gesture.

Interviewer: So do you speak Malay?

Chua: Not anymore, I did take the first grade examination, but I have forgotten all of it by now.

Interviewer: It is the same with my father ...

Chua: We did not get to use it. The government stipulated that to become a civil servant, you must pass grade one of the Malay language examination. I learnt from Mr Lim Chin Kiat (Singapore's renowned Malay language expert, eldest brother of Lim Chin Siong and Lim Chin Joo) and passed my grade one examination. After that, I stopped using it altogether. Come to think about it, it was quite a shame, a real pity. Malay is a language we should have studied seriously. As a result of my childhood experience and the respect Malays had for my grandfather, I have never discriminated against the Malays. In school, whenever I meet teachers who looked down on Malays, I would feel very unhappy as I feel that it should not be the way.

Interviewer: When you attended Sin Min High School, were there Malay language classes you could attend after school?

Chua: We had Malay lessons at that time. As part of our regular curriculum, there was a subject called "national language" which was taught for two periods every week, this stopped after I went to senior middle school. It was when I attended junior middle school that I took "national language classes". For our generation, we were made to study grade one Malay in order to confirm our post, that is to confirm our teaching job.

Passion for Popular Culture

Interviewer: Can you tell us, among the topics that you and your schoolmates discussed, did it include books, songs, movies or other recreational activities that reflected the mass or popular culture?

Chua: Of course. During our secondary school days, movies from mainland China had an immense influence on us, we all watched Chinese movies or documentaries like *Cheng Feng Po Lang (Riding the Wind and the Waves)*, *Bing Shang Jie Mie (Girls on the Ice Track)* and *Nü Lan Wu Hao (Female Basketball Player Number 5)*. For our Teochew classmates, they enjoyed local performing arts like

Teochew opera. During social gatherings, some would even sing a few lines. In the early days, I was a big fan of Teochew opera and watched early Teochew movies such as *Su Liu Niang* (*Soh Lak Neo*) and *Chen San Wu Niang* (*Tan Sa Ngo Neo*) five times; in fact, it wasn't just Teochew opera that mesmerized me, I was also a fan of other local opera. Beijing opera films such as *The Yang Female Warriors*, *Wild Boar Forest* and Shaoxing opera *Dream of the Red Chamber* and *The Jade Hairpin* were some that I watched numerous times. Only after I started learning classical music, did my interests slowly veered towards that. We were all crazy about movies of these local opera. It can be said that we were deeply influenced by mainland China's culture, the songs we sang were also influenced by left-wing cultural and recreational activities. What kind of songs? Take for example the leftist students would often sing songs from movies like *Riding the Wind and the Waves* (Hums), I can still remember the song's melody. When I was young, we sang a lot of folk songs, my eldest brother was a huge influence. For instance, there was a popular song then which was later banned. "How carefree is it to be in the jungle and the field, oh my dear friends..." (Hums) It was actually no big deal, the song was banned because of the word "jungle" and we all thought it was absurd. Naturally, my eldest brother also taught some folk songs in school. There was an African folk song that affected us deeply, (Hums) "The lovely sunlight shines over our endearing hometown, this summer the black people are singing..." We were exposed to such songs, and these were the songs our teachers taught us.

Interviewer: Your family was not well off, how did you get to watch the movies or buy the records?

Chua: I was influenced by my brother when it came to listening to records. I could still afford to go to the movies as watching a film in the countryside cost less than a dollar. I would watch at Guohua Cinema (next to the old Kong Yiong High School). With less than a dollar, I could also get a ticket at Xingguang Cinema; there was also the open air cinema, these were the places I saw my movies. I would usually go with my elder brother or sister to the rural cinema which sold each ticket for a few cents. My family, or perhaps I should say most of the Chinese medium school students were influenced by Chinese movies, but of course, there were also some schoolmates who were not. As for other recreational activities, there were schoolmates who enjoyed playing the harmonica or the flute. They would bring their instruments, exchange opinions on the different styles of playing after class, explored around on their own and learnt from there. I was also influenced by my brother who was a music lover, he too bought some records.

Interviewer: Did you get to watch the movies after school? Or did you have to wait till evening or night time?

Chua: Usually, it was at night, but there were also shows in the day time. Besides the folk songs, I feel that the songs of Chinese movies were also well written as they were very evocative. These were not really Cultural Revolution songs. That was during the initial years of China's founding and the songs were very positive and reflected their ideals. Take for example, *"Riding the Wind and Waves"*, *"Girls of the Ice Track"* and *"Female Basketball Player Number 5"*, they reflected real ideals. I often talked to my uncle in Guangzhou, he felt that those were the golden years of Chinese film, compared to what we see today, they (those movies) were not so commercialised.

Interviewer: When you were in school, where did you get leisure reading materials? There probably weren't any libraries and you could not afford to buy too many books — so how did you get books to read?

Chua: My eldest brother had many books, but he was the serious and earnest kind, quite unlike me in my later days. Besides Chinese and Western literature (works of Western literature mainly included Chinese translations of novels by Ivan Turgenev, George Sand and other writers), I also read a lot of martial arts novel; which I borrowed from my classmates. We had a senior who was Hainanese, and goodness me, he had so many martial arts novels at home! I borrowed the books from him, one set after another.

Interviewer: Did you all like to read martial arts novels?

Chua: Yes, we were all reading and influencing each other. Martial arts novels were quite popular. Most of us read them, and the authors were Liang Yusheng and Jin Yong (also known as Louis Cha). Gu Long had yet to become well-known. Those with leftist inclinations read more of Liang Yusheng, but subsequently we also read Jin Yong's books.

Interviewer: At that time, besides martial arts novels, what other books did your classmates enjoy reading which became subjects of conversations?

Chua: In this respect, no. I think what we talked and discussed about mainly revolved around these martial arts novels.

Interviewer: Were there also entertainment magazines? Otherwise, how would you get information about the movies?

Chua: There were entertainment magazines, which can be divided into two types. Firstly, there was the China-style entertainment magazine, and secondly, those that were influenced by Taiwan. I really enjoyed reading them and collected some of them; it was a real pity that I threw them away for I had too many. One Hong Kong magazine that I really liked and had a very deep impression of, its title should be *Xin Zhong Hua* (*New China Magazine*), and there was also *Chang Cheng Hua Bao* (*Great Wall Pictorial*). Right, I forgot to mention, entertainment magazines from Hong Kong. Among my classmates, a majority of them watched movies by Shaw Brothers. In other words, we were divided into two camps: those who preferred "*Chang Feng Xin*" (this is short for three film companies; *Chang Cheng* (Great Wall Movie Enterprises Ltd.), *Feng Huang* (Phoenix Motion Picture Company) and *Xin Lian*) and this was our camp, and those who preferred movies produced by Shaw and Cathay. Take for example, I had watched movies by Chen Hou and Lin Dai, but did not really enjoy them. Honestly speaking, I felt that the movies by *Chang Feng Xin* were of really high standard, especially *Great Wall* and *Feng Huang*, and their actors were better too. The early day artistes such as Xia Meng and Shi Hui were both beautiful and great actresses. Xia Meng was the one Jin Yong fancied, I felt she had an air of elegance that neither Shaw's Lin Da, Le Di nor any others can match, her elegance was very much like Audrey Hepburn, and she acted very well in a lot of movies. *Chang Cheng* and *Feng Huang* had first class actors, for example veteran thespian Shi Lei who acted in *Liang Shang Jun Zi* and comedian Li Bing Hong. I always felt that Shaw's actors like Chen Hou and Zhao Lei were not very good at acting, and there was no any outstanding actress either. *Great Wall* and *Feng Huang*, on the other hand, had a better pool of talent. Amongst our classmates, there were some who preferred *Chang Feng Xin*, some preferred Shaw, and each camp remained steadfast in their support. As for movie magazines, they had *Nan Guo Dian Ying* and we had *Chang Cheng Dian Ying Hua Bao*. On top of that, *Xin Zhong Hua* and *Xing Fu* were both good magazines in which their content encompassed more than movie news but also included write-ups about China's customs, culture and traditions; the content was rich but also rather pro-leftist. Taiwan's pictorial magazine *Liang You* was pretty good too and I would occasionally read that.

Interviewer: There probably weren't many Taiwanese publications at that time? From what I understood, there were only more of them later; and that was probably after the Cultural Revolution.

Chua: You are right. In the early days, we were more exposed to materials from China and Hong Kong, later on, a lot of publications, from these two areas could not get into Singapore, for example the extreme leftist publications from

Hong Kong; that was when we started accepting those from Taiwan. Even when we were in primary school, we were deeply influenced by Hong Kong's children's magazines, for example *Er Tong Le Yuan* (*Children's Paradise*) and *Nan Yang Er Tong* (*Children of Nanyang*), there was also a very successful magazine… Yes, it was called *Little Friends*! They are not around anymore, what a pity. I had a very deep impression of *Little Friends*, at that time, I would even try the handicraft that was taught in the magazine. The magazine had an impact on many people, including those who eventually became writers.

Interviewer: Did you have classmates who went pursuing movie stars after school?

Chua: Yes. When Hong Kong artistes came to perform, I followed my elder sister to show support, there were actors who were inclined to the left, such as those from *Great Wall*, *Feng Huang* and also those who were inclined towards Shaw. In the 1960s, didn't the Movie Stars Arts Troupe come here to perform? They were already very pro-leftist by that time. Zhang Zheng was one of those who came and performed. I went to watch. North Korean troupes also came and performed shows like "*Kumgang San*", we saw that too. Basically, we were influenced through this avenues. At that time, even entertainment activities were split into distinct camps.

Interviewer: Did you watch Western films?

Chua: Occasionally, I did but comparatively fewer. This was another big mistake. Our command of English was bad because we lacked the exposure in this aspect. I was deeply influenced by my family, my siblings were all Chinese educated and saw very few Western movies.

Interviewer: In the rural cinema that you mentioned, did it screen Western films?

Chua: Yes, it did. The open air cinema also screened Western films.

Interviewer: Was the movie dubbed?

Chua: It was dubbed and had Chinese subtitles. I had very deep impression of an open air cinema in Charlton School's big field. That was the first time I saw Charlie Chaplin's silent film *The Great Dictator*. I fell in love with his films later on and saw other movies like *Modern Times*.

Interviewer: You probably had less opportunity to interact with English school students during your days at Sin Min High School? We interviewed some people who went to the cinema in the city and they said, both Chinese and English school students saw Western films together in the cinema. Opportunities like these were probably fewer in the village?

Chua: Very rare; and we seldom interacted with the English school students. Because of our financial situation, we did not dare to go watch a movie in town as we could not afford the tickets. We can put it this way: Chinese medium school students in the early days were generally poorer, they belonged to the poorer class; the English school students, however, came from a different environment. PAP's policies worked well because they saw this point — you have to address the poverty problem and raise living standards in the villages. As your horizon widened and you interacted with them (English school students), you will realize a lot of things were not what you had imagined them to be. As a Chinese school student of the early days, we were indeed partial in our judgment, as if we had voluntarily trapped ourselves in some stereotypical mindset. We were seldom exposed to and did not have the opportunity to interact with Western culture. In fact, some Chinese schools even sub-consciously neglected English language and deliberately not learn it well. I was an example. That was a mistake, we should have mastered the language.

Interviewer: In the 50s, there was a social movement known as the "Anti-Yellow Culture Campaign", did you hear about it in school?

Chua: Yes, I heard about the "Anti-Yellow Culture Campaign". That was the kind of environment we were living in.

Interviewer: What did the concept of Anti-Yellow Movement and the Yellow Culture refer to?

Chua: Yellow culture meant degeneration. Even movies by Shaw were thought to be "yellow" (i.e. unhealthy, almost pornographic). Sexy stars like Diana Chang Chung Wen (described as "the most beautiful animal" then) were thought to be unhealthy and decadent. The concept also extended to movies and books. For books, it would be those that described sexual scenes… come to think about it now, using our standards today, those were nothing. Take for example Yao Zi, he was a great writer, but his novels like *The Temptation of Coffee* was too daring and labelled as a "yellow" novel. But if you read it today, that was nothing.

Part III

Appendix

THE SINGAPORE CHINESE MIDDLE SCHOOL STUDENTS' UNION
A LOST ECHO OF AN ERA

Lim Chin Joo

Translated by Melissa Gay

Introduction

Formed in 1955, the Singapore Chinese Middle School Students' Union (SCMSSU) was the biggest in its set-up and greatest in its impact amongst the Chinese school students' organisations in the history of Singapore and Malaysia. Born and later destroyed amidst the stormy turmoil of its time, documented historical sources about the SCMSSU have not survived. Based on materials I have at hand as well as personal memories, I shall endeavour to piece together my fragmented memories of the SCMSSU in hope that historical sources may speak for themselves.

Historical Background and the Formation Process of the SCMSSU

After World War II, the tides of social and political movement rose and surged to its height in Singapore, bringing about the emergence of various anti-colonial organisations. In 1948, the colonial government imposed the Emergency Regulations Ordinance which extensively crippled the operations of the anti-colonial movement. Student activists were arrested and put under indefinite detention without trial, while the self-help groups and other organisations in different schools were disbanded. The May 13 Incident in 1954 broke this blockade down. Chinese middle school students came to the forefront by opposing military conscription imposed by the colonial government and questioning the legitimacy of colonial rule. Having in common the goal of ending colonialism and achieving independence, various organisations and groupings re-emerged.

After the May 13 Incident, the SCMSSU was conceived by the students during their camp-in in the Chinese High School beginning 2 June 1954. At a tea-party in honour of the Queen's Counsel D.N. Pritt who had come over to act as the defence counsel for the students arrested on May 13, the formation of the SCMSSU was announced for the first time by the "Singapore Chinese Middle Schools Students' National Service Exemption Delegation" (the Exemption Delegation). The Prep. Committee appointed Lee Kuan Yew and Tann Wee Tiong as legal advisors and presented the application for registration in October of the same year. On 15 January 1955, the Registry of Societies sent a letter to Lee, refusing registration of the SCMSSU on the ground that "this organisation will be detrimental to the public welfare and good order of the country."

The Prep. Committee was not happy with the reply and sought to reason strenuously through Lee Kuan Yew, but their appeal was rejected once more instead. Thus, the Exemption Delegation initiated a boycott of classes by the students on 30 March. Nearly ten thousand students from seven male and female Chinese middle schools participated in this action. At the same time, the Prep. Committee released a statement announcing their intention to gather en masse in front of the Governor's Residence on 2 April when the general elections under the Rendel Constitution would be held. The government immediately declared that it was not prepared to receive any delegation. The Ministry of Education then called up all the principals and instructed them to ask the students to refrain from demonstrating and presenting their petition. The Prep. Committee then decided to present a written petition to the Governor through the schools' management Boards.

The Pan-Malayan Students' Federation sent a letter to the Governor as well, requesting that the SCMSSU be allowed registration. Meanwhile, the general elections saw the victory of the Labour Front which in advocating a "pro-people and pro-workers" stance, went on to form the government. The Labour Front government decided to allow registration of the SCMSSU on the condition that the SCMSSU's constitution must stipulate explicitly that it would not be involved in any activity of a political nature. The Prep. Committee felt that this condition was too vague, and that it was a trap laid out for them, such that the Registry of Societies could easily find excuses to harass the union in future. Thus, with Lee Kuan Yew leading them as their legal advisor, the Prep. Committee met with the Minister for Education, Chew Swee Kee, several times, but these meetings proved to be futile. At one point, the Prep. Committee counter-proposed that the constitution would explicitly "forbid the conduct of any activity against its objectives and aims". This counter-proposal was rejected. After many rounds of contestation, the Prep. Committee finally agreed to provide in the SCMSSU's constitution that there was to be "no direct or indirect involvement in political activities and strikes."[1]

The SCMSSU was officially registered on 7 October 1955.[2] When the news spread, schools responded enthusiastically with firecrackers, gongs and drums, and it can be said that they were overwhelmed with joy.

In order to herald the birth of the SCMSSU, the Prep. Committee published a special booklet entitled "The Founding of the SCMSSU", complete with various illustrations. A union logo was also decided upon. As for the design of the union's flag and the drafting of the union's anthem, there was no final decision despite discussion on these issues.

The Organisational Structure of the SCMSSU

The constitution of the SCMSSU stipulated that each school would elect a number of representatives in proportion to the number of its students registered as union members to form the School Representatives' Assembly from which the Central Supervisory Committee and Central Executive Committee would be selected. The Central Executive Committee was the core of the leadership of the SCMSSU, formulating the guiding principles and policies for the SCMSSU's activities. Apart from the posts of the President and the Vice-President, there were other divisions such as the Secretariat, the Treasury, Organisation Matters, Welfare, Academic, Recreation and General Affairs in the Executive Committee. The President and the Heads of the various divisions formed the Standing Committee, with a separate Central Steering Committee for Publicity. In every [member] school, the SCMSSU established a [union] branch, which was led by a School General Affairs Committee. In turn, every school's General Affairs Committee was responsible to the Organisation Matters Division in the Central Executive Committee, and the various other sections [of the school union branches] coordinated their work with the respective corresponding divisions in the Central Executive Committee.

As soon as the union was officially registered, the Prep. Committee completed the registration of over nine thousand members and the election of school

---

[1] *Sin Pao* 1-11-1956 page 4.
[2] Interviewee had earlier mentioned that the SCMSSU was set up on 6 October 1955 (see page 95). He later clarified by making the distinction that 6 October was the day when the government approved of SCMSSU's registration, while the student today received the news of its official status on 7 October.

representatives within the span of two to three weeks. The first meeting of the School Representatives' Assembly was held in the newly-built Hokkien Huay Kuan at Telok Ayer. The meeting elected the members of the Supervisory Committee and the Executive Committee, followed by the election of office-bearers. Many members of the Exemption Delegation and the Protection of Chinese Education Committee were "pioneers" who had pushed for the creation of the SCMSSU, but they did not join the leadership of the SCMSSU because they were graduating in 1955 and would be entering Nanyang University (Nantah) the following year. Soon Loh Boon was a talented and widely-recognised leader. He was also a central figure in the student movement at that time. Although he would graduate from Chinese High at the end of 1955 and enter Nantah in 1956, he nevertheless stayed behind to lead the SCMSSU. The union's constitution allowed school-leavers to retain their membership for two years.

List of SCMSSU's Office-bearers

The First Executive and Supervisory Committees:

President: Soon Loh Boon, Vice-Presidents: Li Shuhui, Wu Youfa, Ong Gwo Chyun. Head of the Secretariat: Zheng Yushu. Vice-heads: Tan Kok Chiang, Chen Zaicong. Head of the Organisation Matters Division: Chen Ziquan, Vice-heads: Mo Naijiang, Chi Yifen. Head of the Mutual Aid Division: Liu Chunji, Vice-heads: Cai Shijun, Lin Delai. Head of the Academic Division: Lim Chin Joo, Vice-heads: Feng Yihua, Loh Miaw Ping. Head of the Treasury: Xue Jituan, Vice-heads: Chen Qingji, Zheng Minna. Head of the Recreation Division: Lin Yunjie, Vice-heads: Xu Tongying, Chen Ruijian. Head of the General Affairs Division: Chen Ruihua, Vice-heads: Chen Miaohua, Chen Bijuan. Executive Committee members: Xu Shengwan, Chen Yaping, Huang Pingqing, Yang Baozhu, Zhang Yunteng, Zeng Meirong, Su Libin, Huang Cuifang, Cai Xiushan, Huang Qingxin, He Ziai, Huang Rou'an. Alternate members of the Executive Committee: Lin Chunmei, Zhang Guoliang, Huang Changwen, Li Yongji, Sun Guangjing, Jiang Shugui. Head of the Supervisory Committee: Fu Sunmin. Vice-heads: Li Weizhen, Huang Baofeng. Secretary: Chen Shicong. Auditors: Huang Sumei, Zeng Yunying, Liu Jinlong. Alternate members of the Supervisory Committee: Su Bingfa, Lu Hongzhang.

The Premises of the SCMSSU

While seeking the registration of the union, the Prep. Committee frequently held meetings and activities on the premises of the Arts Research Association at Cairnhill

Road. After the SCMSSU was permitted to be registered as a society, it was decided to house the union at Tanjong Katong, at 14 Wilkinson Road, which was the property of the former head of the Chung Cheng High School Management Board, Lim Soo Gan. Lim himself lived next door. I could not remember if we paid him rent. The union's premises was not only the centre for our activities, to some of us, it was also our home. The building was built on stilts above the ground and the space beneath the building was where we spent our nights together. Although it was far from Chinese High, we travelled to and fro on bus number 15 without feeling tired.

Inauguration of the SCMSSU

The Prep. Committee had originally planned to hold the inaugural meeting of the SCMSSU on 23 October at Happy World Stadium. However, the date happened to coincide with the Singapore Traction Company bus workers' island-wide strike which would make transport a problem for the students. Furthermore, the issue of the police's permission for the inaugural meeting was also delayed by a few days. Eventually the date for the inauguration was changed to 30 October, and the venue was Happy World Stadium along Geylang Road.

Other than approximately 10,000 SCMSSU members, those in attendance at the inaugural meeting included teachers, parents, members of the public and representatives of other student bodies. The chairperson of the meeting, Feng Yihua declared in a solemn and resolute voice, "Now, I hereby declare that the SCMSSU has been successfully established!" She went on to say, "The birth of the SCMSSU represents a glorious chapter in the history of the Malayan student movement. We are honoured by the presence of everyone here today and on behalf of the SCMSSU, I pay our utmost respect to everyone present. In the course of its birth, the SCMSSU suffered a great deal in the hands of those who harbour evil motives, but this has not disheartened us. We shall stand at the frontlines in protection of Chinese education and we will fight for ethnic education. We will eradicate completely 'yellow culture' and promote healthy recreation. In line with what we share in common with various races, we will strive to attain equal treatment for vernacular education from the Labour Front government. Finally, let us cheer out loud and clear: Long live the SCMSSU, long live the unity among students from all races in Malaya!"[3]

Other speakers included representatives from the Pan-Malayan Students' Federation, the Pan-Malayan Peninsula Malay Students' Federation, the Kuala Lumpur Technical College, the Singapore-Malay Students' Alliance and the Singapore Chinese Middle Schools Parents' Association. The legal advisor of

---

[3] *Sin Pao*, 1-11-1956, page 4.

SCMSSU, Lee Kuan Yew, spoke in Chinese, "Fellow students fought through thick and thin for the founding of the SCMSSU. I hope that everyone will love and nurture it so that it may truly become a giant." He urged the students to love and defend Malaya, and to banish racial hatred and segregation so as to form a big family together. Finally, Lee led the students in a loud cheer: Long live an independent Malaya! Long live the SCMSSU!

In his speech, President Soon Loh Boon declared that the SCMSSU was committed to fight for a peaceful and stable environment for the students so that they can improve their studies. The SCMSSU would focus on implementing the following: cultivating the right attitude towards learning, integrating what was learnt in and beyond classrooms, with a special emphasis on enhancing students' interest in current affairs, as well as strengthening the unity among different ethnic groups.

The members of the First Supervisory and Executive Committees then went through the oath-taking ceremony. The Principal of Chung Cheng High School, Chuang Chu Lin and the Dean (Administration) of the Chinese High, Huang Fangkui, were witnesses to the ceremony. Principal Chuang said in his speech, "The formation of the SCMSSU is testimony to the unity of the Chinese middle school students. I hope that this will contribute to the unity among various communities. As mentioned in its constitution, the SCMSSU's most important task ahead is to unite students of different races. The image of a book in the union's logo signifies learning. From now on, teachers ought to do their best to teach and students ought to learn to the best of their abilities so as to improve their standards. Many countries experience shortages of talented people after attaining national independence. Government departments would need specialised talent to run. In all democratic countries, it is the specialists or experts who dominate the society. Malaya will soon be independent. For the talent the country needs, we place our hope on all of you."

Message by Dean Huang Fangkui

At the inaugural meeting, the Dean Huang Fangkui offered the following incisive advice:

"Firstly, I hope that the SCMSSU will adhere to its spirit of independence. The SCMSSU has unparalleled strength; well-wishers would assist it, but evil forces would like to make use of it. The SCMSSU should therefore remain vigilant at all times. The May Fourth movement in China was a glorious deed on the part of the students in China. Unfortunately, it was not spared from partisan politics. The SCMSSU should henceforth adhere to its four basic guiding principles. Its paramount principle ought to be the pursuit of truth. Whatever it does would have to be consistent with this principle. Secondly, I hope that all political parties will bear in mind the interests of the students. The members of SCMSSU are students, and students must be given a conducive environment to concentrate on their studies. Thirdly, I hope that the present government will fulfill its promises relating to education. Talking about education, one is bound to have a lot of grievances to air. However, let us treat the past as experience. Since the Labour Front government came into power, it has made many promises on education, the most important one being equality in education. I hope that this promise will be honoured so that each ethnic group can develop its education in accordance with its own cultural ethos.

Some people say that the communists have infiltrated the Chinese schools. This is simply unfounded. It seems that some people have seriously misunderstood the Chinese schools' students, and the root cause lies with the colonial education policy. Even if we are to concede that there are a few students who like to talk about communism, the phenomenon is simply a product of modern society and not something that falls from the sky. Furthermore, there are countries which have recognised the Communist Party as legitimate. I therefore hope that the government will look at the Chinese school students in a new light.

Schools and society are now practically two separate worlds. What the students have learnt as truths in school are debunked as lies in the real world. Students will naturally become disillusioned and would attempt to find their own way out.

The government ought to realise that young people are the country's backbone in the future. No country in the world can afford not to place great importance on the education of its youth. It will be a tragic mistake and an obstacle to nation-building if the government maintains its prejudices against the students and treats them as outlaws. I hope that the government will correct its perception and only then can it formulate a fair policy on education."[4]

The Guiding Principles for SCMSSU's Tasks Ahead: Excelling in Studies and Strengthening Unity

The SCMSSU's Executive Committee formulated the guiding principles for the year's activities, setting the theme as "Excelling in Studies and Strengthening Unity".

---

[4] *Nanyang Siang Pau*, 31-10-1956, page 5.

The Standing Committee then proceeded to divide the year's work into three phases. The first phase would start in February, with "Drumming up Enthusiasm for Learning" as the core activity. The theme of the second phase was "Consolidating the Results of Learning and Enriching the Content of Study", and it started after the term examinations. The core work of the third phase was designated as "Enriching Study Life and Improving the Results of Learning". It started in July and lasted for six months, until the final exams at the end of the year.

In order to fulfill its objectives as well as the declared guiding principles for its tasks ahead, the SCMSSU led students all over the country in carrying out a series of meaningful programmes during the course of its short existence.

I. *Publicity Week to Drum Up Enthusiasm for Learning*

A Publicity Week was held in various schools, with forums involving teachers and students, topical lectures by teachers, the publication of wall posters and bulletin board news, as well as various kinds of competitions to drum up enthusiasm for learning among students and build a sound perspective on learning. Various schools held forums to examine the reasons behind the lacklustre learning atmosphere in the past. The conclusions were: (1) the government's bias against Chinese education, over-crowded classrooms, inadequate teaching staff and other facilities; (2) prior to the formation of the SCMSSU, the students did not have their own organisation. As a result, they failed to cultivate the habit of staying focused on their studies and were lacking in the spirit of mutual help.

During the forums, Huang Fangkui, the Dean (Administration) of Chinese High, pointed out that students should help one another, persevere and engage in self-directed learning; Chen Weijing of Chung Hwa High School advised students to be more observant and comparative. In response to requests from the Academic Division of the SCMSSU, teachers from the Chung Cheng High School produced broadcasts on special topics for students during their breaks. For example, Mr Liu Yuji did a broadcast lecture on "Why We Should Pay Attention to Current Affairs", Mr Chen Yizheng spoke on "How to Study Mathematics" and Mr Zhang Shoushi spoke on "Some Issues in Learning Languages". These lectures were warmly received by the students.[5]

After the "Publicity Week for Learning", an excellent and positive atmosphere of learning began to prevail in various middle schools. Students' passion for knowledge ran high. All this was unprecedented. Some classes even laid down the

---

[5] *Sin Pao*, 22-3-1956, page 4.

following conventions for themselves: (1) Hand in homework on time; (2) No cheating; (3) Be attentive during lessons.

Many students stayed behind in schools after classes. They grouped themselves into small clusters to revise their homework together either in the classrooms or under the shelter of the trees.

II. *Cadres' Training Classes*

The Standing Committee regularly reviewed the work of every stage and came up with a summary of the work done. The Summary Report for the first stage pointed out that ever since the "Drumming up Enthusiasm for Learning" campaign, the students' study mood was relatively calm and settled, and there was a relative improvement in their morale. There was also a great improvement in teacher-student relations, and the group-study approach was popular with students. In all these changes, the [union] cadres in the various schools played a very big part. Besides leading various activities, they also continuously spotted and groomed new cadres. The Report also pointed out the following flaws: (1) Some cadres were lacking in enthusiasm and could not grasp the thrust of the task to be done, causing difficulties in coordination amongst the various sections; (2) Cadres were not competent enough and lacked in creativity; (3) Cadres lacked understanding of the contemporary political situation which affected their analytical ability and judgement on problems in their work.[6]

In order to improve the working capacity of the cadres, the Standing Committee held a Cadres' Training Class in April at the union's premises, with participants selected from various schools. The lessons included current affairs, work reports, work methods and the cultivation of one's outlook on life. Instructors were senior students who were accomplished in their studies, exemplary in their behaviour and possessed strong leadership ability. After assembling for training at the SCMSSU, the cadres returned to their schools and further held cadres' training classes within their schools. This greatly increased the cadres' morale, corrected bad work attitudes, as well as cultivated the enthusiasm and capabilities of the cadres.

III. *Group Excursions, Spring Camps, Summer Camps*

On New Year's Day of 1956, the SCMSSU organised a group excursion. Approximately a thousand students took a railway trip to Johor Bahru, had a picnic in the Sultan Park and participated in cultural performances. The exciting

---

[6] *Sin Pao*, 19-4-1956, page 4.

performances and high level of discipline displayed were striking and left a deep impression.

The SCMSSU Standing Committee also held a Spring Camp after the term examinations at the Zhang Jinling Villa in Pasir Ris. Several large buses transported students from different locations to assemble at the Villa. Two to three days of collective life quickly fired up many young students, filled them with enthusiasm, expanded their horizons and let them experience the (collective) power of being in a group. They were thus awakened. In June, the various branches of the SCMSSU jointly held another Summer Camp.

IV. *Commemorating International Women's Day and the March 30 Student Protest*

On International Women's Day (8 March) of 1956, the SCMSSU held a grand commemorative event at the Happy World Stadium, with approximately 3,000 male and female students attending the event. In his speech, President Soon Loh Boon reprimanded the police authorities for obstructing the event by imposing many restrictions. He strongly criticised the colonial government for interfering with and standing in the way of interaction between students of different races and linguistic backgrounds.

In order to commemorate the mass boycott of classes by all Chinese middle school students which took place on 30 March 1955, after the colonial government refused to allow registration of the SCMSSU, a commemorative assembly was held by the union's cadres on 31 March 1956 at the Hokkien Huay Kuan. The commemorative assembly described the mass boycott of 30 March 1955 as a glorious milestone in the history of the Malayan student movement. This historical move came through a series of repression in the colonial era and paved the way for the founding of the SCMSSU. The SCMSSU's Central Steering Committee for Publicity released a bulletin for the celebration, as well as an open letter to fellow students, calling upon them to collectively strive and realise the guiding principle of "Strengthening Unity and Excelling in Studies".[7]

V. *The Commemoration of May 13 by Various Schools*

"We commemorate May 13 because we wish to uphold the courageous spirit in the face of the violence perpetrated by the colonial authorities in this incident! Uphold the spirit of May 13, and Chinese schools will live forever; uphold

---

[7] *Sin Pao*, 31-3-1956, page 3.

the spirit of May 13, only then can we attain independence and eradicate colonialism; the spirit of May 13 means unity and courage in the face of violence." This was what a student passionately and fervently spoke about at the "May 13 Commemorative Assembly" held by students of Chinese High.

The students of six other middle schools held separate commemorative meetings and passed the following resolutions: (1) Designating May 13 as the day of commemoration for Chinese school students; (2) Only in a truly independent Malaya do we, as Malayan citizens, have the duty to undertake national service; (3) The assembly requests that the SCMSSU present a memorandum to the forthcoming Afro-Asian Students' Conference and a complaint about the plight of students under colonial rule; (4) Authorising the SCMSSU to establish amicable relations with Asian and African middle school students; (5) The assembly requests that the government conducts an open trial of fellow student Lim Woon Kiat and all other innocent students who are under detention.[8]

At the same time, the SCMSSU also held a "May 13 Historical Materials Exhibition" at its premises. Consisting of three parts in all, the exhibition displayed historical materials starting from the declaration of the National Service Ordinance on 1 May 1954 to the bloodshed of the May 13 Incident and the camp-in at Chinese High on 2 June 1954. The exhibited materials included newspaper clippings on the events leading up to the formation of the SCMSSU and all that it had gone through prior to its formation. There were also pictures written statements, proclamations, bulletin board publication, blood-stained clothes, songs, comics, letters of support from members of the public, signed letters from parents, as well as telegrams from the following groups: International Union of Students, Overseas Malayan Students in Indonesia and Overseas Chinese Tuition Students in Guangdong etc., as well as signatures of the first SCMSSU Supervisory and Executive Committee members and etc.

VI. *The Debate: Malaya as our Country*

With the establishment of the People's Republic of China, quite a number of students chose to return to mainland China for their higher education, especially during the period of the May 13 Incident. However, that was actually a one-way trip. The possibility of their return to Malaya after graduation was extremely slim. In order to cultivate a Malayan identity, as well as to encourage young people to stay behind and join in the anti-colonial and independence movement, the SCMSSU held a debate at its premises in May 1956. The topic was "Malaya is Our Country"; participants were union cadres from various schools. Soon Loh Boon said in his

---

[8] *Sin Pao*, 15-5-1956, page 4.

opening speech, "The focus of the second stage of SCMSSU's work is enriching the content of learning. Presently we have to shoulder the duty of safeguarding truth and justice. We need therefore to build up the capability of our leaders to express themselves, build up their knowledge, train their analytical ability, as well as enhance their ability to exercise judgment, so that when we want to advocate the truth, we can provide clear justifications. All debates aimed at promoting the correct viewpoints on any issue are constructive activities. As Malaya is on its way to be independent, the issue of dual citizenship needs to be resolved."[9]

VII. *A Letter to Fellow Students: Strive to Do Well in the Term Examinations*

In May, the Academic Division issued a "Letter to Fellow Students":

"In response to the call of 'Consolidating the Outcomes of Learning, Enriching the Content of Study' which underpinned the SCMSSU's second stage of core activities, fellow students have embarked upon the passionate acquisition of knowledge in various fields, including current affairs. The essence of the 'Excel in Studies' campaign is to establish the right atmosphere for learning and to promote the integration of classroom and extracurricular learning. Thus, we place great importance on the upcoming term examinations, because these examination results will affect our fellow students' chances of academic promotion. In the same vein as all other acts of justice, this campaign of 'Excel in Studies', we want to bring out fully our fellow students' excellent qualities of unity, mutual aid and fraternal love. Thus, we promoted the approach of group-study, and from this year, the practice of group-study has already become widespread. In order to attain good results in the coming term examinations, we call upon fellow students to have a good understanding of the nature of group-study, to be resolute in your will, to bravely and enthusiastically strengthen the practice of group-study, as well as to popularise it even further, so as to go a step closer to attaining good results in the coming term examinations. There is something which we have to point out, that in the March examinations this year, a handful of teachers who did not understand the SCMSSU and/or who were hostile towards the SCMSSU tried to use the examinations to obstruct the 'Excel in Studies' campaign, for instance, by raising the standard of the test papers in an unreasonable manner, which caused fellow students to do badly and thus to lose faith in learning. However, the efforts of this group of people have in fact proven to be futile. They have not only failed in their efforts but also betrayed their true colours. Thus, we would want to remind them that the

---

[9] *Sin Pao*, 10-5-1956, page 4.

'Excel in Studies' campaign is in the best interests of all students in Singapore. Any schemes to disrupt this campaign will not only be futile but will also be condemned by all. We sincerely call upon our respected and beloved teachers to cooperate with us fully to enable fellow students to attain good results in the term examinations, and to be one step nearer to successfully carrying out the 'Excel in Studies' campaign."[10]

Students from various schools responded to the call of the SCMSSU and consequently showed an improvement in their mid-year examinations across the board. In order to help fellow students to achieve better results in their studies, the Academic Division encouraged the union branches to conduct tuition classes for various subjects during the school holidays, with students from senior classes and/or those with excellent academic results in charge as teachers. Students from various schools signed up enthusiastically for these classes.

VIII. *External Relations: The Pan-Malayan Students' Cultural Festival and the Afro-Asian Students' Conference*

Ever since it was formed, the SCMSSU was pro-active in strengthening its interactions and unity with students from various ethnic groups in the whole of Malaya. At the end of 1955, the SCMSSU became a member of the Pan-Malayan Students' Federation and sent a large delegation to Kuala Lumpur to participate in the Pan-Malayan Students' Cultural Festival. The SCMSSU also cooperated with the Pan-Malayan Students' Federation in publishing a Chinese edition of the periodical, the *Malayan Student*.

The Afro-Asian Students' Conference was held in June 1956 at Bandung. The SCMSSU was invited to send an observers delegation. It was an invitation which they took up, with Soon Loh Boon leading the delegation in its attendance. The SCMSSU presented a memorandum to the Conference, which described the plight of the Chinese schools' students in Singapore, their struggle in the face of oppression by the colonial government and the pursuit of equal treatment for vernacular education.

IX. *Protesting Against the Federation Government's Travel Restrictions*

In June 1956, the Malayan Government suddenly invoked the Emergency Regulations Ordinance to restrict students from Chinese High, Chung Cheng,

---

[10] *Sin Pao*, 22-5-1956, page 1.

Nan Chiau and Chung Hwa middle schools from travelling in groups to Malaya, unless they first applied for permission from the Malayan state in question. Even the number of people allowed to travel as a group was restricted.

On 15 June, several hundred students from the four schools held a general meeting at the SCMSSU's premises and protested against the unreasonable measures taken by the Malayan government. After the meeting, the SCMSSU released a statement denouncing the Malayan government for blaming the SCMSSU for staging "undesirable performances at the 1955 Pan-Malayan Students' Cultural Festival and also for alleging that the SCMSSU group outing to Johor Bahru on New Year's Day of 1956 was a "demonstration of strength". The statement pointed out that the colonial authorities were brazenly obstructing the interaction among students of all races and expressed deep concern that the unity among students of different races was being undermined by the colonial rule.[11]

X. *The Wholehearted Support of SCMSSU for the 1956 Merdeka Talks*

Ever since the Labour Front Government came into power, the Chief Minister, David Marshall, felt deeply about the limitations of the Rendel Constitution and clashed a few times with the Governor, which led the Legislative Assembly to resolve to conduct negotiations with the Colonial Office in the United Kingdom. On 18 March 1956, the Cultural Association of Singapore held a rally at the Badminton Hall to show support of the various cultural organisations for the negotiations. Several thousand students attended the rally in response to a call by the SCMSSU for students' support. At the rally, SCMSSU President Soon Loh Boon strongly denounced colonialism and urged fellow students to go to the old Kallang Airport after the rally to join the All-Singapore Mass Rally for Independence and to show the visiting colonial officials present at the rally the wish of the people for independence.

As arranged by Lim Chin Siong pursuant to SCMSSU's request, representatives from the SCMSSU paid a visit to David Marshall's official residence at Coleman Street before the Merdeka Delegation left for their mission to London, in order to express the support of all the Chinese school students in Singapore for the delegation. During the meeting, the SCMSSU representatives offered to mobilise students to send off Marshall and the other delegates at the airport. Marshall was grateful for the students' support but indicated that it was unnecessary for the students to send off the delegation.

---

[11] *Sin Pao*, 16-6-1956, page 1.

From its inception, apart from its participation in the Mass Rally for Independence, the SCMSSU did not involve itself with any political parties or participate in any political activities.

On the Eve of the Storm

During the 1956 constitutional talks, the Colonial Office adopted a hardline approach and was utterly insincere. The collapse of the talks and the resignation of David Marshall were welcomed by the British, as well as by the right-wing elements in the Singapore delegation. It was clear from subsequent developments that the British was determined to destroy the left-wing forces in Singapore first, and then make arrangements to transfer power to people approved by them.

Well before the departure of the Merdeka Delegation, there were already signs of the coming storm. In April 1956, colonial government officials used the excuse of "poor health" to revoke the registration of eight teachers from Chinese schools. This drew dissatisfaction and protests from the school management boards, teachers and students. It was obvious that the colonial officials in Singapore were working with the Colonial Office in London in the hope of stirring something up.

On 18 September, the Singapore Women's Federation and the Brass Gong Musical Society were dissolved by the government. The government also detained Lin Zhenguo of the Singapore Farmers' Association, Chen Mong Hock of the Singapore Women's Federation, Chen Guangfeng and Chen Yuxing of the Singapore Primary Schools' Teachers' Union, as well as Peng Zhuishang and Chen Menghui of Chung Cheng High School under the Banishment Ordinance. On 22 September, approximately 1,200 cadres held a meeting at the SCMSSU to discuss these latest suppressions. Everyone had the same sense of foreboding about the frenzied crackdown that was to come.

Dissolution of the SCMSSU

Indeed, at noon on 24 September, the government announced its decision to dissolve the SCMSSU via a radio broadcast. At that time, those of us who used to stay overnight at the SCMSSU premises had just returned from schools and were resting in the quarters at the back. When we heard the news, we were completely dumbfounded and became so confused as not to know what to do. At that particular moment, we did not seem to see any government official or the police around yet and it did not occur to us that we should move away some of our documents and funds; it would have been very easy to do so through the side gate into our neighbor, Lim Soo Gan's house. Not long after, officials from the Official Assignee arrived with a written notice to officially seal off the premises. Then came President Soon Loh Boon together with legal advisor Tann Wee Tiong, followed by the government officials. We watched helplessly as they began to take away everything, including funds, documents, tables, chairs, and even the portraits of Sun Yat-sen and Lu Xun from the wall. The next day, they went to the union's branch offices in Chinese High and Chung Cheng to remove everything there.

The government soon came out with a statement accusing the SCMSSU of violating the stipulation of "no involvement in politics" and of actively participating in political demonstrations with other organisations aligned with the Communist front. Such an accusation was completely absurd. Although the government followed up with a lengthy "White Paper on the Dissolution of Singapore Chinese Middle Schools Student Union (SCMSSU)", it failed to produce any evidence to prove that the SCMSSU had ever "organised and participated in political demonstrations". The SCMSSU participated only once in an activity of a political nature, which was the rally in March to support the Merdeka Delegation organised by all the political parties and civil organisations. It must be noted that the Minister for Education had once openly acknowleged that students' participation in the independence movement could not be regarded as involvement in politics. Whatever the SCMSSU did during its short life span was conducted openly and can be listed in full detail, there should not be any cover-ups, distortion or fabrication.

The White Paper identified the SCMSSU as a Communist front organisation pursuing policies of the Communist front. However, other than disclosing that two or three SCMSSU officials were found to be in possession of documents distributed by the Malayan Communist Party (MCP), the White Paper failed to explain categorically the kind of purported relationship between the SCMSSU and the MCP, or as to how the SCMSSU followed MCP policies. The White Paper also reproduced a great amount of materials written by communists on the learning or study of Communism with a view to casting aspersion on SCMSSU's learning campaign. It was an obvious exercise to find an excuse for dissolving the SCMSSU.

The Formation of the "Anti-Persecution Delegation"

President Soon Loh Boon gathered all the members of the Supervisory and Executive Committees that very night for an emergency meeting at Chinese High. Thereafter, Soon Loh Boon informed the press reporters that he would instruct the union's legal advisers Lee Kuan Yew and Tann Wee Tiong to appeal against the de-registration of the SCMSSU. He called upon fellow students to remain calm and to continue to return to schools for classes pending further development of the situation. Soon also indicated that he would send a telegram to the SCMSSU's former legal adviser, D.N. Pritt, to inform him of all that had happened so far.

That night, the People's Action Party (PAP) also released a statement to condemn the Labour Front government for destroying the SCMSSU before it could mature. The statement called upon the government to reverse its policies henceforth or else it would soon be isolated from the people whom it wished to represent.

The next day students from seven Chinese middle schools in Singapore held a series of meetings and elected representatives to form the "Committee of Singapore Chinese Middle Schools Students for the Protection of Human Rights and the Restoration of Registration of the SCMSSU" (abbreviated as the "Anti-Persecution Delegation" or the "Delegation"). The members were: Ong Gwo Chyun, Chen Zaicong, Chen Yaping, Chen Ruijian, Su Libin, Sun Guangjing, Huang Changwen, Cen Ruihua, Cai Shijun, Low Miaw Ping, Lin Chunmei, Chi Yifen, Zheng Yushu, Lim Chin Joo, Li Weizhen, Chen Qingji, Mo Naijiang, Su Bingfa, Liu Chunji, Zhang Guoliang, Wu Youfa, Zhang Yunteng, Cai Xiushan, Huang Qingxin, Lin Delai, Chen Miaohua, Chen Bijuan, Jiang Shugui, Zeng Meirong, Huang Rou'an, Zheng Minna, He Ziyuan, Zeng Yunying, Huang Cuifang, Yang Wanqing, Jiang Jingcai, Chen Hanquan, Xu Shengwan, Li Yongji, Yang Baozhu.[12]

The students had originally planned a camp-in within their school campuses from 25 September to protest against the government's dissolution of the SCMSSU. However, in view of the warning given by the Minister for Education to the Principal of the Chinese High School, Cheng An Lun, and the Principal of Chung Cheng High School, Chuang Chu Lin, that further action by the students would lead to the closure of the schools by the government, the "Anti-Persecution Delegation" decided after due deliberation to accept the advice of the schools and withhold action.

More Students Arrested

On 1 October, after attending a meeting held by the Delegation at the premises of the Arts Research Association at Cairnhill Road, Soon Loh Boon was forcibly taken away near the Pavilion Cinema at Tanglin (Orchard Road) by plain-clothes

---

[12] *Nanyang Siang Pau*, 26-9-1956, page 5.

policemen. The news of Soon's arrest spread and white terror loomed over all schools in Singapore.

Very soon the Delegation was quickly informed by their legal advisors that the Ministerial Meeting had outright rejected the appeal against the dissolution of the SCMSSU. On 8 October, the students in all the Chinese middle schools in Singapore held general meetings to protest against the arrest of Soon Loh Boon, as well as to demand the government to set up a public inquiry investigating the charges laid by the government against the SCMSSU.

Upon arrival at the Chinese High School for classes in the morning of 11 October, a fellow student who was my room mate at a rented room at Keng Lee Road came running to me to tell me that the police had turned up at our place the previous night to look for me. Clearly, the police had moved out last night to conduct mass arrests. Many students managed to evade arrest, but those who were unfortunate enough to be taken away included Zheng Youling, Zhang Guoliang, Loh Miaw Ping and She Wentong. Then came the news that the Ministry of Education had announced the sacking of two teachers and the expulsion of one hundred and forty-two students from various schools. I was on the list.

Obviously the students had been driven to the wall. The Anti-Persecution Delegation had no choice but to organise a camp-in at Chinese High and Chung Cheng from that very day (11 October). Those assembled at Chinese High included fellow students from Nanyang Girls', Nan Hwa, Nan Chiau, Tuan Mong and etc. Besides students from Chung Cheng (Main) and Chung Cheng (Branch), those who assembled at the campus of Chung Cheng (Main) included fellow students from Chung Hwa and Yock Eng. Altogether about 8,000 students in total gathered at both schools. Most of the members of the Delegation were at Chinese High.

The Management Boards' Refusal to Close Down Chinese High and Chung Cheng High

The government surely knew that the students had already been forced to the end of their tether and would no longer remain silent. In the morning of 11 October, the Minister for Education Chew Swee Kee called up the management boards of Chinese High and Chung Cheng, told them to close down their schools voluntarily and loan their teachers to the Ministry of Education. The Ministry of Education would conduct classes for Chinese High and Chung Cheng students at designated English schools. The Minister wanted a reply by 4:30 in the afternoon. The management boards of the two schools arrived at the Ee Hoe Hean Club at 2:00 p.m.

to convene an emergency meeting. Those present were Lim Soo Gan, Kang Zhenfu, Lin Bangyan, Sun Deqi, Zhang Jianjin, Liu Murong, Cheng Fuxing and Chuang Chu Lin of the Chung Cheng Management Board, as well as Yeo Chan Boon, Tan Lark Sye, Huang Guinan, Ye Qinghe, Guo Shanhu, Pan Guoqu, Lin Shouming, Tan Long Teck and Huang Fangkui from the Chinese High Management Board.

Principal Chuang Chu Lin and Dean Huang Fangkui briefed those present at the meeting on what had transpired and stressed that until the recent development, the atmosphere within the schools during that year (1956) had been relatively peaceful. The students' camp-in was the result of the arrest of Chinese school teachers and students, as well as the closure of the SCMSSU. Furthermore, the government had announced the expulsion of over a hundred students and the dismissal of two teachers. A succession of events had taken place within such a short time. The students felt that they were left with no alternative.

The meeting decided to send a reply to Minister Chew, informing him that they would go along with the matter of the loan of teachers since that was an order. As for the voluntary closure of their schools, the management boards regretted not being able to comply and could not be held accountable for that. If the government ordered both schools to be closed or otherwise declared the schools to be illegal, that would entirely be the government's business and all consequences would have to be borne by the government.[13]

Tan Lark Sye's Impassioned Speech

The Vice-Chairperson of Chinese High's Management Board, Tan Lark Sye, spoke fervently at the emergency meeting of the two schools on 11 of October. He said:

"The recent incident involving the two schools was, in fact, the result of the rivalry among political parties, instead of really putting local education at the heart of considerations. The Chinese schools currently receive a small amount in subsidies from the government, but this is what the government ought to do in the first place, as the money is derived from taxes by the Chinese community. The management boards of the Chinese schools donated money and made all efforts to establish the schools. They should have autonomy over the schools and their work by reason should not be interfered with. Even if the government does not collect taxes and [even if] the schools do not receive this small subsidy from

---

[13] *Nanyang Siang Pau*, 12 October 1956, page 5.

the government, the schools can still be run well. Most of the board members present are not local citizens, but they are in effect grooming talent for the local government. This is a point which should be made clear to everyone. Do not merely listen to the government in everything; you ought to have your own stand on the issue. The incident involving the two schools is in reality the result of incompetence on the part of the government and its inability to deal with the students. It is not the fault of the schools' management boards."[14]

In response to Tan Lark Sye's speech, Education Minister Chew Swee Kee alleged that Tan was trying to defend the students and free them from any blame for his personal interests. The Minister further alleged that Tan was partly trying to exonerate the subversive elements. Tan Lark Sye came out with a strong rebuttal:

"I suspect if it's the case that Mr. Chew does not know Chinese. As such, he could not comprehend the resolutions and written documents passed by the meeting, resulting in the erroneous views which distort the true picture.

I have not given as much attention recently to the problems relating to Chinese education. No doubt I am the Vice-Chairperson of the Management Board of Chinese High and the Chairperson of the Hokkien Huay Kuan. In the case of Chinese High, it is the Chairperson [of the board] who is in-charge. As for the Hokkien Huay Kuan, there is an Education Division to look after the five schools. There isn't much that requires my personal attention. The reason that I am expressing my views this time round is because I attended the combined meeting of the two schools yesterday.

Mr. Chew took issue with my statement that 'the recent incident involving Chung Cheng and Chinese High was the result of the rivalry between political parties' was unfounded. I think what Mr. Chew has said is even more groundless. Did this incident arise from political rivalry? According to the radio stations, the newspapers and the statements issued by the government, the recent arrests have mostly been linked to a certain political party in our country. I believe that many of our people could see with their discerning eyes and get to know the true picture. Does Mr. Chew claim to have unique views that are different from everyone else's observation?

Furthermore, Mr Chew's accusation that I am 'trying to defend the students and free them from blame' must be considered sensational. As the Education Minister, Mr. Chew should be extremely cautious, and not be casual, in making his statements. The truth is that I have never defended the students. Why should I? The chaos in the Chinese schools today is the result of Mr. Chew's policies.

---

[14] *Ibid.*

Mr. Chew's accusation that I am doing this for my 'personal interests, and partly to exonerate the subversive elements' is a serious one. I have lived here for over forty years. My work has always been for the welfare of the community and the people. Members of the public can judge for themselves as to what has been my record. I have never acted out of self-interest. May I ask Mr Chew as to what he has done to benefit the people before and during his tenure as the Education Minister? I have no connection whatsoever with any political party. Whatever community service rendered by me was for the benefit of the government and the people. Have I ever defended the students? Why should I defend the subversive elements? I would like to request Minister Chew to be prudent when making his statements in future and to give careful consideration to my rebuttal. I await his reply."[15]

The Anxious Management Boards

When handing over the management boards' official letter to the Education Minister and conveying to him that the management boards have decided not to initiate voluntary closure of the two schools at 4:30 in the afternoon of 11 October, representatives of the four management boards — Yeo Chan Boon, Huang Fangkui, Lim Soo Gan and Chuang Chu Lin — must have felt heavy and unsettled in their hearts. The representatives headed back to Chinese High and met student representatives at the Haw Par Building in the school. The Dean (Discipline) of Chinese High, Sun Huanxin, and the Chairperson of the Singapore Chinese Middle Schools' Parents' Association, Woo Chye Tang, were also present. Looking back, the setting was so dismal and helpless that it demoralised everyone. There had been no quarrels so far among the management boards, the teachers and the students. Together, they strove for the protection of Chinese education. But in the face of the crisis, there was bound to be disagreement as to how best it could be dealt with. Yeo Chan Boon was domineering and kept blaming the students for wasting all their time on worthless activities instead of concentrating on their studies. He wanted the students to disperse immediately or face all the consequences [by themselves], causing Woo Chye Tang to argue with him out of a sense of righteousness. Chuang Chu Lin and Huang Fangkui knew deep in their hearts that the students had actually been driven to the wall.

The Students Stood Firm

On 12 October, the Governor announced in the gazette that Chinese High and Chung Cheng would be relocated and that their students would attend classes in twelve

---

[15] *Nanyang Siang Pau*, 13-10-1956, page 5.

appointed English schools. The entire staff and faculty members of Chinese High immediately held a meeting. They decided to call for a meeting with student representatives and advise them to resume classes before discussing other issues. At 5:00 pm, Huang Fangkui, Chuang Chu Lin, Lim Soo Gan, Chen See How and Sun Huanxin returned to the Haw Par Building in Chinese High to meet with the Delegation. They advised the students to prioritise the interests of Chinese education and cherish the glorious past of Chinese High and Chung Cheng. They appealed to the Delegation to disperse immediately so that the schools could resume classes as normal. After some internal negotiation, the Delegation felt that the matter should be decided by the whole student body at a general meeting, though it expressed the reservation that it would be very difficult for them to convince the students unless the government made some concessions. The Delegation repeatedly made it known to the management boards that the majority of students in both schools supported the SCMSSU, as well as the actions and demands on the part of the students then occupying Chung Cheng and Chinese High. The students would never respond to the Ministry of Education's call to move to the English schools. The Delegation also stated that as long as the management boards, the teachers and the students stood together, any attempt to destroy Chinese High and Chung Cheng would be doomed to failure.[16]

On 14 October, the Singapore Chinese Middle Schools' Parents' Association held a parents' rally at the Hokkien Huay Kuan which was attended by approximately 1,000 students' parents. The meeting supported the actions and requests of the students and also called upon the Chinese Chamber of Commerce to help solve the crisis. With regard to the Education Minister's criticism against parents providing food and clothing for the students then occupying the two schools, the meeting's Chairperson, Woo Chye Tang retorted, "Will it only satisfy Minister Chew if we let our children starve and freeze while they camp in at the schools? That would be inhumane and unacceptable."[17]

Intervention and Mediation by the Pan-Malayan Students' Federation

From the very beginning, members of the Delegation knew that politically the situation then was very delicate. They knew it would be very difficult to expect the release of the students who had been detained and the re-registration of the SCMSSU. From the start, the Delegation had requested the SCMSSU's legal advisor, Lee Kuan Yew, to arrange a meeting with Chief Minister Lim Yew Hock to see

---

[16]*Ibid.*
[17]*Nanyang Siang Pau*, 15-10-1956, page 5.

if tension in the situation could be defused. As some of the students representatives were wanted by the police, the Delegation also requested that a group of students be allowed to accompany the representatives to the meeting to offer protection. Lim Yew Hock informed us through Lee Kuan Yew that he was prepared to see ten members of the former SCMSSU Executive Committee on 17 October, but he would not acknowledge them as student representatives, much less allow a large group of fellow students to accompany them.

In the evening of 16 October, the Delegation made two requests through Lee Kuan Yew, namely for a guarantee that the representatives would have an opportunity to speak and also, a guarantee for their personal safety to ensure that none of them would be arrested on the way to the meeting or back to the schools. The Delegation was concerned because yet another two students had been arrested the previous night. Lim Yew Hock replied to Lee Kuan Yew that he could not give any such assurances as he knew neither the identities of the representatives nor anything that each of them had done before. The Delegation thereafter instructed Lee Kuan Yew to inform the Chief Minister that they would not attend the meeting.[18]

The Ministry of Education's plan to move Chinese High and Chung Cheng students to several English schools for classes proved to be an embarrassing failure. The students who responded to the Ministry's proposal numbered merely three hundred or thereabouts. Consequently, everyone began to hope that the situation would soon return to normal. The Pan-Malayan Students' Federation organised a team to investigate the arrest of students and the dissolution of the SCMSSU. Members of the team included P.S.G. *Oorjitham*, Jimmy Yong and Agoes Salim. For several days they went around visiting and talking to various quarters. In the end they arranged for the Delegation to meet with Chief Minister Lim Yew Hock and Education Minister Chew Swee Kee on 20 October. The Pan-Malayan Students' Federation guaranteed the safe passage of the student representatives. As arranged, Oorjitham and his colleagues personally accompanied nine student representatives to the Chief Minister's office on that day. The nine student representatives were: Ong Gwo Chyun, Wu Youfa, Lim Chin Joo, Cai Shijun, Chen Zaicong, Li Weizhen, Chen Bijuan, Lin Delai and Lin Chunmei. Lim Yew Hock's press officials, Lee Siow Mong and Yet Ruitan, were present at the meeting as interpreters.

Dialogue with Lim Yew Hock and Chew Swee Kee

At the meeting, the spokesperson for the Delegation, Lim Chin Joo, presented the following requests: (1) to retract the decision with regard to students' expulsion and

---
[18] *Nanyang Siang Pau*, 18-10-1956, page 5.

teachers' dismissal; (2) to guarantee that there would be no more arrests of students and teachers; (3) to respect the basic rights of the people and immediately re-instate the registration of the SCMSSU, cancel all unreasonable restrictions on Chinese schools, and either conduct open trial of the teachers and students arrested or release them unconditionally; (4) to acknowledge that learning was the basic task of the students.

Another member of the Delegation, Wu Youfa, went on to raise the following questions:

(1) The aim of our "Excel in Studies" campaign was to improve our studies and enhance our morale in learning. Why couldn't we embark on campaigns like these? Which article or clause in Singapore's law did we breach by undertaking such projects?
(2) During the constitutional negotiations with the Colonial Office in London, Chew Swee Kee issued a statement in his capacity as acting Chief Minister to say that "students' participation in the Merdeka movement does not amount to participation in political activities". Why does he now find fault with us for participating in the Merdeka Rally? What, may I ask, does the Government hope to achieve? Does it not heap praises on us when we suit its purposes, but when we are not needed, ban all organisations and arrest those who could contribute to the Merdeka movement?
(3) Is the attempt to impose on the schools' management boards the "voluntary closure" of the two schools an act in protection of Chinese education?
(4) The SCMSSU have 13,636 members. Yet Minister Chew claimed we have only 3,000 members. This can sufficiently show that the government does not know much about the SCMSSU. May I know how the Minister would then explain to the people its decision on dissolving an otherwise lawful organisation without any idea about its membership?

Lim Yew Hock made it clear that his government would certainly not allow students to form student associations. He was therefore seeing them as individuals and not as student representatives. Chew Swee Kee indicated that the government was prepared to reconsider the students' expulsion on a case-by-case basis, but the students must register for classes first. He even went on to say, "as students, your duty is to study in the right manner under the guidance of teachers. It is not the students' business to conduct meetings, because that is the business of the adults". When one of the representatives asked for further clarification, the Minister replied angrily, "I am not here to debate with you, but to tell you a few things. Accept them if you like, otherwise do whatever pleases you!"

As for the arrests of students and teachers, Lim Yew Hock's reply was officious. "All those who were arrested will be dealt with according to the law, and anyone who has not done anything wrong need not fear arrest. If anyone does anything to endanger public interests, the government will definitely take action."

This meeting lasted three hours. The government was only interested in getting us to yield unconditionally and disperse on our own accord. The representatives felt it would be useless to go on talking. Eventually, the spokesperson Lim Chin Joo had only this to say, "We are extremely disappointed by the Chief Minister's responses. The government has not been sincere in wanting to solve the problems. We strongly protest against this."[19]

Although nothing came out of the meeting, the Delegation nevertheless sent another open letter to Lim Yew Hock appealing for his government to demonstrate sincerity by stopping forthwith its persecution of Chinese school teachers and students, as well as to respect the rights of Chinese school students.

Dispersal of the Students by Force

It was already very obvious that the series of oppressive measures was well-planned beforehand. More people were arrested and more civic organisations were struck off the roll. By 25 October, those taken into police custody included activists within the Chinese cultural circles like She Ruiji, Xu Hanjie, Yang Zhizhen, Huang Chensi, Chen Zhuyan, Lin Naiyan and etc. The civic organisations dissolved included the 1953 Singapore Chinese Middle Schools graduating cohort's Arts Research Association, the Singapore Chinese Middle Schools' Parents' Association, the Chung Cheng High School Alumni and the Singapore Primary School Teachers' Union etc.

Lim Yew Hock and Chew Swee Kee went on a radio broadcast in the evening of 24 October to announce that if the students did not disperse themselves by 8:00 pm the next day, they would be dispersed by force. Both of them called upon the parents to bring their children home. The situation turned very tense from the next morning. Thousands of parents thronged both schools. They held successive assemblies, speaking fervently and appeared resolved to face the worst scenario. As the evening approached, a huge crowd gathered at the entrance to Chinese High. The people were there to offer support and protection for the students. There was also news that large groups of workers from the factories along the Upper Bukit Timah Road had clashed with the police on their way to Chinese High.

The police failed to move into Chinese High by the evening of 25 October as the Chief Minister had threatened. We thought that they would pull back and retreat.

---

[19] *Nanyang Siang Pau*, 21-10-1956, page 5.

However, much to our surprise, a great number of anti-riot police with loaded rifles broke into the school early morning the next day. They came into the school by cutting through the school's barbed wire fences or by simply climbing over walls. They moved in groups and within a short time, succeeded in encircling the key areas like the library, the canteen, the auditorium and the clock tower. Approximately 3,000 students then in the school found themselves completely trapped within the auditorium. In anticipation of the use of tear gas by the police, we had arranged for buckets of water to be placed around the auditorium and told the students to carry a handkerchief or a piece of cloth. From experience we knew that covering one's eyes with a wet cloth could reduce the pain inflicted by tear gas. As expected, bouts of tear gas rained on the auditorium. With batons in their hands, the police lost no time in charging at the defenceless students, forcing them to run about aimlessly. In the end everyone moved in the direction of the school field. With the police getting closer, the students and their parents, several thousands of them, had no alternative but to rush out of the school and start to march along Bukit Timah Road towards the city.

A Great Setback to the Student Movement

Members of the Delegation re-grouped themselves during the procession, but had absolutely no idea as to what to do next. Someone suggested marching to the Hokkien Huay Kuan downtown to re-assemble before deciding on the next course of action. Some of the members of the Delegation then forced their way to the front to be in the very first row of the procession. When arriving at the junction of Bukit Timah Road and Balmoral Road, we could see the anti-riot squad taking position before the traffic lights at Newton and looking poised for a fight. Members of the squad were lifting up their rifles and one of them was heard yelling in Malay at us to stop moving any further or else they would start firing. The procession was unfazed and kept moving forward. As tension ran high, some parents who were in the procession, as well as some bystanders, suddenly forced their way to the forefront of the procession. They lined up to stop the procession from moving any further while continually engaged themselves in conversation with members of the anti-riot squad. What followed was a stalemate for quite a while. In the end, the Delegation accepted the advice of the parents to arrange for all the students in the procession to be led away by them. Secretly, the students knew that they were to proceed separately to the Hokkien Huay Kuan at Telok Ayer Street.

Some representatives of the Delegation were escorted by parents to arrive shortly at the Hokkien Huay Kuan. (It was only years later that He Peizhu told me it was she who had led me out of the procession that very day.) In late afternoon the government suddenly declared a nation-wide curfew, As a result, all public transport came to a halt. When we did a head-count in the evening, only a few hundred students were able to come to the Hokkien Huay Kuan. We came to know later that the students who were similarly driven out of the Chung Cheng High School (Main) had moved to Kong Hwa Primary School at Guillemard Road though the number was also very small.

That night at the Hokkien Huay Kuan, we learnt from radio broadcasts that the same day on which we were driven forcibly out of Chinese High, the police carried out a series of oppressive measures island-wide against the trade union movement. The influential Singapore General Employees' Union, the Singapore Bus Workers' Union, the Farmers' Association and few others had been disbanded. Leading trade unionists like Lim Chin Siong, Devan Nair, Fong Swee Suan, S. Woodhull and Puthucheary were also arrested.

The next day, during the brief period when curfew was temporarily lifted, the students dispersed from the Hokkien Huay Kuan.

Lim Yew Hock was so politically naïve that he willingly played the role of an executioner for his colonial masters. He must have thought that if the next constitutional talk proved successful, he would be the one to reap the fruits. He was grossly mistaken as he did not realise that someone else was then lurking at his back for the opportune moment to claim the spoils. He would only have himself to blame for the tragic end of his political life.

The Lost Echo of an Era

The crack-down on the anti-colonial movement in 1956 was a repetition of what had taken place in 1948 when the colonial government imposed the Emergency Regulations Ordinance in Singapore and the Federation of Malaya. The difference, however, was that in 1956, it was the Chinese school students and the cultural sector who were made to bear the first blows, with the SCMSSU being the first target.

What the SCMSSU had done in its short span of life which lasted only 352 days was the propagation of time-honoured traditions of Chinese culture and the infusion into young people a passion for knowledge. Through the combination of learning in and beyond the classrooms, the SCMSSU sought to inculcate the young people with the right values so that they can think and act independently. The Chinese schools students who came under the tutelage of the SCMSSU in the 1950s had, in fact, become the main pillars of all historical developments involving the masses over the past decades.

Through the way it had conducted itself, the SCMSSU had demonstrated utmost self-discipline on the part of Chinese-medium school students and destroyed the colonial rulers' malicious propaganda which portrayed the Chinese school students as scourges. Through interaction with young students of different races, the SCMSSU contributed considerably towards racial harmony in our society.

The year 1954 witnessed the May 13 protest against military conscription, while the year 1955 marked the students' camp-in resulting from the Hock Lee bus workers' strike. Those were relatively turbulent years. However, as pointed out by Principal Chuang Chu Lin and Dean Huang Fangkui on several occasions, since the formation of the SCMSSU at the end of 1955, the atmosphere in all the schools had been calm and stable and the students demonstrated an impressive and unprecedented passion for learning. At that time, the Nantah had just commenced classes as well. Teachers and students in the Chinese middle schools, as well as people at the management level, were extremely optimistic and confident in the belief that henceforth they would be free to undertake in their own way and in reliance upon their own resources a more balanced yet comprehensive development of Chinese education in the context of a multi-racial society. However, the colonial rulers who had always been hostile to and contemptuous of Chinese education had obviously found this state of affairs very unpalatable.

The Chinese students' unparalled ability to organise themselves and the extent of influence they had over the community under the leadership of the SCMSSU surely must have displeased the colonial rulers and made them uneasy. Hence the decision to get rid of the SCMSSU before it could fully mature.

The SCMSSU — the lost echo of an era!

Thoughts of Exhibition Visitors

Transcribed by: Lynn Ong

> Nice Gallery!
> Looking forward to a similar event for primary school life as well!
> I enjoy these informative pictures…
> I enjoy these video clips too!!! 赞!
> ~ Phyllis Tan Yixuan
> XXX primary school

> A great start for our younger generations to learn about "English-medium" and "Chinese-medium" schools in Singapore between WWII and Independence. Such terms are very distant to them, (and myself too ☺)
> ~ Sunny Chong 9/11/07

> Good exhibits!
> It's wonderful to have these information provided to the public
> ~ Christina

> 很有意思的展顾，往事只能回味！
> 希望下一次的展览更大、更多。
> ~091107中正校友（1972）林秀珍

> 前辈先烈
> 反英反战
> 可歌可泣
> 万古流芳
> ~XXX

> Great exhibition — thank you for helping some Australian tourists understand more about Singapore's History!
> ~ Daniel & Cindy 15/11/07

> 50's的年青人原来是这样子的。
> 纯情，合群，豪情到再把"青春"献出来。
> 历史不是已经发生过的事。
> 历史是影响今天的事。
> 绕场一圈，又呆了许久，
> 我还再想这个空间所展示的
> 青春岁月，
> 留到今天，
> 其字是以什么样的形式，
> 影响着接下来的事情。
> Good Effort! Tangent
> ~ WY
> 6.12.2007

> 很好！
> 很用心。
> 回首过去是关心未来。
> ~ 陈XX
> 2007年11月11日

> 难得的资料展览
> 富教育意义
> 也回味无穷
> ~ 陈先生

> 干得非常好
> 继续干下去。
> 莘莘学子需要这些。
> 有干的勇气不容易哪
> 星星之火，可以燎原。自焚吧！
> ~ X先生
> 2007.11.11

> 佩服你们的先知先觉，亲自亲为，为
> 被忽略这一段华校生——当年反殖
> 民地主义、反对服务于英国的兵役、
> 反黄色文化运动，波澜壮阔等史迹的
> 收集，这一切的努力、有利于构建历
> 史，并对主流历史有更深沉的认识；
> 虽然通过多样化的资料展览，仍然有
> 所局限，但如何培养新一代具有民族
> 精神，多元种族，多元文化，和谐共
> 处建设家园的这一课题——让我上了
> 一节由你们青年人编写的历史课，得
> 盖良深，谨此向您们再三致敬！
> ~ 石叻坡民俗文化馆
> 陈来华
> 12.11.2007

> 历史哟历史，
> 何时方才返真？
> ~ 陈女士
> 12/11/07

> 展现不老的历史！
> 温馨的回忆。
> 努力加油
> ~ 陈XX
> 18/11

> 用心经营　令人动容
> 祝展览成功！
> ~ 莉蓉
> 13/11

> 给后代的一个历史的见证！
> ~ 红兵

> 不错的展览，让人追忆往事如烟。
> ~ 刚 11.15

> 岂有豪情似旧时，
> 花开花落两由之；
> 如今再见旧时雨，
> 泪水依然夺眶流。
> （前两句是直录鲁迅的诗，后两句我瞎凑。）
> ~ 韩山元
> 15/11/07

> 为圆切线叫好！加油！

> 给我了解到五一三事件与排华513的
> 不同点。希望有更多历史提供给
> 年轻人去了解
> 加油
> ~ 陈女士
> 15/11/07

> 看了展览后，真的被感动了
> 谢谢你们
> 办了这次的展览，
> 干得好！
> ~ '子X 07

> 星马历史有太多的官方叙述，需要
> 挖掘多一些民间资料以反应历史的
> 真相。五十年百年后，世人将会
> 记得你们的努力和功劳！
> 干得好！感激你们的辛劳！
> ~ XX
> 16/11/2007

> 恍如隔世
> ~蔡欣于零七年十一月十六日

> 收集这些资料非常不容易，圆切线却
> 办到了，干得好！这让我们知道过去
> 发生的一些事，如五一三事件等。我
> 们更应该珍惜一切。希望年轻人应该
> 多学习。
> ~ 廖美莉
> 2007.11.17

> An extremely useful and informative
> exhibition. Makes history comes
> alive for us. Thank you.

> A commendable effort!
> It's very heartwarming to see the
> dedication in documenting student
> life in Singapore. I definitely learnt
> a lot more about Singapore history
> and what it was like to be a student
> in those turbulent times. You should
> be proud of yourselves.
> ~ Gretchen
> 18/11/2007

> 感谢圆切线，让一个年代跳脱平板，继续发声。微弱的声音，更需细心聆听。加油！
> ~ 胡爱妮
> 18/11/2007

> 很有意义的展览！从中，我学到了以前小和中学的事情。
> ~ 王嗣词11岁
> 醒南小学
> 18/11/07

> 很感谢圆切线为我们设制了一堂活生生的历史课。从展览中，我们可以看出上一代人的执著，有理想、有生命力。
> 应把此展览物变成流动式，让历史课继续传下去。
> ~ 余立信
> 2007年11月18日

> 非常有意义的展览，让我回想起几十年以前的学生生活，此时我年青起来了。谢了。
> ~ 钦永
> 18/11/2007

> Enjoyed this exhibition immensely. Thank you for piecing together an invaluable bit of S'pore's history
> =) Karen

> 深受启迪
> 深深感动……
> ~ 慧心

> Congratulations on
> A Successful Exhibition!
> ~ Yinghui

> 很有意义的展览，再接再励！
> ~ 梁炳章 19/11/2007

> 谢谢你们对历史的真诚。
> ~ 林国文 11月19日

> Congratulations. I was active in student activities in 1950s.
> Arthur Lim
> ~ NUS graduate in Medicine 1956

> Thank you for this informative exhibition
> ~X

> Thank you for the initiative!
> ~Tan Wai Lan
> 20 Nov 2007

> 今天的观展收获不少！多谢！希望更多的朋友们能下来感受你的这份诚意
> ~ XX
> 20/11/2007

> Congrats on your successful exhibition. Enjoyed it! Very informative also.
> ~ Magdalene
> 20 Nov 2007

> "难得的回忆"
> ~周庭芳
> 22/11/07

> 感谢有这样一个回忆，至少肯定了当时华校生对社会，国家的关心与参与，总算没有留下空白！
> ~ 中正中学校友（4人）上
> 22/11/07

> As a student, the whole process of completing this project had been very meaningful and it had also allowed me to review the school's history in a totally new perspective.
> Thank you for giving me this wonderful chance!!
> 谢谢！ ☺
> ~陈秋琳
> 2007年11月23日

❛在这忙碌的社会里，学生们能够停下脚步，观察以前学生的生活，是值得我们骄傲的。在制作与摄影中，我获得的收获不少。参察了展览后，对以前学生的生活更加的了解。希望今后的学生，也能够对历史有同样的兴趣与认识。
～沈佩瑾
2007年11月23日

❛匆匆路过，在繁忙的街市边独有的一抹风景，无比的沁人心脾。祝活动成功！
～许晓勇（中国）

❛参观了这次展览会，所收集的图片，只是一部分。但"圆切线"已费了好多时间与精力。让我在那时代求学的中学生回顾以往殖民地时代。居民的苦难与祈求……总之，新加坡独立自主了。人民应感庆幸。感谢"圆切线"。
～颜清波
（1950–1955）
中正中学分总校生
24-11-2007

❛用心良苦
搜集与展示那段历史所需要的应该不只是热情，时间与体力。
展览意味着什么，
对当年的经历者，
现在制作者和参观者来说，
只能说冷暖自知。
～咏红

❛历史是抹不掉的！
不能遗忘的！
～XX
25-11-2007

❛谢谢你们……
让我更进一步了解新加坡的过去，
更让我发现自己多幸福 =D
~Lynette

❛往事不堪回味
回味却又甜酸苦辣
要回首，只因为它是
历史的沉淀
～过来人
27/11/07

❛很好！谢谢…
～连慧
29 Nov ' 07

❛回忆起我那物资缺乏
精神丰富的年代

❛愿历史长留！
～张平
2007年11月29日

❛感恩圆切线的用心。这是一个很好的展览，温故知新。回溯历史，是一种有意义的学习。感恩您
～翠莲
2007.11.29
340pm

❛历史需要多方面
和多元的呈现
感谢并赞赏你们的努力！
～任君
29/11/07

❛唤起年青同学的反思，建国的过程走来不易！
～廖宝强
7/12/2007

❛这段宝贵的资料，值得与目前中学生分享。意义深长。
～陈士X
7/12/07

❛难忘当年华文、华校生的被排斥，一句话"语文"
还是经济挂帅。
中国强，华文就吃香！
～中正，老林（1968年毕业）
08/12/07

Thoughts of Exhibition Visitors

❝ 看了展览会，使我感触良深。
往日的中学活动多姿多彩。
往日的生活尝尽辛酸苦辣。
往事只能回味。
慧玲，你们的展览会成功，
我替你们高兴。
干得好！继续努力！
希望下次有机会与你们分享往日的趣事。
～ 过来人 吴珍 8/12/07

❝ 虽然无缘参与当时的种种活动（年龄太小）但身为"纯华校生"的一分子，以我们的华校前辈为荣。因为当时我们的父母把我们送进华校求学，主要的目的就是华人必须懂华文华语，不要当"二毛子"。
～XX
09/12/07

❝ 看到了母校以往的情况，看到了珍贵的历史画面，还看到了来自不同"世界"（英校、华校生）的结合。很有诚意的展览。谢谢tangent的努力！
～ 能端
9/12/07

❝ 再接再励！
愿鼎力支持！
～ 中正校友
09/12/2007

❝ 谢谢圆切线！
不一样的"知识分子":)
加油！
～ 丽玲
9.12.2007

❝ 很有意义的展览会，让我了解了当时的中学生。满腔热血，自动自发的参予了活动，关心身边发生的人与事。
～ 秀凤
06-12-07

❝ 很快乐！很高兴！
能够更深入地了解当时学生的生活以及更加认识我的母校——中正中学（总校）。
谢谢你们！谢谢！
～ 陈彬红
中正校友（2002）

❝ 很高兴能参与这项活动，让我们回顾过去学生们积极地参与争取独立和推动整个社会的自由民主运动，他们不惜牺牲了学业和前途。大无畏的精神很可嘉。
～ 沈月草

❝ Congratulations on a fantastic exhibition!
~ Sandree

❝ 这个展览让我获益不浅！！没想到40-50年代的中学生生活也如此有趣、精彩。
感谢有着一次的展览！辛苦了！
感谢你们举办这次的展览，
真的开拓了我的视野。
加油！=-)
～ 莹与铃
Dec'07

❝ 很珍贵的展览会！
让我们年轻一辈有机会认识新加坡的教育历史！
谢谢！:)
～ 惠惠&兆伟
12月3日07年

❝ 展览让我觉得很幸福。
幸福，现在有良好的学习环境。
也让我觉得很遗憾，遗憾，
我们少了当时的热诚。
～嘉
08Dec07

❝ 你们这个展览使撩起无限的感触是非常难得的。
～ 我王思群
22/11/07

❝ 谢谢圆切线负责人办逍遥游展览。
让我想起60年代在识字班的点点滴滴。祝你们成功。
～ XX

❛ Thank you for the well designed
and interesting exhibition.
We are traveling from Australia and
found it very interesting and
useful to understand
a bit more about Singapore's history.
Great work :)
Thank you
~ Daniel & Cindy

❛ 今天来到这里，让我回想起六十年代
的我。感觉非常亲切。
非常感谢圆切线举办逍遥游这个活动
让我有机会重新体会当年所经历的一切。
谢谢
~ 陈淑卿

❛ Nice Gallery…
Good visual resources…
Keep up the Good
Work…
Keep the Chinese history
Alive…

❛ tangent and forum is a progressive
one, though thinly layered but
the willingness to engage in
many traces of socio-historical
fabrics is a good faith indeed!
I truly believed more of such
spontaneous dialogues with
history and collective memories
will benefit many more.
It is after all what Singapore was,
is and becoming.
~Kuo-wei, Chiu
research scholar from miao-li city, taiwan

❛ 感谢圆切线成员的努力奉献，
让我感受到关怀新加坡社会
文化的热切心火并没有在
建国之后熄灭。
在新加坡管理大学的展览会场，
听见年长人士经由参观亲身经历
的时代剪影，联系起彼此的记忆，
建国之前"仿佛生于不同国度"
的英校生与华校生，
于四五十年后，
有了共同的话题。
~ 衣若芬
2002年11月12日

❛ Good Job! I will ask
more people to come and
take a look.
~ November 18, 2007

❛ 谢谢……
~ S
December 11, 2007

Participating Schools

CHIJ St Nicholas Girls School (Secondary)
Teachers-in-charge: Soh Chungwei, Chen Fang
Students: Elissa Teo Shiting, Olivia Tan Ying Ling, Lim Hui Qi, Loh Si Jun Shauna, Foo Chuan Ping, Chng Yu Ting Krystal, Ong Lynn, Foo Hui Min, Kwek Keng Yi, Wong Jia Qi Melissa

Chung Cheng High School (Main)
Teachers-in-charge: Hsin Shu Han, Wong Peng Kwee
Students: Li Shao Bo, Yu An Qi Angela, Hannah Tjoa, Chenn Yi Kang, Ho Bing Hong, Yong Jin Kai, Chua Joshua, Caleb Tay

Raffles Girls' School (Secondary)
Teachers-in-charge: Koh Bee Ha, Thern Siew Huay
Students: Wang Qi, Sun Ying, Shi Zhihua, Michele Koh En Bei, Ong Gee Ru, Wang Yuqing, Zhang Yifan, Luo Ling Yan

Raffles Institution
Teachers-in-charge: Cheryl Yap, Sunny Chong, Tan Puay Hock
Students: Zhu Hanfei, Khoo Jun Da Benjamin, Ong Woo Sheng, Subramaniam s/o Singaram, Wong Khai Cheong, Kenneth Tan Kai En, Kenneth Chew Zi Yang, Leonard Yap Quan Feng, Brandon Yow Jie Wei

Singapore Chinese Girls School

Teachers-in-charge: Kavita DKH, Florence Tan
Students: Serene Cai, Nicole Ng, Katrina Liao, Abigail Leong, Natalie Sim, Roxanne Loh, Sibyl Seng, Kong Eng Hong, Cheryl Cheong

St Margaret's Secondary School

Teachers-in-charge: Chong-Yeo Chiu Peng, Wang Li
Students: Ong Ser Lee Linette, Tan Chew Lin, Tan Wan Yan Victoria, Sim Pei Jin, Chen Zhi, Brenda Lee Xin, Yeong Huei Deen, Miyuki Saito, Lin Jia Huan, Lim Rui Fen Eunice, Theresa Low Li Yee, Christina Tjen, Fiona Yap Shiow Jean, Leng Su Yee, Ong Xiang Yu Belinda, Mabel Lim Yi Jun, Tan Lijia Gloria

Xinmin Secondary School

Teachers-in-charge: Joan Chia, Karen Ang
Students: Wan Xin Yi, Seah Qing Xuan, Una Hsu Xin Ying, Gasper Chan, Gilbert Toh Wei Han, Nur Nasuha, Jefferson Ng, Tan Kok Hwee, Kelly Ho, Chen Wenqi

Editors' Notes
A Collective Imagery of Youth in the Island-State

Chan Cheow Thia

When the publication project finally saw a real possibility of fruition, we — the three editors in-charge — decided to include a postscript to record the intentions, encounters and goodwill that had gone into its making. In the final assembling of the materials for publication, we also hoped to reflect on a particular phase of the Tangent as a group.

The exhibition took place in 2007, but this book did not materialise until 2012. If we consider how the whole project began with the idea of an exhibition, this book actually took seven years to complete. If one may say that the history elucidated within was really an involuntary passage of destiny, this "exhibition cum publication" project undertaken by the Tangent was more of a conscious relay of shared beliefs. The genesis of the project was not unlike that of the group — the idea came out of a gathering over food and drinks. And in retrospect, the circumstances now seem to be even more coincidental in that it was also the three of us (now bound by the editing of this book) who met in 2005 for dinner. I had then just moved to the Ministry of Education to participate in the national-level planning for Chinese language curriculum. Siao See had just returned from the United Kingdom, and during the meal, she spoke about Lai He, the father of modern Taiwanese literature, as well as how she was presented with a music album produced by a group of young Taiwanese commemorating Lai and his works. As she happened also to be browsing through Malayan Chinese fiction at that time, Siao See found a stark contrast over the awareness of local literature in Taiwan and Singapore and lamented that Singapore's own early local writers who attempted to express their concern for the local society are hardly known to younger Singaporeans. The topic somehow shifted from literature to history, and we started talking about student activities in the 1950s and the 1960s. At some point during the conversation, Huay Leng suggested that The Tangent organise an exhibition to explore the different facets of student life of those times. Siao See and I both thought that it was a good idea as our journal readership is limited. Putting up an exhibition would enable the group to reach out to a wider audience.

The idea really took off after other members of The Tangent responded enthusiastically. Each of us subsequently committed ourselves to different tasks in our spare time outside work: Sy Ren led the way in liaising for venue sponsorship and organised discussions for the overall conceptualisation of the exhibition; he also fronted a press conference with Francis and Siao See to appeal for the donation of relevant artefacts. Chang Woei moderated a public forum; Huay Leng, Weili, Siao See and I conducted oral history interviews, as well as contacted schools that might potentially contribute to our exhibition content. Sin Hwee took charge of producing the short video clip... That the exhibition — one we would occasionally call "The Unofficial History of the Scholars" in jest, after the famous premodern Chinese novel — eventually came into being was nothing short of an extraordinary feat, for we were extremely short-handed, and had to rely heavily on many friends outside The Tangent to render assistance, especially Celine, Zhaocheng, Cheng Tju, Chun Meng and Pin Pin. The stage of publication entailed complex coordination as well. Oral history recordings had to be transcribed; the interviewees and speakers had to be contacted to confirm their willingness for their contribution to be published; translation and reviews of the translation had to be scheduled. (In the end, there was still a transcript edited by Wai Fong that was eventually excluded after the interviewee changed his mind.) There were times when morale was low, it would be untruthful to say that we never thought of aborting the work, but fortunately, there was always someone willing to continue overseeing the job and share the burden in time. What is now presented in the form of a book is veritably a product of a persistent collaboration.

All along, "Education at Large" was meant to be a journey to inquire about the history before the island-state became independent. As Huay Leng mentioned in her foreword of the exhibition pamphlet, "...to complete our understanding of how we got here, we can then claim to fully appreciate the context of our present circumstances. It [The journey] is also a means of ensuring that we are adequately responsible, in light of the choices and decisions we make in our present age." The intent underpinning the exhibition is therefore neither memorial nor nostalgic in nature. Rather, it stems from a wish that through layered comparisons, more people would develop a sense of ownership for the past and the future of the island-state. Globalisation today has caused bodies and memories to be in a state of continual flux. Experiences of such drifting subjects will find permanent refuge and anchor if inter-generational discourses can be preserved in written form, and only then will it be possible to imagine a more plural history of mentalities. Taking after the spirit of the exhibition, this book does not intend to purvey any exotic content. Instead, we hope that a heterogeneous state of historical discourses will become normalised, and that the island-state will face up and get used to the heteroglossia in the society, before learning to manage the different voices within.

From another perspective, what the Tangent has realised through this publication is a certain desire to inscribe. The collective youth imagery emerging from this inscription constructs a mental snapshot of the society in the past, as well as embraces an array of alternative imaginations. Measured contemplation and passionate action existed side by side, just as the sense of self blended with an allegiance towards a larger cause in those times. We shall remember how this place and its future were rich with possibilities then. As the island-state finds itself ushering in a new political climate and historical period, the polyphonic history represented in this book will engage other discourses in the negotiation of social energies amongst a fresh ensemble of actors. Amidst the contest enacted by different forces, regardless of how the future turns out, The Tangent will continue to observe the development of history and culture in this island-state.

ABOUT THE EDITORS

Teng Siao See

Born in 1975, Siao See obtained her first degree from the National University of Singapore and has a PhD Sociology degree from the University of Essex, United Kingdom. She is presently a researcher on educational and cultural issues at the Nanyang Technological University.

Chan Cheow Thia

Born in 1978, Cheow Thia received his Bachelor's degree in Chinese Language and Literature from Fudan University and has an M.Phil. in Chinese Studies from University of Cambridge. He is currently pursuing his PhD at the Department of East Asian Languages and Literatures, Yale University. Cheow Thia was previously an educator who taught Chinese language and participated in the development of the national curriculum.

Lee Huay Leng

Born in 1971, Huay Leng graduated from the Department of Chinese Studies, National University of Singapore, with a Bachelor's degree and obtained her Master's degree from the School of Oriental and African Studies, University of London. She has been working with Lianhe Zaobao as a journalist since graduation. Huay Leng is a Tangent founding member.

Organising Committee

Chairpersons	Lee Huay Leng, Quah Sy Ren
Project Manager	Celine Choi Poh Heng
Secretary	Ong Chang Woei
Treasurer	Ho Sheo Be
Oral History Interview	Chan Cheow Thia, Chiu Wei Li, Lee Huay Leng, Teng Siao See, Zhou Zhaocheng
Copywriting	Chan Cheow Thia, Lee Huay Leng, Francis Lim, Lim Cheng Tju, Quah Sy Ren, Teng Siao See, Zhou Zhaocheng
School Outreach Programme Coordinators	Chan Cheow Thia, Francis Lim
Translation	Chiu Wei Li, Chan Cheow Thia, Lee Huay Leng
Programme Editor	Low Chun Meng
Short Film	Tan Pin Pin, Goh Sin Hwee

The Tangent Committee (2010–2012)

President	Lee Huay Leng
Vice-President	Ong Chang Woei
Secretary	Ho Sheo Be
Vice-Secretary	Teng Siao See
Treasurer	Chan Cheow Peng
Committee Members	Chan Cheow Thia, Chiu Wei Li, Goh Sin Hwee, Quah Sy Ren, Francis Lim Khek Gee